A Sunset Travel Book

Islands of the
SOUTH PACIFIC

LANE BOOKS · MENLO PARK, CALIFORNIA

Foreword

Behind the popular image of the South Pacific—white sand beaches and coconut palms that Somerset Maugham called "the perennial pennants of Polynesia"—much can be discovered by today's tourist: history, legend, an intriguing kind of life, a surprising variety of scenic beauty, a tremendous range of things to do.

In this book, we have brought together information in guide form that will help in your own discovery of this storied part of the world. Some approximate prices are given to aid the reader in planning; however, since prices change constantly, we urge you to accept these only as approximations. Hotels are named in the more remote areas where only one or two hotels exist, but no attempt has been made to list all the hotels in each group. You should know also that new hotels and other facilities are under construction and on the planning boards throughout the area. For up-to-the-minute details, we suggest you contact your travel agent or the appropriate government tourist office listed in each chapter.

Many persons helped in the collection of information and checking of the manuscript. A special acknowledgement should be made for the help and cooperation provided by the following: Gerard Gilloteaux and James Boyack of Papeete, Tahiti; Rory Scott and J. Cokanasiga of Suva, Fiji, and Thomas Talamini of San Francisco, California; Bruno Tabuteau and Antoinette Kidney of Nouméa, New Caledonia; Lloyd Clark of Pago Pago, American Samoa, and Stanley S. Carpenter of Washington, D. C.; Vensel Margraff of Apia, Western Samoa; Peter D. Wallis of Nuku'alofa, Kingdom of Tonga; Joe Mulders of Vila, New Hebrides; H. Creighton of Honiara, British Solomon Islands Protectorate; Christopher D. Copeland of Port Moresby, Papua New Guinea; Bert Unpingco of Agana, Guam; Mike Ashman of Saipan, Mariana Islands, Trust Territory of the Pacific Islands; Raul S. Kristian of Los Angeles, California; R. Teiwaki of Bairiki, Tarawa; Harry Mercer of Los Angeles, California; and Charlotte Hyde of Los Angeles, California.

Supervising Editor: Frederic M. Rea, Publisher, Pacific Travel News

Research and Text: Frances Coleberd

Coordinating Editor: Sherry Gellner
Design: Joe Seney

FRONT COVER PHOTOGRAPH, by Jack Fields, shows lagoon off Majuro atoll in the Marshall Islands.

BACK COVER PHOTOGRAPH (upper, by Fiji Visitors Bureau) is of street scene in Suva, and (lower, by Don Normark) pictures Tahitian dancers in Papeete.

Executive Editor, Sunset Books: David E. Clark

Second Printing March 1973

Contents

THE ISLANDS OF THE SOUTH PACIFIC . . . **5**
High islands, born of volcanoes . . . and low
islands, tediously created by coral polyps
. . . but all enchanting

**TAHITI AND FRENCH POLYNESIA . . .
WHERE THE LEGEND BEGAN** **13**
Storied islands with lofty peaks, studded with
vegetation, circled by necklaces of coral,
inhabited by enchanting people

FIJI . . . KNOWN AS THE HAPPY ISLANDS . **39**
A fascinating blend of cultures, a tantalizing
collection of islands begging to be explored

**NEW CALEDONIA . . .
THE ISLE OF LIGHT** **65**
Pine-clad heights, snow-white beaches,
protected by offshore reefs . . . Melanesian
but with a touch of *la vie française*

THE SAMOAS . . . CRADLE OF THE RACE . . **85**
Purest Polynesia . . . with high chiefs and
talking chiefs and a plethora of churches

TONGA . . . WHERE TIME BEGINS **99**
A benign set of islands . . . with gentle people,
a towering king, and a royal tortoise

**NEW HEBRIDES . . . A RARE
CONDOMINIUM** **109**
Primitive rituals, dramatic land divers,
smoking volcanoes that rise out of the sea

**SOLOMON ISLANDS . . . BEYOND THE
TOURIST ROUTES** **115**
A mountainous chain, fringed with coastal
villages, a primitive landscape scarred with
the battlefields of World War II

**PAPUA NEW GUINEA . . . LAND OF 700
CULTURES** **121**
Second largest island in the world, land of
sing-sings, wig men, and mud men

**GUAM AND MICRONESIA . . . A CORAL
NECKLACE** **133**
2,141 specks of land, traces of ancient
civilization, deep scars of World War II battles

**NEWCOMERS . . . ISLANDS YOU CAN
HELP DISCOVER** **153**
The Cooks, Easter, Gilbert and Ellice, Lord
Howe, Nauru, Norfolk—previews of coming
attractions

SUPPLEMENTARY READING **158**

INDEX **159**

SPECIAL FEATURES

INTRODUCTION
The coconut palm is a providential tree **9**
Captain Cook . . . remarkable map maker
of the South Seas **11**

TAHITI AND FRENCH POLYNESIA
Say it in Tahitian **18**
Shopping surprises **21**
Gauguin's Tahiti . . . "A sky without winter" . . **24**
Tamaaraa in Tahiti . . . pig and poi, music
and motion **32**
Bastille Day—South Pacific version **37**

FIJI
Fijian pronouncing primer . . . mind your
B's and Q's **44**
Shopping in Fiji . . . cameras to kerosene
lamps **49**
Take the sugar train . . . it's a
free ride **50**
Firewalking: the mystifying ritual **53**
Yaqona . . . it's a drink and a ritual **60**
A calendar of events . . . from Fijian
fireworks to Indian firewalking **63**

NEW CALEDONIA
Ladies' cricket . . . in Mother Hubbards **70**
The Melanesian hut . . . it's like a beehive **73**

THE SAMOAS
Etiquette, Samoan-style **87**

TONGA
Moby Dick . . . revisited **103**

PAPUA NEW GUINEA
Sing-sing in the Highlands **126**

GUAM-MICRONESIA
An island hopping adventure . . . on
field trip vessels **142**
Nan Madol . . . artificial islets in a
world of islands **144**
Palau's rock islands . . . the locals
call them chalbacheb **149**

THE MANY FACETS of the South Pacific: a tiny church isolated amid palm groves and edged by a deepwater bay; Tahitian natives engaged in a javelin throwing contest during Bastille Day; the schooner Seaspray *on a day-cruise to one of Fiji's offshore islands.*

The Islands of the South Pacific

HIGH ISLANDS BORN OF VOLCANOES AND LOW ISLANDS FORMED BY CORAL—ALL ENCHANTING

Scattered between the Tropic of Capricorn and the Tropic of Cancer lie thousands of islands—some barely more than patches of coral exposed at low tide, others craggy islands with towering peaks, high valleys, broad plains, rushing streams, tumbling waterfalls, and villages and towns.

These bits of land were discovered and explored by Captain Cook, Abel Tasman, Ferdinand Magellan, Louis Antoine de Bougainville, and a host of other early-day explorers. These are the lands painted by Gauguin, the places described in poem and prose by Stevenson, Melville, London, Maugham, and Michener. So splendid are the pictures these artists have created that the South Pacific evokes among us all a quickened pulse, a myriad of images—romantic, peaceful to a point of languor, adventuresome to a point of intrigue.

Among these thousands of islands, a few are easily accessible today to travelers. Many more have become the province of the boat owner who can island hop for months on end without retracing his route, and the adventurer who drifts with the tides of occasional transportation. In this book we'll explore the islands that can be reached by regularly scheduled air and steamship lines, islands that have hotels and other facilities providing creature comforts for the traveler.

POLYNESIA, MELANESIA, MICRONESIA

The three general regions of the South Pacific are Polynesia, Melanesia, and Micronesia. *Nesia* means island. Polynesia translates as *many islands*, Melanesia means *black islands*, and Micronesia, *tiny* or *small islands*.

Almost as varied as the topography of their islands are the people who make the different islands their home. Each island group has racial

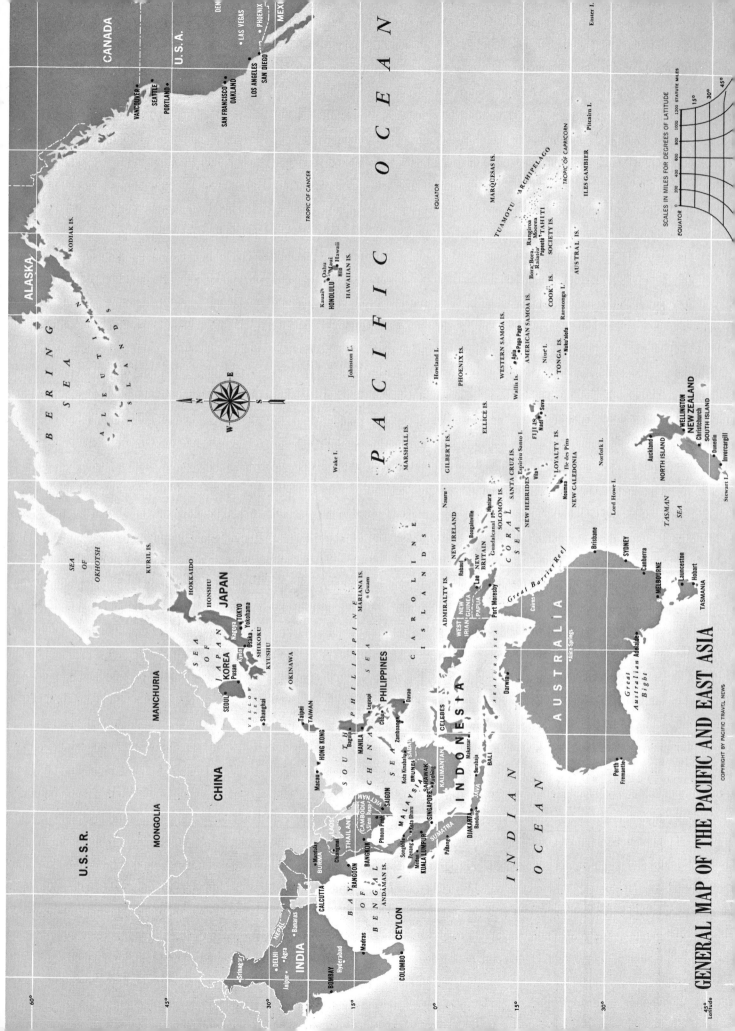

GENERAL MAP OF THE PACIFIC AND EAST ASIA

COPYRIGHT BY PACIFIC TRAVEL NEWS

FASCINATING FACES of the South Pacific: a New Caledonian in costume, a New Caledonian youngster, a Tahitian dancer, a Fijian school boy, a Fijian chief's daughter, and a Papua New Guinea wig man.

characteristics, physical appearance, languages, social systems, and dress different from those of its neighboring island groups. Yet all of them have one thing in common—the sea. The winds and the tides and the abundance of the ocean harvest influence their attitudes, their ways of life.

Most islanders live a communal type of existence in thatched villages, their concept of family going beyond that of blood relationship. Few of them covet material possessions. Although many have embraced the Christian faith, they enjoy the ritualistic songs and dances of their ancestors. Most islanders have great dignity, an appreciation of ceremony, and a respect for tradition.

Polynesians. Justifiably romanticized in legend and art, the Polynesians dwell in the vast archipelagoes of the Polynesian triangle. The points of this triangle are Hawaii on the north, New Zealand on the south, and Easter Island on the east. Within these approximate boundaries, you find the Samoas, Tonga, Tahiti, and the Ellice and Cook islands. Polynesians are brown skinned, straight haired, and usually quite handsome—as the voyagers of the past often testified.

Melanesians. The Melanesians are Oceanic Negroids, occupying islands of the western fringe of the South Pacific: Papua New Guinea, New Caledonia, Fiji, the New Hebrides, the Gilbert Islands, and the Solomons. Melanesians are dark skinned, fuzzy haired, and artistically creative. The Melanesians found in Papua New Guinea and New Caledonia—smaller than the Melanesians of Fiji—are thick lipped and show Australoid strains similar to those of the Australian aborigines.

THE HIGH ISLAND with serrated peaks (left) is of volcanic origin; the low island (above) is a reef or atoll formed of coral.

Micronesians. Finally, there are the islands and people of Micronesia. These islands include the Marianas (Guam, Rota, Saipan, and Tinian), the Caroline Island archipelagoes (Palau, Yap, Truk, Ponape, and Kusaie), the northern atolls, and the Marshall Islands. The Micronesians as a group have many similarities, but they are not as closely related as either the Polynesians or the Melanesians. They display local differences in social organization, religion, and culture. Generally a sturdy, heavy-set people akin to the Polynesians, they are seemingly more influenced by proximity to Malaysia and the Asian mainland.

Other islanders. Infusing the South Pacific islands with additional color are the non-indigenous residents—among them, descendants of early explorers, adventurers, missionaries, and traders who landed in the Pacific in past centuries. In addition, the islands shelter a great number of newcomers—migrants from India, for instance, who have come to Fiji, as well as sizable populations of Chinese and many Europeans and Americans who have chosen to live in the islands.

Low and high islands

There are two kinds of islands in the South Pacific: *low* and *high*. Regardless of how they vary in size and topography, all islands fall into one or the other categories.

Low islands are coral reefs or atolls built by coral polyps and isolated in the open ocean. Ring or horseshoe shaped, most of them enclose salt water lagoons. Some low islands are nearly submerged; others, such as Tongatapu Island, are uplifted coral masses. All these circular reefs have coral gardens housing a diversity of marine life. Many are fringed by coconut palms, their roots in salt water, and by wide beaches—a familiar island image of the South Seas in fiction and photography.

High islands are exposed summits of partially submerged volcanoes. Some thrust jaggedly up out of the sea to heights of several thousand feet. Most are drained by rushing rivers that tumble into dramatic waterfalls. Spectacular examples of high volcanic islands include Bora Bora and Moorea.

How to get there and get around

The islands of the South Pacific may be reached from virtually any point on the compass: from Honolulu and the West Coast cities of the United States; from the Orient, Southeast Asia, Australia, New Zealand, and Chile.

By air: Nine major airlines presently operate regular flights from Honolulu and West Coast cities—Los Angeles, San Francisco, Portland, Seattle, Vancouver, B. C.—to the South Pacific islands: Air New Zealand, American Airlines, British Overseas Airways (BOAC), Canadian Pacific Airlines, Continental Airlines, Pan American World Airways, Qantas Empire Airways, Trans World Airlines, and UTA French Airlines.

THE COCONUT PALM IS A PROVIDENTIAL TREE

That symbol of the South Pacific—the coconut palm tree—is much more than just a supergraphic that fringes many picture postcard views of a tropical island.

The coco palm contributes substantially to a sustenance economy throughout the South Pacific. No other tree or shrub or plant can match its multiplicity of uses. In its scope, it suggests a tropical supermarket—supplying everything from food and drink to household hardwares, building materials, and articles of personal adornment. In addition, the coco palm produces copra (dried meat of the coconut) for an industry that is the economic mainstay of the South Pacific. The coconut palm is indeed a providential tree.

Actually the coconut palm, although found throughout the South Pacific, is not believed to be indigenous. Its origin remains something of a mystery. No truly wild coco palm has been found; all such groves seem to stem from man's presence. Some botanists believe the tree may have originated somewhere in the Indo-Oceanian area. They speculate that it was probably dispersed by human migrations and by natural means, such as drifting on water.

In any event, the coconut is a kind of South Pacific staff of life which now grows in large commercially planted plantations, as well as in natural groves. In the culinary department, it is an ingredient in native recipes for cakes, puddings, and poi-like concoctions. Fresh coconut, generally grated, is virtually a staple and no farther away than a climb up a tree.

You'll find the milk of the coconut—a rich, creamy liquid—in fish cream sauces and other recipes. Many South Pacific restaurants serve heart of palm salad. And coconut pudding is a simple but elegantly tasteful dessert. The watery liquid of the green immature coconut, slightly sweet to the taste, is used instead of water by natives of arid islands and atolls. Try a sip—it's surprisingly cool and refreshing.

Since the trunk of the coconut tree is a hardwood, it is used for uprights and rafters of buildings and for masts and other spars on boats. Palm fronds are used to thatch roofs (and to rethatch them every five years or so) and as a weaving material for a variety of products: hats, baskets, floor mats. The coconut shell is used as a bowl, a cup, or a cooking vessel. The nut is also carved into buttons, bracelets, and other ornamental objects. Many coconut products end up as souvenirs you'll find sold throughout the area. The fibers of the coconut husk are twisted into a cordage called sennit, once used for fishing nets but now replaced by nylon netting.

The same providential coconut palm tree produces copra. It is harvested by halving the nuts, then drying them. This is done either naturally, in the sun, or artificially, in kilns using hot air or smoke. The dried meat is then taken to the nearest port, where it is shipped to a crushing mill and the oil (about 70 per cent of the meat) is extracted. As a high grade vegetable oil, it is used in the manufacture of soap, margarine, cosmetics, and other products.

In the island way of life, even the small white flowers that grow along the branching stalk come into the picture: they're used to make a kind of coconut brandy.

NATIVES SPLIT coconuts by hand and toss them on the ground to dry.

CRUISE SHIPS and airlines make regularly scheduled trips to many of the islands of the South Pacific.

By sea. One steamship company, Pacific Far East Line, operates the two luxury liners, *SS Mariposa* and *SS Monterey*, on regularly scheduled sailings out of San Francisco to South Pacific islands. In addition, PFEL and four other steamship companies (P & O Lines, Royal Viking Line, Swedish American Line, and German Atlantic Line), schedule occasional cruises throughout the year from West Coast ports to the South Pacific. Several Australian and New Zealand-based steamship lines provide service to many of the islands. Cargo passenger vessels of various lines, sailing out of West Coast ports bound for Australia or New Zealand, carry a limited number of passengers. Other options involve traveling part of the way by air, part by sea. As a sea leg for this kind of travel, the Westours vessel, *West Star*, offers eight-island cruises between Tahiti and Fiji during the winter months. Another sea leg of this type is offered on occasional trips of the Linblad Travel Inc. vessel, *MS Linblad*.

Regional services. You will find a host of regional airlines operating on inter-island routes. And there are many shipping lines and small trading vessels with space for a few passengers. Some of these ships call on islands that are otherwise inaccessible. Most regional services are covered in the separate chapters of this book.

Island-hopping. Cruise ships usually make stops at several island ports in the South Pacific. Although much of the fun of a cruise is being on board ship, if you are a dedicated island-hopper, you can usually leave your ship in one port and, traveling by air, catch up with it at the next, seeing a variety of islands and peoples while your ship is at sea.

The secret of working out an island hopping trip as part of a longer journey by air is to find out how much mileage the airlines will allow on a one-way trip to your farthest destination, or between the points used for calculating the fare. The maximum mileage allowed one-way between the West Coast of the United States and Sydney, Australia, for instance, is 9,050 miles. This means you can route yourself to Honolulu (2,397 miles), to American Samoa (2,612 miles), to Western Samoa (94 miles), to Tonga (554 miles), to Suva (466 miles), to Nadi (77 miles), to New Caledonia (788 miles), and then on to Sydney (1,231 miles), with miles to spare—the mileage adds up to only 8,219 miles—for the price of a direct ticket to Sydney. You can return home by way of New Zealand or Tahiti on a similar mileage basis.

Guam, a crossroads island in the central part of the western Pacific, is a logical stop if you are on your way to the Philippines and Southeast Asia or if you are making a circle tour of the Pacific. A round-trip tourist fare allows you to fly as far as Taiwan on a Pacific circle route that includes Honolulu, Guam, Japan, the Philippines, Singapore, Indonesia, Australia, and the Pacific islands of your choice on the way home.

CAPTAIN COOK...REMARKABLE MAP MAKER OF THE SOUTH SEAS

Of all the explorers who ranged the Pacific following Magellan's voyage in the early 1500's, the man who ranged the widest and left the most lasting marks was Captain James Cook.

On his three voyages that lasted almost nine years, he touched on nearly every island group in the South Pacific: Easter, the Marquesas, Tahiti, the Cooks, Tonga, Fiji, New Caledonia, Norfolk, Niue, Hawaii, New Hebrides, Pitcairn. In addition, he charted 2,000 miles of Australia's east coast, circumnavigated and charted New Zealand, charted the west coast of North America, and was the first European explorer to cross the Antarctic Circle.

By the end of his second exploration in 1775, he was internationally acclaimed for his discoveries, for his superb charting of the oceans and mapping of the lands he visited, for the immense amount of scientific data collected by the scientists who voyaged with him, and for his own shrewd observations of the people who inhabited these new lands. Using sextant and chronometer and refinements in nautical astronomy, he also developed a method that was to become standard for estimating longitude.

Today, some 200 years later, Cook is still a name to be reckoned with in the South Pacific: you'll find islands, straits, mountains, coves, beaches, headlands, streams, hotels, and streets named after him.

The son of a Yorkshire farmhand, Cook was born in England in the remote village of Marton in 1728. After four years of school, six years as a merchant's apprentice, and nine years at sea on small barkentines carrying coal to London, he joined the Royal Navy. After being promoted to non-commissioned warrant officer at age 29, he became master of a ship deployed to North America. There he sounded and surveyed the course of the St. Lawrence River and charted the coasts of Labrador and Newfoundland. On this same trip he also found time to make meticulous scientific observations, involving mathematics and astronomy, of an eclipse of the sun. Compiled into a paper, his observations were submitted to the prestigious Royal Society in London, an action that was to trigger the events that brought Cook to the Pacific. As it happened, the Royal Society was mounting an expedition to Tahiti for the purpose of observing the transit of Venus in a "favorable location." Cook was selected to head the expedition, commissioned lieutenant, and given command of the small bark *H.M.S. Endeavour.*

So began, at age 40, a remarkable decade in the life of a Yorkshire farmhand's son. In the years from 1768 to 1779, Cook led three expeditions into the vast, uncharted areas of the South Pacific. His expeditions were noteworthy for one other reason: in the course of nearly three years at sea, he lost not a single member of his ships' companies from scurvy. Up to this time, the disease had decimated crews and had been considered an unavoidable liability. Cook prevented it by applying the cure and prevention recommended by Scottish naval surgeon, James Lind: fresh fruits and vegetables.

For all his accomplishments, Cook was known as a kind and gentle person, a considerate commander, and a courteous and understanding student of the native inhabitants of the lands he discovered. Ironically enough, however, he met his death at the hands of Hawaiians at Kealakakua Bay in 1779—the result of a fracas that ensued after the theft of one of his small-boats. Now a Hawaiian village at this site bears the name "Captain Cook."

To the lords of the Admiralty, he had been a source of amazement: a man who overcame "the social handicap of lowly birth" to rise to the rank of Post Captain in the Royal Navy; a man proclaimed by a contemporary, Admiral John Forbes, as "the ablest and most renowned navigator this or any country hath produced."

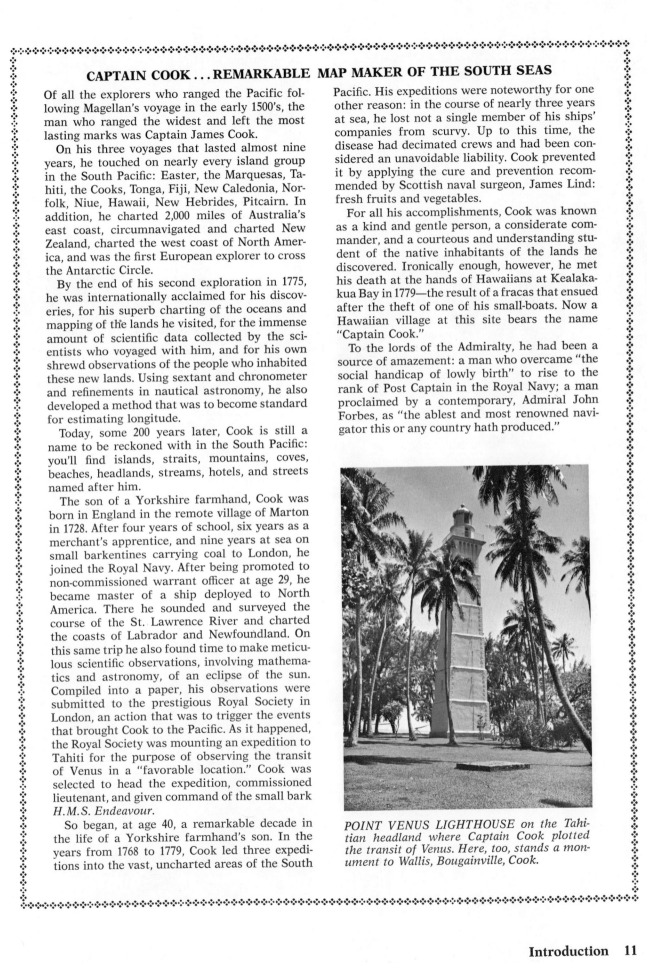

POINT VENUS LIGHTHOUSE on the Tahitian headland where Captain Cook plotted the transit of Venus. Here, too, stands a monument to Wallis, Bougainville, Cook.

IN THE WATER WORLD along Tahitian shores, a sightseeing boat docks at Moorea's Aimeo Hotel pier (above); youngsters set out for a Saturday sail in outrigger canoe (right); passengers in glass-bottom boat peer at coral gardens in Bora Bora lagoon (far right).

Tahiti & French Polynesia... where the legend began

ISLANDS WITH LOFTY PEAKS AND NECKLACES OF CORAL, INHABITED BY ENCHANTING PEOPLE

Anyone in search of an island paradise might well pause to wonder whether there's need to look farther than Tahiti and her sister islands in French Polynesia. These are the islands that achieved a legendary allure from the early-day chronicles of such men as Wallis, Bougainville, and Cook; the writings of Melville, Stevenson, London, Nordhoff and Hall; the paintings of Gauguin.

They are beautiful, even spectacular islands. Lush and mountainous, they plunge into an ocean that's every shade of blue. They mix the deep greens of rain-fed tropical forests with a profusion of flowering shrubs and trees. They're ringed with coral reefs that enclose shimmering lagoons.

The climate is balmy, tempered by practically constant tradewinds. The population is friendly, attractive, and hospitable. The atmosphere is at once distinctively Polynesian and distinctively French.

For the visitor, Tahiti is far away yet within easy reach by air. It lies roughly mid-way between the United States and Australia, 3,700 miles from Los Angeles and 3,300 miles from Sydney. It's about 5½ hours from Honolulu by air, about 8 hours for the direct flight from Los Angeles.

Once in Tahiti, you find yourself within easy reach of some of the smaller jewels of French Polynesia that are part of the Society Islands: Moorea, Bora Bora, Huahine, Raiatea, Rangiroa, Ua Huka, Maupiti, Tubuai, and Manihi.

By air, Moorea lies not more than 10 minutes away from Tahiti, Bora Bora not more than an hour, and Huahine and Raiatea from half to three-quarters of an hour. Their remoteness is not measured so much by flying time from Tahiti, however, as by prevailing atmosphere. They are farther removed from the influences of civilization, with none of the urbanization that marks Tahiti, where about one third of the island's population now lives

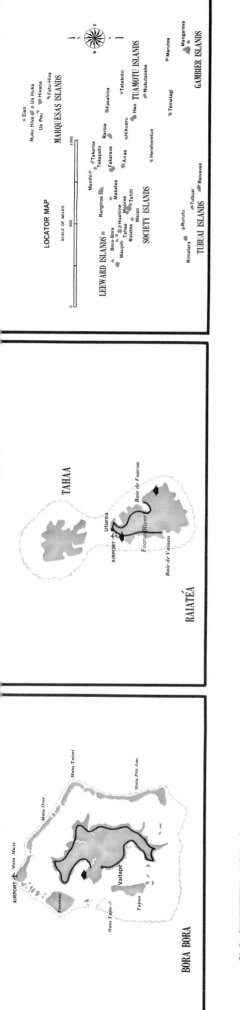

SOCIETY ISLANDS

SOUTH PACIFIC OCEAN

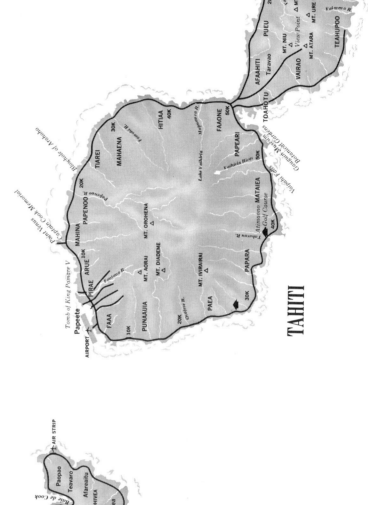

TAHITI

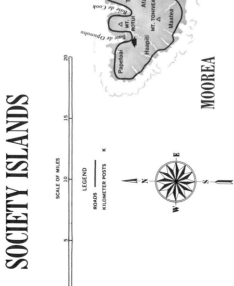

MOOREA

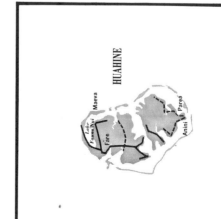

HUAHINE

TAHITIAN LIFESTYLES appear in a young girl weaving pandanus into leafy-brimmed hat (above); fishing nets hung up to dry (upper right); house with lacy woodwork fringing roof (lower right).

in Papeete. The outer Society Islands are to many visitors more true to the idea of an island paradise.

Geography

More than a hundred islands make up the five separate archipelagos of French Polynesia. These island groups include the Windward Islands (5 islands)—Tahiti, Moorea, and three smaller islands; the Leeward Islands (9 islands)—Raiatea, Huahine, Tahaa, Bora Bora, Maupiti, and several atolls; the Australs (5 islands); Gambiers (20 islands); Marquesas (14 islands); and Tuamotus (81 islands). The Windward and the Leeward groups comprise the Society Islands. Of these, Tahiti is the most important socially, politically, and economically.

Tahiti is one of the high islands of the South Seas (see page 8). Its land mass consists of several craggy-topped cones of extinct volcanos joined by a narrow isthmus. Its figure-eight shape somewhat resembles a floating sea turtle with protruding head. The large body is Tahiti-Nui or Tahiti proper; the smaller head, the peninsula of Taiarapu or Tahiti-iti (Little Tahiti). Together they comprise 402 square miles. The interior of the island, practically uninhabited, is an area of jagged peaks and deep gorges. Tahiti's highest peak is 7,321-foot Mount Orohena. A coral reef makes a fringe of foam around the island, protects the lagoons and beaches, and strikes a dividing line between the indigo of the deep ocean and the myriad lighter shades of blue and green in the lagoons. At a few intervals where the waters of mountain streams empty into the sea, the cooler waters inhibit the growth of coral. Some of these passes in the reef are large enough for ships to sail through.

THE SPECTRUM of Tahitian types ranges from men strumming guitars on the beach and a priest bicycling down the street to women stitching appliqued tenture on the grass; and everywhere, Tahitians wearing flowers on the hat or in the hair.

History and government

Tahiti was first sighted by Europeans on June 19, 1767, when the *Dolphin*, under the command of England's Captain Samuel Wallis, anchored in Matavai Bay off Point Venus. He was followed in short order by France's Louis Antoine de Bougainville in 1768, by England's Captain James Cook in 1769, by Spanish Captain Domingo Boenechea from Peru in 1772, and by Captain William Bligh aboard the *Bounty* in 1779.

Boenechea returned a second time in 1774, bringing two priests as missionaries, but they stayed only a year. It wasn't until 1797 that missionaries landed in force: 30 men and their families, sent by the London Missionary Society.

Each of the islands in the archipelago had its own government headed by local chiefs until 1793, when Pomare I, an ambitious chief on Tahiti, began capturing his neighbors' lands. By 1791 he had Tahiti, Moorea, and Huahine under his control and had established a dynasty that was to last for almost a century.

In the first half of the 19th century the islands were torn by wars brought about largely by rival Protestant and Catholic missionaries and their supporting governments (England and France). Tahiti became a French protectorate in 1846 during the reign of Queen Pomare IV, remaining so until 1880, when King Pomare V made a gift of his kingdom to France.

Now the Territory of French Polynesia, the islands are administered locally as a single unit by a governor appointed by the French Republic, assisted by a 5-member council and a local Territorial Assembly of 30 elected members, who have wide legislative powers. They meet in Papeete, the capital, in the Territorial Assembly Building on Avenue Rue du Général de Gaulle (see page 20).

Each archipelago has its own administrator, and there is a gendarmerie post on each large island. Municipal and district councils are responsible for the settlement of local disputes.

Lifestyle

Tahitian life is capsuled in their phrase *aita peapea* —a kind of happy "Who cares?" A telling insight to the island's lifestyle comes when you visit the final resting place of the last of the Tahitian monarchs, that tippler King Pomare V, whose tomb is appropriately topped with a reproduction of a Benedictine bottle.

Originally the basic social unit in Tahiti was the family and beyond that, the tribe. Each tribe was identified with a separate region, either a small island or a portion of a larger one. The tribal chief was usually the first-born of the ranking family, one that could trace its descent back to the founder of the tribe. The concepts of *mana* (supernatural power) and *tabu* (restrictions imposed upon those infused with *mana*) were widely prevalent.

Today Tahiti and the other islands of French Polynesia form a more dynamic society which combines its early Polynesian beginnings with more than 200 years of contact with the outside world. The social and economic scene fuses with European, American, and Asian influences. On Tahiti alone, some 80,000 Tahitians, French and Chinese, a few Americans, and people of other nationalities live and work together.

As is true in so many of these tropical islands, the Chinese are the industrious ones. The European, Tahitian, and tourist alike depend upon the Chinese for French bread and most of the meat and vegetables that go into the fine French cooking. But Chinese restaurateurs look to the Tahitians for fish and fruit. And the French, of course, furnish the wines.

Formerly the traditional Tahitian home was the thatch-roofed *fare*, a compound of separate living, sleeping, and cooking areas. In Papeete, the *fare* has given way to a conventional-type home built of wood or concrete blocks. Elsewhere on the island you still see numerous dwellings with roofs of thatch or corrugated iron, windows and doorways curtained in bright *pareo* prints. (*Pareo* is the cloth; *pareu* is the traditional Tahitian garment.) As a rule, the kitchen unit is still a separate structure, although Tahitians now use butane as a cooking fuel rather than the once commonly used hot stones in hole-in-the-ground ovens. The usual dwelling in villages outside Papeete does not use electricity because the electric lines only run about 10 miles either side of Papeete. In Tahiti, where the gathering of food is possible only in daylight hours, the islanders rise early and retire early.

Religion

Basically Tahitians are a church-going people; worship has an important place in their lives. Protestant churches, first established after the missionaries disembarked in Matavai Bay from the *Duff* in 1797, claim more than 40,000 members. The Catholics have the same number of worshippers at the Cathedral of Place Notre Dame in Papeete and at churches in other parishes. Among other religious sects are Mormons, Seventh Day Adventists, and Buddhists.

PAPEETE

Papeete is a sprawling waterfront town with a city beat that belies its subtropical location. Languor

SAY IT IN TAHITIAN

In Tahiti, French is the official language, and most islanders speak—or at least understand—English as well. But the Tahitians also speak Tahitian.

You'd have to be something of a linguist to learn enough Tahitian to carry on a whole conversation, but anyone can learn some simple basics of pronunciation and a few common phrases. If you do, it not only makes your Tahiti adventure more meaningful, but Tahitians will be pleased by your attempt to learn *their* language.

The Tahitian language had no written form until early missionaries attempted to put it down. They used a simple 13-letter alphabet, and it has survived as such to this day. There are five vowels (a,e,i,o,u,) and eight consonants (f,h,m,n,p,r,t,v). First let's tackle pronunciation. The vowels are pronounced the same as in Latin, but if you don't remember much Latin, memorize the following:

a—pronounced as in father

e—usually pronounced as a in may but sometimes a shorter *eh* sound

i—pronounced as e in be

o—pronounced as o in go

u—pronounced as u in dude

In such languages as Italian and Hawaiian, much more emphasis is placed on vowels—especially on *pronouncing* vowels—than in English. This is also true of the Tahitian language.

Each syllable in Tahitian ends with a vowel. Each vowel, when following another vowel, should be pronounced as a separate syllable.

Frequently three will be grouped together, in which case all three should be distinctly pronounced. As an example: in the word *Faaa* (the international airport), each of the three a's is distinctly pronounced (Fah-AH-ah). It means "burnt valley."

In general, Tahitian words are accented on the next to last syllable. The conspicuous exception to this occurs when an apostrophe separates the last vowel and the vowel preceding it. Then both vowels, or syllables, are given equal emphasis. For example: *mataura'a* (meaning "custom") is pronounced: mah-tah-oo-RAH-AH.

Consonants are easy because they're pronounced the same as in English. The Tahitian language has no silent letters. Two consonants never occur without a vowel separating them.

Now for a few words and phrases:

Hello! . . . *Ia-ora'na* (ee-ah-oh-RAH-NAH)
How are you? . . . *Maita'i oe* (mah-ee-TAH-EE OH-ay)
I am fine . . . *Maita'i vau* (mah-ee-TAH-EE VAH-oo)
Thank you very much . . . *Mauruuru roa* (mah-oo-roo-OO-roo ROH-ah)
Goodbye . . . *Parahi* (Pah-RAH-hee)
To your health! . . . *Manuia* (Mah-noo-EE-ah)
Please repeat . . . *Tapiti* (Tah-PEE-tee).

Now go back and practice saying Papeete (Pah-peh-AY-tay) a few more times, and it will all come naturally.

---

is not part of its charm. People are out on the sidewalks before 7 in the morning, and by 7:30 most businesses are open. The narrow streets become choked with automobiles and open air buses, motor scooters, and motor bikes. Riders, wearing bright *pareo* prints and with flowers tucked in their hair, fly by, only to become tangled in the next block's traffic jam. As long as you're not in a hurry, this early morning confrontation is an interesting kind of spectator sport—a traffic jam of Gauguin models on motor scooters. If you miss seeing the tangle of traffic in the morning, you can be sure there will be another in the afternoon between 4:30 and 5:30.

Papeete is not waiting for the arrival of the jet age—it's already here. The skyline is changing because of a rash of new buildings. Even the celebrated Quinn's—"most famous bar in the South Pacific"—is slated for displacement. Papeete-town is fast becoming a city, decked out with stop lights and divided traffic lanes. Its population is about to go over the 25,000 mark.

The village appearance is still here on Sundays, though, when almost everything is closed. Then it's a town reminiscent of a stage setting with the new and the old, the exotic and the ordinary, all crammed together. When Monday arrives, this stage setting comes to life; the play is on.

If you arrived in Tahiti by air, you would have landed at Faaa International Airport, about three miles from Papeete. But if you arrived by sea, your ship would have nosed through the shimmering lagoon to tie up close to Papeete's main street that runs along the waterfront. Papeete means "basket of waters"; the main street is the rim of the basket. This rim street is a series of *quais*, starting on the southwest with Quai de l'Uranie, which merges into Quai Bir-Hakeim, then Quai du Commerce, and lastly Quai Gallieni.

In the past few years, Papeete's waterfront has changed. This rim road, which used to be a hodgepodge of old shacks and souvenir vendors, is now a wide boulevard, divided by a grass strip, edged with sidewalks. Where old warehouses once stood, handsome new buildings have been built (among them the offices of the Tahiti Tourist Development Board). An important part of the waterfront color remains, for you can still stroll by the yachts that tie up right to the edge of the sidewalk, their sterns toward you bearing markers that read like a roll call of world ports. Equally fascinating is the hodge-podge of yachtsmen, passengers, and crews.

On the land side of the *quais* are sidewalk cafes, large stores, mercantile houses, the post office, shipping and airline headquarters, and tourist offices. Farther on are the small shops, the famous early-morning Papeete market (also the starting point for buses and taxis), the Governor's Residence and the Territorial Assembly Building, the cathedral, and the Musée de Papeete, the town museum. The residential areas stretch along the coast on each side of town and toward the hills.

In Papeete, stop and see and do ...

Art galleries. Two galleries have changing exhibits of local art; they welcome visitors: Galerie Winkler, on Passage Vaima, and Noa Noa, on Place Notre Dame. Call ahead for the exact hours of each gallery.

Camera events. For the avid photographer, there are special tours and events scheduled during daylight hours that offer a glimpse of island life. Some hotels schedule a weekly program of dances especially for the visitor with camera. Local travel agents offer a tour by *Le Truck*, taking you to a beachside home in one of the rural districts outside Papeete. Here you can photograph such traditional activities as dancing, coconut tree climbing, coconut husking, and net casting. Inquire at your hotel for information about these events.

Churches. Visitors are welcome at Tahitian churches. Typical services contain a rich program of music, highlighted with hymns sung by *a capella* choirs of splendid voices. Tahitian women attending church wear delicately woven Sunday hats and white frocks; men generally dress in suits, white shirts, and ties.

The Protestant Temple de Paofai, on Quai de l'Uranie, has an English language service at 8 a.m. and one in Tahitian at 10:30 a.m. every Sunday. A second Protestant church, Temple Bethel, is on Rue Edouard Ahnne. Papeete's Roman Catholic services are held in the Cathédrale Notre Dame, at Place Notre Dame, and in Église Sainte Thèrese, on Cours de l'Union Sacrée. Offering other services are the Mormon Chapel on Avenue du Commandant Chesse; Sanito Temple (related to Mormonism); and Temple Fare Ute, on Fare Ute. In addition, Buddhists, Seventh Day Adventists, and Jehovah's Witnesses all have houses of worship.

MOTOR BIKE, SCOOTER, *and automobile pass Cathédrale Notre Dame in the center of Papeete.*

Food and drink. Given time and a little local gourmet counsel, you'll find a number of excellent restaurants in Papeete serving French, Chinese, and Italian cuisine. If you forego the expensive wines, most meals will cost less than five dollars. A few small Chinese-style restaurants in the area of the market serve good meals for about a dollar.

Wines and liquors are plentiful, and the local beers (Hinano and Manuia) are inexpensive and very good. Tahiti, of course, harvests a wealth of shellfish and other seafood, served in fascinating concoctions. Fruits and vegetables are in glorious abundance; your breakfast tray is sure to have on it a papaya, mango, or grapefruit, if not all three and more. Hearts of palm salad served with fresh watercress makes a good starter for a lunch of *mahimahi* (dolphin), prepared with a butter sauce and served with a dry Sauterne. Try these other Tahitian tantalizers: rock oysters served on the halfshell; coconut water in the shell, served as an afternoon refresher; marinated raw fish salad.

Besides the first-class hotels which usually offer excellent French cuisine, many enjoyable French restaurants are scattered throughout Papeete and the immediate environs: Le Belvédère and La Chaumière (both a few kilometers out of town on a hilltop with fine views); Le Bougainville, Chang Feng, Pitate, Restaurant de l'Aéroport, Chez Jean, Le Maori, and Routiers de Mer. Other restaurants serve Chinese cuisine: A la soupe Chinoise, Le Dragon d'Or, Prince Hinoi, Waikiki, Pitate Mamao, Te Hoa, and Liou Fong.

Glass-bottom boat ride. A tour of Papeete's lagoon in a glass-bottom boat will reveal a huge, natural aquarium with fascinating coral formations and brightly colored fish. Boats leave from the Papeete harbor front (near the Post Office) in the morning, and from the Maeva Beach Hotel in the afternoon every day except Thursday and Sunday. The *Manurere*, a 36-foot craft which carries up to 30 passengers, cruises out to the barrier reef and back in two hours. Check with your hotel desk for scheduled departure times.

Government Center. The buildings comprising the seat of the French Polynesian government are located just a block off the waterfront Quai Bir-Hakeim at Avenue Bruat. Flanking the avenue are the executive and judicial offices of the Territory, and to the east are the handsome Governor's Residence and the Territorial Assembly Building standing on a park-like expanse. In the latter building, the 30 elected members of the Assemblée Territoriale of French Polynesia meet at least twice a year.

BUSINESS BUILDINGS with second story verandas still line Papeete's shorefront avenue.

Scheduled sessions begin in mid-May and mid-October and continue for about two months. The government buildings are relatively new and are of particular architectural interest.

Marché Papeete. Papeete's municipal market may well be the best show in town any day of the year. The earlier you go, the better the spectacle. The marketplace is a block inland from Quai du Commerce, and the curtain goes up at 5 a.m. at the open-air, roofed market place. It's then that the serious business of buying and selling fish, fruits, vegetables, flowers, and a hundred other kinds of merchandise begins. The fish are exotic, and so are the fruits and vegetables: *fei*, a red banana that is cooked; taro root, used in *poi*; *ate tamarin*, which looks like a bean; *uru*, a breadfruit. It's one of those places where you're prompted to ask, "What is it?" every time you move to a different stall. Friendly Tahitians, pleased that you ask, smilingly answer.

Sunday is the principal market day of the week. Tahitians come to town from villages all around the island to sell their products, traveling on Saturday, sleeping at the market that night, arising before dawn on Sunday. Many of Papeete's housewives do their week's shopping that day; others shop during the week—especially around 4 in the afternoon on Friday. So the "best" day at market might be any day you can make it. The visitor who can't get to Marché Papeete at 5 a.m. can go at 6:30 or 7. It's a good show as long as it lasts (activity slacks off by late morning except on Sunday when the market closes at 8 a.m.).

Museums. The Musée de Papeete is located on the Rue Brea, two blocks up from Quai Bir-Hakeim. Operated by the Societé des Etudes Océaniennes (Society of Oceanic Studies), it contains many archeological and ethnological artifacts of Polynesia. Tapa cloth, stone statues, weapons, canoes, and wood carvings are all displayed in the space-cramped *musée*. Outdoor areas are utilized for displays of large-size artifacts. Hours are 2 to 5 p.m., Tuesday through Saturday.

Tahiti's two other museums are outside Papeete. The Musée Gauguin is located 30 miles southeast of Papeete in the Papeari District. The Musée de la Découverte (the Museum of Discovery) is located about eight miles northeast of Papeete at Point Venus.

Night life. For a first-time visitor to Tahiti, the best way to get an extended view of night life in swinging Papeete is to take an after-dark tour. Most of the travel agencies in Papeete offer such tours. A typical tour includes visits to the most popular clubs—Quinn's, of course (while it lasts), Pu'o'oro

SHOPPING SURPRISES

American shoppers tuned to the merchandising rituals of Fifth Avenue or Wilshire Boulevard find a Polynesian adjustment needed in Tahiti. For here, both the shops themselves and the goods they sell create an atmosphere of surprise. In Papeete there is no "shopping district." Here, there, and everywhere, little shops are tucked between big businesses and various other kinds of enterprises. You come across a shop when you least expect to. Walking inside, you'll discover anything from canoe paddles and Melanesian masks to hand-screened fabrics, jade carved miniatures, grass skirts, or maybe even an umbrella for that rainy day. Discovery is half the fun of shopping. But a few general directions can help the fun along.

About shopping hours: stores open at 7:30 a.m. and generally close between 11 a.m. and 2 p.m. and then re-open until around 5 p.m. On Saturdays, shops usually close around 11 a.m. They remain closed on Sundays. There are exceptions, of course. The Chinese-operated stores tend to stay open longer and later. Some are even open on Sundays, but don't count on it.

About bargains: everything is fairly expensive in Tahiti. Being situated a good distance away from almost anywhere helps to push up prices. "Bargains" are only relative. For instance, Paris perfumes are less expensive in Tahiti than they are in the U.S. but more costly than in Paris.

Chinese-operated stores generally sell merchandise that is lower priced than merchandise in Tahitian and French operated shops. But the Chinese generally stock goods that cover a wider range in quality, so the price spread is greater.

Numerous shops inside and outside of hotels stock ready-made Tahitian wear and almost anything else you might want.

Looking for something special? Here's a sample list of exotic and semi-exotic items sold at some Papeete shops. (If you're in a hurry, ask your hotel to direct you to the right shop.)

Dressmaker shops: Augustine, Celina Femina, Heloïse, Liliane, Marie Ah You, Rose Marie, Vogue; **grass skirts:** Christine, Elma Dexter, Manuia Curios; **hand-wrought jewelry:** A. Mouraueau; **Marquesan masks, carvings:** Jean Jacques Laurent, Manuia Curios, Polynesian Curios; **musical instruments:** Rony Tchia; **Oriental art:** Shangrila; **Paris styles:** Caprice de Paris, Chiffons, Elle et Lui, Femina, Sin Sing; **Polynesian printed fabrics:** Essor, Tahiti Art, Tapa; **shells:** Le Nautilus; **imported shoes (Italian, Spanish, French):** Bata; **skin diving gear:** Marine Corail, Tahiti Sport; **tapa:** Celina, Christine, Manuia Curios; **Tahitian records and tapes:** Celina, La Discothèque, Le Sagittaire; **umbrellas:** Select.

Don't forget the post office. If you have a philatelist on your list, Tahiti has exotic stamps, too.

FABULOUS FABRICS—some hand-blocked —delight many shoppers in Papeete. Below, woman sells strings of sea shells, woven hats, big baskets, smiling the easy Tahitian smile.

Plage, Zizou, Whiskey a Gogo, and after-hours spots such as Lafayette. In these places dancing is uninhibited, elbow room is at a premium, and the decibel count is on the high side. If it's atmosphere you want, you won't be disappointed. However, if your tastes run to less swinging establishments, choose a hotel bar or seek out a place like La Taverne.

Around the island

To discover the idyllic charm of Tahiti, take the 72-mile *Route de Ceinture*, or Belt Road, that encircles the larger portion of the island. This route reveals the island perimeter in all its green and flowering beauty. Flamboyant trees, spreading broad, colorful branches, flag your attention. Hibiscus towers higher than your head, with flowers that measure five or six inches across. The pink cassia sends down a shower of pale pink petals. Towering Malay apple trees mix with banana, papaya, avocado, tree fern, and the handsome breadfruit tree.

Trees aren't the only visual delight along the Belt Road. It goes past black sand beaches and outcrops of lava rock that thrust into the sea. It passes deep ravines cutting far inland and high peaks pushing up into the clouds. Every few kilometers you see a native village with churches, a school, and habitations. Landmarks at several places will bring island history into focus. Early on the trip you'll notice "mailboxes" filled with just-delivered French bread (the number of loaves usually being a good indication of family size).

To make this trip, you can hire a guide-driven car, drive a rental car, take a tourist bus, or have an adventure on *Le Truck*. The road is paved, has two lanes, and is not heavily traveled. If you start by 9 a.m., it's an easy one-day trip. You will have time for stopping at places of interest and a leisurely lunch and swim mid-way along the route.

If, in addition, you want to see some of Tahiti-iti, allow two days for the trip. You can stay overnight in a bungalow at the Te Anuanua Hotel in the village of Pueu on Tahiti-iti's north coast. It has 12 bungalows.

Driving clockwise from Papeete, points of interest along the Belt Road include the Tomb of Pomare V, the last monarch of Tahiti; the King's Burial Ground; One Tree Hill, the point of Tahiti that Captain Samuel Wallis first sighted in 1767; Point Venus, the site where Captain James Cook and his expedition observed the transit of Venus in 1769 (here also is the Musée de la Découverte with its wax figures of discoverers Wallis, Bougainville, and Cook, along with a fine collection of early day memorabilia); the Blowhole of Arahoho, where waves surge through a nozzle in the basalt rock; the three waterfalls of Faaruumai; the anchorage of Count Louis Antoine de Bougainville, who reached Tahiti in 1768 (the second European to do so); the Cascade de Vaiharuru on the Faatautia River (you can see the thin stream of water from the bridge); the Isthmus of Taravao, where roads to Tahiti-iti turn off from the Belt Road; the Harrison Smith Botanical Gardens and Musée Gauguin, adjacent to each other; the Cascade of Vahipahi, another lovely waterfall that spills into a small pool (the short walk up to it from the road gives you a better taste of the island's lush vegetation); Marae of Arahurahu, part of an ancient open-air temple or place of worship; and Maraa Grotto, a cool, fern-grown cave, the largest on the island.

Highlights of this island circling trip are the Musée Gauguin and the Botanical Gardens. The Harrison Smith preserve, now a public park, is an impressive collection of trees, shrubs, and flowers representing the contributions to Tahiti's vegetation from the rest of the tropical world. Towering trees, great stands of bamboo, smoke-like vines, lovely flowers—from Ceylon and India, the Malay world, South America and Africa.

If you make the circle trip in a day, stop for lunch at Le Rotui Restaurant (excellent buffet), Restaurant Felix Garbutt (good seafood), or the Taiarapu (French cuisine). A small pier at Rotui Restaurant has a *pareo*-walled dressing room where you can change for a refreshing swim before lunch. Sightseers who begin the circle island trip along the east coast will find any of the three restaurants convenient lunch spots. Those beginning on the west coast may find it easier to eat at the Musée Gauguin Restaurant (grilled steaks, chops, fish). You can also drive out along Tahiti-iti's north coast road to the Pueu district and have lunch at the Hotel Te Anuanua, situated on a beautiful bay.

If you like to explore and have the time, don't limit the trip to a day or two. Some fascinating trails lead into the island's interior—into the beautiful Papeuoo Valley in the north, to the top of 4,100-foot Mt. Aorai, to Lake Vaihiria at 1,420 feet, to Pierre Loti's pool. The roads that run along the north and south coasts of Tahiti-iti lead to small villages and areas most tourists don't see. At the end of each road, you can arrange for a boat ride to isolated villages, a tiny satellite island, some ancient ruins. Papeete-based travel agents can make arrangements for these adventure trips.

Active sports

Tahiti offers almost endless opportunities for both active and spectator sports enthusiasts.

Deep sea fishing in Tahiti rose to worldwide prominence in the 30's when Zane Grey hooked

STOP AND LOOK, on a drive around the island, at the Blowhole of Arahoho (right); the huge stone tiki outside Musée Gauguin (lower right); Marae Arahurahu, an ancient place of worship (lower left); Musée Gauguin, in effect, an illustrated chronicle of the artist's life (below).

GAUGUIN'S TAHITI..."A SKY WITHOUT WINTER"

To the world at large, the blazing canvases of Paul Gauguin epitomize the Tahitian people and their land. To those who visit Tahiti, the canvases of this bold colorist come to life.

Paul Gauguin left a comfortable livelihood as a Parisian stockbroker to become a virtually penniless painter. He led a tempestuous and frequently tormented life—that of an eccentric, lonely, proud, and arrogant man who had turned his back on the Bourse in favor of paint brush and palette.

In 1891, at the age of 42, Gauguin first sailed for Tahiti. Why did he point toward Tahiti—an island half-way around the world from France and, in the 19th century, not too far removed from being a terra incognita? For one thing, he was influenced by the writings of a contemporary, Pierre Loti (the pseudonym of Louis Marie Julien Viaud). His novel *Le Mariage de Loti* painted an ecstatic picture of Tahiti as a terrestrial paradise. In addition, Gauguin was moved by the descriptions recorded by French explorer Louis Antoine de Bougainville. And there were other compelling arguments in favor of Tahiti, among them a pronouncement by Vincent van Gogh: "The future of painting is in the tropics."

So it was that Gauguin came to Tahiti, to live for two years at the village of Mataiea on the coast south of Papeete. Then after a sojourn in France, he returned to the island and lived at Punaauia in Tahiti, and then at Atuona in the Marquesas for the last eight years of his life.

Today much of the world knows of Gauguin's Tahiti, where "pure and ardent colors dazzled and blinded." The impressions of Tahiti that he went on to record in heightened colors — on canvas, paper, burlap, and wood — have fired the imaginations of people who have never seen Tahiti. Gauguin's paintings can also vividly heighten one's own impressions of the Tahitian scene.

In retrospect, Paul Gauguin's years in Tahiti had tragic aspects. He was almost always penniless. Though he was accepted by the natives and lived with them, he was a lonely man — vain, proud, conceited, self-willed, ambitious. He reaped little of the sweet spinoff of success and public acceptance. That was to come after his death at age 54.

Now there is a museum at Papeari not far from Mataiea. Adjacent to the Botanical Gardens, the building consists of a series of rooms, open to the breezes, designed in the handsome Tahitian style, and set in a spacious, subdued tropical garden. A memorial dedicated to Paul Gauguin, it contains no original works. Instead, by means of photographs, maps, reproductions, and other graphic devices, it recreates the triumph and tragedy of this great artist.

LARGER THAN LIFE reproduction of self portrait of Paul Gauguin (left) in airy Musée Gauguin, where background and events in the life of the artist are depicted (below).

record and near-record game fish in these waters. (His record catches included a 63-pound dolphin, a 1,040-pound striped marlin, and a swordfish said to have been 30 feet long.) Since then deep sea fishing has continued to rouse fishermen's enthusiasm. In fact, professional anglers feel that Tahiti will one day rival Mexico and Florida.

You don't need a license to fish in Tahiti, nor are there any seasonal limitations. November through March are the best fishing months, December being prime time for the big ones in Vairao Bay off Tahiti-iti. The least productive months are August and September.

Among big game fish caught are black marlin, sailfish, mahimahi (dolphin), wahoo, tiger and thresher sharks, ocean bonito, barracuda, and several species of tuna (big eye, Allison long fin, yellow fin, and dog-tooth). Offshore game fish caught outside the reef include jack crevally, permit, rainbow runner, pompano, red snapper, red bass, giant sea bass, and bonefish. To introduce you to a fisherman's dream, consider the mahimahi: they grow to much larger size than those in U.S. waters, averaging 35 to 70 pounds and running four to six feet in length. When hungry, the mahimahi strikes at spoons, and—fasten your seat belts—since mahimahi run in pairs, often the catch is two at a time.

Fishing boats are available for charter at charges starting at $170 for a 10-place craft, $100 for a 4-place one. The charge generally includes bait, tackle, and beer or soft drinks; lunch is extra. The dedicated deep sea fisherman might do well to get in touch with Tahiti's Haura (meaning "marlin") Club (c/o Dave Cave, P.O. Box 582, Papeete, Tahiti). The club is affiliated with the International Game Fish Association and stages two fishing tournaments each year. Available to the public are the services of the organization's three scales and two weigh-masters. In addition the club will make boat reservations and provide prospective fishermen with information.

Skin diving attracts many visitors to Tahiti. Since the waters are warm, divers won't need wet suits. The chief attractions are coral formations and an abundance of tropical fish. For many skin divers, primary targets are the waters around Moorea and around Bora Bora.

In Papeete, you can rent diving equipment from Marine Corail on Quai Gallieni and Tahiti Sport on Rue du Commerce. Marine Corail also provides instruction, gives information, and takes groups on diving excursions.

On Tahiti two of the best skin diving areas are the black sand beach at Pirae, just north of Papeete, and the Isthmus of Taravao, between Tahiti and Tahiti-iti.

Although diving is possible at various places around the island any month of the year, conditions are best in the waters around Tahiti from June through September.

Spearfishing with aqualung is prohibited; so if you're stalking the big fish and can't free dive more than 60 feet, better set your sights on waters away from Tahiti.

Swimming is possible in hotel pools, ocean, and rivers. The best beaches are at Pirae, just north of town, and in the Punaauia area to the south. Water temperatures run about 72 to 75 degrees, and the view of Moorea from either area is superb. River swimming is best in the Punaruu and Paueuoo rivers; but hiking up any of the other river valleys, you'll find many more enticing spots.

Water skiing is good around the harbor off Papeete, in the Punaauia-Paea area, and along the beaches at Arue (just northeast of Papeete), and in the lagoons off Bora Bora and Moorea, Raiatea, and Huahine. Ask at your hotel about equipment and ski boats. Most hotels have them for rent.

Surfing is considered good along the north coast near Arue, along the beaches in the Papenoo district, and along the west coast in the vicinity of Paea. Boards can be rented in Papeete or obtained from the Surf Club.

Golfers can enjoy a relatively new golf course at Atimaono, opened in 1970. It's the island's first 18-hole course. (A 9-hole pitch and putt course is in operation at the Hotel Tahara'a.) The 6,355-meter, 72 par course of the Atimaono Golf Club has elevated tees, plenty of traps and water hazards. Greens fees are $5 a round, $2.50 for a second round on the same day. Weekly rates are $15. Players under 20 pay half these fees. Local boys and girls in *pareus* act as caddies. Golfers appreciate the modern clubhouse with restaurant and bar, as well as the well-equipped golf shop which has clubs for rent for visitors.

Tennis players will find courts and a tennis club one mile northeast of town at the Fautaua Stadium. Racquets are sometimes hard to come by, so it's best to bring your own.

Hikers learn early that Tahiti's mountainous interior (however beguiling it may appear) is rugged enough to warrant the help of a guide. The best way to arrange for one is to inquire at your hotel (ask them to contact Monsieur Jay in Mahina). Without a guide, it's advisable to stick to the trails in the valleys, resisting the urge to climb higher.

Horseback riders can push back into the untrammeled hinterlands of the valleys that lie beyond the belt road circling the island. Two stables in Pirae near the race course are Ranch Ker Breiz and Circle Equestre, both on the Route de Fare Rau Ape. At both, guides are available.

Spectator sports

The volatile Tahitians turn almost any spectator sport into a colorful performance.

Soccer, for instance, attracts vocal, enthusiastic crowds on Sundays at Fautaua Stadium, northeast of Papeete.

Horseracing, Tahitian style, is bareback, with amateur jockeys at the track in Pirae wearing *pareus* and *coronnes* of flowers. During the season running from April to November, races are held once a month, usually on the first Sunday. The biggest races are part of the Bastille Day celebrations (see page 37). Pari-mutuel betting adds some spice and excitement.

Cockfighting is another spirited crowd-pleaser. Young and old gather around the fighting rings, cheering and sometimes nearly upstaging the fighting cocks. Cockfights are held at certain private residences in Tahiti; your hotel can tell you where in the Paea district they are taking place.

Other regularly scheduled spectator sports are track, archery, volleyball, bicycling, boxing, and sailboat racing.

BORA BORA

Some, including James Michener, feel that Bora Bora is the most beautiful island in the world. It may well be. In any event, such a reputation should be reason enough to visit this reef-fringed, islet-encircled island that lies 140 miles northwest of Tahiti. A relatively small island, it's dominated by craggy mountain peaks that soar more than 2,000 feet above the sea.

Flying from Papeete takes less than an hour on non-stop flights, slightly more on flights that stop at Raiatea. From the Bora Bora airstrip, on a *motu* (or islet) just inside the encircling barrier reef, you go by boat to your destination: about 45 minutes to the Club Méditerranée's Hotel Noa Noa, about an hour to the Hotel Bora Bora.

It's possible to make the trip to Bora Bora and back in one day if you don't mind crowding your day with as many as five to six hours of travel. By taking a morning flight over and returning on a later afternoon one, you'll have time for lunch at the Hotel Bora Bora, a glass-bottom boat ride, and perhaps a spin part way around the island on a motor scooter or a bicycle. Or you can lazily relax at the hotel.

Tourist activities on the island center largely around the 75-room Hotel Bora Bora. Its white sand beach fronts an exquisite lagoon, famous for its underwater coral gardens. Situated 5½ miles from the village of Vaitape, the hotel has 10 acres

of tropical gardens, a boat pier, and a deep-water anchorage for yachts. The hotel is an important part of the island community whose population is just over 2,000. Villagers serve as maids and bus boys, or work in the kitchen and electric plants or on the grounds. On Saturday nights many of the island's residents gather at the hotel for the Polynesian-night activities. These parties often start out slowly as the islanders trickle in—the men dressed in tight white slacks, the women in long Mother Hubbards and bright *pareus*. When music and dancing begin, the atmosphere catches fire.

From a base at the hotel, you can take excursions in outrigger canoes or Polynesian sailing canoes; go on picnics on a *motu;* try lagoon fishing; take boat trips around the island; or see the coral gardens and fascinating marine life from a glass-bottom boat. Similar activities, but on a more restricted scale, are offered at the Hotel Noa Noa, a quarter-mile from the village of Vaitape and at the Oa Oa Yacht Hotel (8 bungalows) situated on Vaitape Lagoon.

You can also hop on a bus for a tour of the island. The 17-mile trip takes about 3 hours. Running along the sparkling lagoon, the road cuts through groves of coconut palms and passes the tiny village of Faanui, alongside the old seaplane base where American ships anchored in World War II. Here

PROFILES OF BORA BORA: a lone sailboat skirts the shore (above, center); church steeple soars above the village of Vaitape (upper right); deck of a bungalow hangs over the lagoon (lower right); a white-sailed outrigger rests on sandy shore of Bora Bora lagoon (above).

French Polynesia   27

APPROACHING HUAHINE. One of French Polynesia's most unspoiled islands; it now has a new small hotel.

you will see *maraes* (ancient altars) and pass a monument to Gerbault, who sailed around the world in a small boat. In the environs of Vaitape, you pass long tables loaded with curios and souvenirs for sale—skirts, baskets, shell *heis*, cultured pearls, and other jewelry.

However long you stay, you'll come away with a particular feeling for the serenity of this island: it's as calm and quiet a place as you can find. Bora Bora means "fleet of canoes with silent paddles." Once you've been there, you understand.

HUAHINE

By air Huahine is 80 miles northwest of Tahiti. Three 50-minute flights per week are scheduled in each direction. Huahine is the most unspoiled island of all; you have to be something of an island adventurer—to a mild degree, at least—to visit it.

The newly opened Bali Hai Huahine, with 12 thatched roof bungalows, is the island's first tourist-type hotel. Fare, the largest village on the island,

has other room rentals, all of a very modest type, available in local *fares* (or residences). For information about accommodations, contact the Tahiti Tourist Development Board in Papeete.

Huahine has a population of less than 3,000; people live by fishing and farming. At high water the island is really two islands divided by a strait: Huahine Nui (big Huahine) and Huahine Iti (little Huahine). Each has a mountain—the 2,331-foot Mt. Turi on Huahine Nui and the 1,495-foot Mt. Moufene on Huahine Iti.

Near the village and lake of Maeva, in the northern part of Huahine Nui are several ancient Polynesian temples and the ruins of 29 *maraes*, some of which are now being restored. You can take a taxi from Fare to Maeva and back for $6. Or if you prefer, you can ride in a modern mini-bus for $10.

Fun, also, is sightseeing by native canoe or motorboat. A canoe ride in a 50-seat canoe from Fare to the village of Haapu is a real adventure. Or there's a longer canoe ride to Parea; the ancient fish traps in the area are fascinating.

THATCHED ROOF fares of new Bali Hai Huahine are situated on water's edge; tree-shaded street on Huahine, deserted at midday is typical of uncrowded nature of French Polynesia's other islands.

MOOREA

From the Papeete area the view of Moorea with its high peaks shrouded in clouds or silhouetted against the setting sun is a memorable sight. It beckons; if you accept the invitation, you'll find Moorea to be a tranquil, small island of 85 square miles. Its population of about 5,000 is scattered around its shores. Beauty spots are two lovely bays, Cook's and Papetoai (Opunohu), separated by 2,884-foot Mt. Rotui. Dominating the whole island are the serrated peaks of Mt. Tohivea, pushing 3,975 feet into the clouds, and Mt. Muaputa, a toothlike peak of 2,592 feet.

You can get to Moorea from Papeete by air (10 minutes and about $10) or by launch (less than two hours and about $5). It's worth going the 11 miles at least one way by boat, even though the crossing can be rough on a windy day.

Most of the island's activities are associated with or arranged by the island's hotels. The two oldest, Aimeo and the Bali Hai Moorea, offer activities ranging from skin diving and sailing to island tours and *tamaaraas*. The newer hotels—the Mahana Village, the Maui Beach, Moorea Lagoon, and Tahiti Safari Club—also arrange activities for guests but generally on a less extensive scale. But all of them provide snorkeling and water skiing equipment. Hotels can also make arrangements for cruising or

for a picnic lunch at some remote beach or tiny offshore island. Some of them have entertainment at night; also worth a try is the bar at the One Chicken Inn, the small hotel in Paopao. At both the Aimeo and the Bali Hai, cottages are built out over the water, so all you have to do is walk down a ladder into that wonderfully warm water for a pre-breakfast swim.

In an entirely different category is the Club Méditerranée's village on Moorea. Part of a chain of resort complexes scattered around the world, the club was started with the younger set in mind. Facilities were kept simple and the prices low. Now the young have been joined at the Club by older travelers and families who also enjoy the informality and appreciate the bargain. Accommodations at the Club are offered only as part of a package arrangement which includes air transportation from Los Angeles or San Francisco, food, lodging, entertainment, and use of all sports facilities, instruction, and equipment.

Around-the-island tour. A 37-mile bus tour around the island takes about four hours and includes visits to small villages and spectacular views of volcanic peaks and coral strands. Stops include Paopao's Catholic Church with Pierre Heyman's impressive mural above the altar, and the octagonal church at the entrance of Papetoai Bay. Built

MOOREA IS THE PLACE to relax at Aimeo Hotel on Cook's Bay (upper left); to strum guitars and sing on board a canopied boat (lower left); to stay in one of Club Méditerranée's thatched bungalows (below).

in 1829, the church is the oldest European structure still being used in the South Pacific. At one of the Chinese stores along the way you'll find *pareo* prints, along with fresh fruits, canned vegetables, plastic dishpans, and bicycle tires. Skin divers will tell you the best diving is at Temae Beach, just east of Cook's Bay.

Interior island tour. You can get a good feeling for the interior of this island by taking the micro-bus trip up the Opunohu Valley. The drive, on a rather primitive road, lasts about half a day. You stop at several recently-excavated *maraes*, and you'll discover from a lookout shelter an absolutely spectacular view of the ocean and bays below and of Mt. Rotui above.

Tahitian feast and dancing. The Hotel Aimeo every Wednesday, the Bali Hai Moorea every Sunday, and the Moorea Lagoon on Fridays and Sundays are settings for Tahitian feasting and dancing. The *tamaaraa* (or traditional Tahitian feast) and the *otea* (or traditional native dancing) are combined into this highly festive occasion. You'll be entertained in exactly the same way Tahitians have entertained their guests for centuries. Don't miss the opportunity to attend while you're in Moorea. If you have only a day to spend on the island, choose a day that coincides with a feast. You can make the round trip by boat; sailing schedules are timed accordingly. Any travel agent in Papeete can make arrangements for you.

RAIATEA

Second only to Tahiti in size, the big island of Raiatea has much to offer a tourist; yet it remains one of the relatively unspoiled islands in French Polynesia. Easily accessible, the island is less than an hour's flight from Papeete; a dozen or more round trips are scheduled each week. The Hotel Bali Hai Raiatea at Uturoa has 24 bungalows (some over the water), serves meals, and provides the basic facilities for enjoying the island: bicycles, island tours, outrigger canoes, scuba equipment (and instruction), deep sea fishing boats, and excursion boats for exploring Raiatea or some of the other nearby islands.

Raiatea and its companion island of Tahaa are ringed with a barrier reef and share a common lagoon. About 30 miles in circumference, Raiatea is approximately twice the size of Tahaa. Each has a mountain peak: 3,389-foot Mt. Temehani on Raiatea and 1,936-foot Mt. Ohiri on Tahaa.

Uturoa, the main village of Raiatea, has a population of more than 2,500, making it the second largest town in the Society Islands. Most of the town businesses are operated by Chinese. Their small shops are crowded inside and out with *pareo* prints, handmade baskets, native carvings, and island necessities such as groceries and motor bikes. You'll find prices in Uturoa lower than elsewhere in the Society Islands. If you can come to Uturoa on a Wednesday, by all means do. That's the town's market day, the day when natives come from all over the island, usually by outrigger or small boat, to sell their produce. Fish and fruit and vegetables, pigs, ducks and chickens all stock the marketplace on Wednesday. Fridays and Sundays are also market days but on a considerably smaller scale.

Raiatea was the original "Havaiiki," the site of the ancient Polynesian civilization. This was the place from which the Hawaiian Islands took their name, as well as the place of origin of New Zealand's Maori colony. Marae Taputapuatea was once the most important *marae* in the South Pacific. A great international temple which figured in the traditions of New Zealand's Maoris, it was the ancient seat of knowledge and religion, known as the home of the island's fire-walking cult—a cult that still exists to this day.

Activities and excursions to historic and scenic points of interest can be arranged through the Bali Hai Hotel. Among the possibilities are these:

Faaroa River. Traveling up the Faaroa River takes you to the original home of New Zealand's Maoris. By motor-canoe or speedboat you pass Polynesian huts hanging on the shores. As you move beyond reach of roads, all signs of habitation disappear. The original homeland of the Maoris is now overgrown with tropical vegetation.

Waterfall of Opoa. Waterfall viewing takes a full day when you start your journey from the Bali Hai Raiatea. The trip includes picnic lunch, swimming

AT A TAMAARAA, *the* tamure, *a spectacular dance is performed to drum accompaniment after island feast.*

FIRE WALKING is a ritual in Raiatea, where barefooted natives stroll across white-hot stones.

TAMAARAA IN TAHITI . . . PIG AND POI, MUSIC AND MOTION.

Tamaaraa, the word for feast in Tahiti, means more than just a meal of baked pig and *poi*. The Tahitian *tamaaraa* is a combination of ingredients: a special Polynesian meal followed by Tahitian music and group dances.

TAHITIAN TAMAARAA *PRELIMINARIES, starting hours before feast begins, include wrapping food in leaves, cooking it on hot stones.*

Excellent *tamaaraas* are offered every week by the hotels on Moorea. You make a day of it, boarding the big launch in Papeete about 9 in the morning and leaving Moorea around 9 in the evening.

When you reach Moorea, you'll be welcomed at the hotel dock by musicians and girls with flower *heis* (like the Hawaiian lei) for the guests. The rest of the morning is free for swimming, snorkeling, bicycling, or just relaxing on the hotel grounds.

Buffet lunch may be followed by a short show for photographers, featuring music and dances and Tahitian net throwing. Another activity might be a sightseeing jaunt by *Le Truck* to Cook's Bay and then back to the hotel to watch some of the preparations for the evening feast. Preparations begin with the placing of the pig in the *ahimaa* (earthen oven). The climax of the day is the feast itself, followed by the *otea* (Tahitian dance) performed by torchlight.

The *tamaaraa* menu usually consists of pig, breadfruit, and big bananas, all cooked in the *ahimaa*. To this basic list may be added chicken and fish, marinated raw fish, taro, and Tahitian *poi*, local fruit (such as papaya, bananas, oranges, Tahitian grapefruit, mangoes), accompanied by iced coconut water.

If your stay in Tahiti doesn't coincide with one of the weekly *tamaaraas* on Moorea, check with a local travel agent or tour operator. Several variations of the *tamaaraa* take place during the week in Papeete and its environs, some at the resorts on the other islands.

---

in clear calm waters, shell hunting, and a 30-minute walk to the Opoa Waterfall, cascading 200 feet into a large pool.

Tahaa. A launch leaves Uturoa every morning for the trip across the lagoon to Tahaa. First stop is Tiva, a small village. Here you visit Chief Tavana's home which has a shark aquarium, a turtle pool, and a museum of sea relics. The boat usually stops for a picnic, and you are treated with spectacular views of Bora Bora and Raiatea.

Visiting maraes. You can arrange at the Bali Hai Raiatea to be driven to the Taputaputea Marae and the Tevaitoa Marae, second most important *marae* on the island, now standing next to a new Protestant church at Tevaitoa.

Fire walking. Ask about the fire walking ceremony at the Bali Hai Raiatea. The ritual, in which some 40 natives of the village of Apoiti participate, is sometimes held on the grounds of the hotel.

RANGIROA

Rangiroa, largest of the 81 fabulous coral atolls of the Tuamotu Archipelago, is accessible by air from Papeete. The flight takes 90 minutes; round trips are scheduled twice a week. At the present time, a small pension with bar and restaurant offers rustic accommodations, and a new hotel, the Kia-Ora Village, will have 20 bungalows. You can also make arrangements to stay in a private home. Many Rangiroa homeowners rent rooms and serve meals to tourists. You can get in touch with these Rangiroans by inquiring at the Rangiroa airport.

Skin divers regard Rangiroa as offering the finest diving in the world. Skin diving groups, either camping out or staying in island residences, generally include it on their South Pacific itineraries.

Only two villages are established on Rangiroa, Tiputa and Avatoru, each with fewer than 500 inhabitants. The island is bordered by white sand beaches and low-leaning coconut palms. At its center is a large lagoon. Natives, wearing goggles and carrying baskets, dive in the lagoon for oysters. Papayas, bananas, taro, arrowroot, and manioc (a tree with an edible, starchy root) are abundant on the island.

PRACTICAL INFORMATION

Entry regulations

Without a visa a United States citizen may stay in Tahiti for 30 days provided that he has a round-trip ticket or a ticket to an onward destination. For longer visits, a tourist visa is required. This is good for three months, extendable for another three for a total of six months only within the calendar year. A tourist visa is available from any French consulate at a modest cost.

A valid smallpox vaccination certificate is also required for those entering Tahiti.

Local regulations

Before luggage is unloaded, aircraft and ship cargo compartments are closed for 10 minutes for spraying. Fresh flowers must be left aboard plane or ship.

For tourists arriving from Fiji or Pago Pago, specific regulations are enforced to protect the coconut trees from certain pests found on some islands in the South Pacific. All baggage except hand luggage must be fumigated on arrival. Goods subject to contamination by fumigation (this includes film, exposed and unexposed) should be carried in hand luggage. Because the fumigation process takes about two hours, it's wise to carry a bag containing clothing and toilet articles for a night's stay. Baggage held in bond normally is left at the airport and can be picked up later the same day or the following day. Ask your hotel clerk or tour guide to take care of this for you.

A visitor leaving Tahiti-Faaa on an international flight pays a departure tax of 400 CFP, a portion of which is for airport taxes and porterage fees.

Customs

When entering Tahiti, you are allowed to bring in 400 cigarettes or 50 cigars or one pound of tobacco, and one quart of liquor. Photographers are allowed two still cameras, one movie camera (but it must be less than 16 mm), and a total of 10 rolls of unexposed film duty free.

Currency restrictions

No limit is placed on the types or amounts of currencies you bring in, and you can leave Tahiti with all the unused foreign currency that you declared on entry.

Currency exchange and banking

The monetary unit in Tahiti is the Coloniale Franc Pacifique, usually written "CFP" (or just "frs") and called "French Pacific franc" (or the shorter "franc"). With a floating dollar, exchange rates will vary, but you can figure approximately 85 francs for one U.S. dollar. One franc equals 100 centimes. In pricing, 50 francs, 25 centimes would be written 50.25 frs.

Banking hours are 7:45 a.m. to 3:30 p.m. Monday through Friday. Papeete has two banks—the Bank of Indochina and the Bank of Tahiti. The Bank of Indochina, with offices at 22 Place Notre-Dame and on the waterfront on Rue Clappier, maintains a foreign exchange counter at Faaa International Airport that is open for all international arrival and departure flights.

Carry your funds in travelers checks. Bank checks—even cashier's checks—can take up to a month to clear.

Climate

French Polynesia has a tropical climate cooled by trade winds during the day. At night a cool breeze (hupe) blows down from the mountains. Warmed to an average temperature of 78°, Tahiti toasts in sunshine about 225 days a year.

Tahiti's climate is at its best during the cool and dry season from March through November, when average temperatures range from 64° to 72° and humidity averages 78 percent. During the warm and moist season from December through February, you can expect from 13 to 18 days of rain during a month. Temperatures will range between 72° and 90°; humidity averages about 78 percent. In August and September, Bora Bora sometimes is subject to southerly winds of high velocity.

Communications

One English language newspaper is published in Tahiti, as well as three daily newspapers in French. Radio Tahiti broadcasts in French and Tahitian. One television station, financed by the French Government and carrying no commercials, broadcasts in French every evening from 6 to 9:30 p.m.

The Papeete post office, located at Quai Bir-Hakeim and Rue Pomare IV on the waterfront, houses the local telephone exchange, radio communications, and general post office. Most of the operators speak English. A three-minute telephone call to the United States costs about $13.

Health and medical

You can safely drink Tahiti's tap water and eat almost anything in the way of foods, including raw fruits and vegetables.

Though the islands have long been free of malaria, in some areas you will find that a mosquito repellent makes your life much more comfortable.

Cuts from live coral *must be treated as soon as possible* to prevent serious infection. Good doctors and dentists, a large hospital, some private clinics, and several pharmacies are available in Papeete.

For information

Two of the best sources of information in Papeete are the Tahiti Tourist Development Board, located off Rue du Commerce at Rue Paul Gauguin, and the Syndicat d'Initiative, on Quai Bir-Hakeim. Both organizations have capable staffs to provide you with maps and brochures and to give information about sightseeing, shopping, hotels, or restaurants.

Other excellent sources of information are travel agents and tour operators in Papeete who can arrange for car rentals or guide-driven automobiles, make reservations for other islands, and line up fishing and hiking guides.

Tipping

Tipping is tabu in Tahiti, a rare situation indeed in the world today! A tourist doesn't have to puzzle over unfamiliar coins and wonder whether he's giving an adequate tip. Not having to tip goes far toward creating a genuine friendliness. You feel people do something for you because they want to, not because they're hoping for a big tip.

Where to stay

In Tahiti there are large hotels and small ones, luxurious ones and simple, unpretentious ones. The two largest in the Papeete area are The Maeva Beach and the Tahara'a Inter-Continental. Each is

HOTELS, old and new, include Hotel Tahiti (right); Maeva Beach Hotel (lower left); and Hotel Tahara'a Inter-Continental (below).

a modern, high-rise structure surrounded by gardens and trees. Both have superb pool areas, access to good beaches, and all of the amenities. Most other accommodations tend to be thatch-roofed *fares* or bungalows, scattered around extensive grounds, usually with larger thatched lounge and dining rooms open to the air. Among the smaller hotels in and around Papeete are the Princess Heiata, Royal Papeete, Royal Tahitien, Tahiti, Tahiti Village Beach, and Te Puna Bel Air hotels.

The only hotel on Tahiti outside the environs of Papeete is the Te Anuanua Hotel on Tahiti-iti, at Pueu village, about 12 miles off the *Route de Ceinture* at Taravao.

A number of the island's hotels provide traditional Tahitian feasts. Many present folk and modern dances and entertainment, as well as facilities for sports and sightseeing. Most hotels in Tahiti are on the European plan. On the outer islands you will find that meals normally are included in the room rates (for where to stay on the outer islands, see details under each island heading, beginning on page 26).

Because the number of tourists to Tahiti is increasing yearly, shortage of hotel space occurs more often these days; so reservations well in advance are recommended.

For help in selecting hotels, check with your travel agent, or write to the Tahiti Tourist Development Board, P.O. Box 65, Papeete, Tahiti, for a list of hotels. With a list in hand, you can mull over the possibilities, selecting a hotel located at the edge of a lagoon or on the side of a cliff, a bungalow over the water or in a garden, a simple room for $8 or a suite in one of the big hotels for $65.

How to get around

By taxi. Any way you do it, getting around Papeete is fairly expensive. For one thing, the biggest tourist hotels are located five miles or more outside of Papeete. Then taxi rates are high. For instance, it's $5 or more, as a rule, to go from Papeete to the Maeva Beach Hotel, five miles out of town. The taxi fare from Faaa International Airport to your hotel probably won't be less than $3 and may be more than $6, depending on the hotel location. Some hotels outside Papeete provide mini-bus shuttles that connect with international flights and also operate on regular schedules to and from Papeete. Between 11 p.m. and 6 a.m., taxi rates double. On taxi trips outside of Papeete, it's advisable to reach an agreement with the driver before starting.

By guide-driven cars. Private cars with English speaking drivers and carrying up to four passengers cost a little less than $10 an hour.

By rental car. If you plan to do at least an average amount of sightseeing, you're money ahead in a rental car. A small Fiat 600 rents for about $8 a day plus 20 to 25 cents per mile. Rates are substantially less on a weekly basis. Some companies have special two-day rates of less than $15 including unlimited mileage.

For your own peace of mind while driving around Tahiti, it's advisable to take the collision insurance. To say that traffic is somewhat wild may be an understatement. It's not that motorized Tahitians are reckless. It's that they drive their automobiles, motor bikes, and motor scooters with an excess of *joie de vivre!*

Best advice for anyone tempted to rent motor bikes or scooters is *don't.* They are too hazardous in Papeete traffic to classify as practical transportation.

By bus (or *"Le Truck").* Public transportation is Tahiti's one great bargain—and beyond that, it's

TAKE A RIDE on Le Truck *for fresh air, occasional surprises and a native's eye view of Tahiti.*

fun. Papeete's municipal transport system is comprised of a large and multi-colored fleet of open air trucks, benches on both sides and baggage racks on top. Passengers can ride any number of miles for a small charge. It's a mild kind of adventure that you shouldn't miss, even if your interests don't run to great bargains. Look for *Le Truck* terminal area at the Papeete public market. Once a trip begins, stops are made wherever passengers choose to get off. Apart from these ground rules, the Tahiti bus system isn't laced with the crisp logic and efficiency of its Parisian counterpart. (In Paris you take a number from a little box and board your bus calmly in numerical order.) Vehicles don't have numbers or letters; no route chart is posted to help you determine where each bus goes. But you can ask. And you can get off when you want, sooner or later catching another bus back. Each *Truck* serves a certain district—with the district marked on the side. If you want to try getting around like a Tahitian, make a note of your hotel district.

By boat. On a daily basis the only regular inter-island boat service runs between Papeete and Moorea. The trip takes close to two hours (and is sometimes a rough one). Sailings leave Papeete between 9 and 9:30 a.m., returning at 5:30 p.m. On feast days (Wednesdays at the Hotel Aimeo and Sundays at the Hotel Bali Hai), additional departures from Moorea are scheduled later in the day so that visitors can attend the *tamaaraa* (see page 32) and still return to Papeete the same day. Almost as great a bargain as a *Le Truck* ride, the round-trip on board either the *Maire* or the *Keke II* is about $5 per person.

For cruising through the wonderful French Polynesian world of the outer islands, charter arrangements are possible. A travel agent can put you in touch with the proper organizations if he doesn't handle this himself.

If you yearn to prowl among the little islands clustered in the archipelagoes of French Polynesia, sailing on a charter craft (either motor or sail) with bunk space for six or more is the next best thing to having your own boat. The diesel driven *Maeva III*, for example, can take passengers to Rangiroa or to Huahine and Tahaa in the Leewards, where the South Pacific still seems a world apart. The charge is $180 per day; this fee does not include food and drink.

Sailing buffs can charter ketches, schooners, and trimarans. On board one of the South Seas Windjammers, you could sail from Tahiti to Moorea, Tetiaroa, Huahine, Raiatea, Tahaa, Bora Bora, and return in two weeks. By adding another week, you could include Rangiroa, Manihi, and Tikehau, all in the Tuamotus. Charter rates for a ketch bunking up to six people are $1,600 per week. Food and drinks cost an additional $10 per person daily. A trimaran with space for 10 persons is available for day-charter. Cost is $23 per person, plus $5 for lunch and drinks.

Intermittent schooner sailings out of Papeete take passengers to other islands, both the well-known and relatively nearby ones and the little known remote ones. These vessels travel from island to island on voyages that take from 5 to 45 days, providing the only way to reach many of the islands in French Polynesia. Costs are very low, but accommodations are spartan. For information write to the Tahiti Tourist Development Board.

By air. Two regional airlines offer regular scheduled air service from Papeete to the outer islands. Air Polynésie has many round-trip flights a day to Moorea. Flying time between Faaa International Airport and Moorea's airfield in either a Britten Norman or a Twin Otter is 10 minutes. To Bora Bora, Air Polynésie schedules 18 round-trip flights per week. On non-stop flights, flying time is less than one hour. (On flights stopping at Raiatea en route, it's an hour and a half.) To Raiatea, there are 14 round-trip flights per week, and flying time is 55 minutes. To Huahine, round trips depart on Monday, Wednesday, and Saturdays; flying time is 50 minutes. To Rangiroa, in the Tuamotus, there are two round trips a week (Wednesday and Saturday), flights lasting an hour and a half. To the Marquesas (Ua Huka), two round trips a month are scheduled, via Rangiroa and Manihi. It's an eight-hour flight.

Air Tahiti flies smaller aircraft (six to nine passengers) between Papeete and Moorea in an "air bridge" shuttle service. The operation runs be-between dawn and dusk (approximately 6 a.m. to 6 p.m.). Planes take off from Faaa International Airport every 5 to 15 minutes, or whenever there is a planeload of passengers. Reservations are not necessary.

Round-trip air fares from Papeete are approximately $12 to Moorea; $44 to Bora Bora; $32 to Huahine; $11 to Raiatea; $54 to Rangiroa; $259 to Ua Huka.

Outer island transportation. You won't have the same options for getting around on the outer islands. Car rentals are available on Moorea (at the air strip) and on Bora Bora at Vaitape, but not on the other islands. Your hotel can usually arrange transportation within general limitations. Hotels generally have motor scooters, motor bikes, and push (or pedal-your-own) bicycles for rent at modest rates. Here you can ride scooters or bikes; there are few if any traffic hazards to cope with. And all of the hotels have boats available.

BASTILLE DAY—SOUTH PACIFIC VERSION

There's nothing like it in all the South Pacific. Bastille Day. It's a unique day, a day that runs into a week, then two weeks, then three . . . the way they celebrate it in Papeete town.

July 14 is the day of La Fête du Juillet, commonly called "the Fête." It gets under way at noon on July 13 at the sound of sirens and artillery shots. All kinds of activities follow: street parades, water floats, sidewalk booths, horse races, and carnival attractions. Special events unfold in leisurely succession—races, games, contests, singing, and dancing. The grand ball is especially opulent.

This may read like the description of a Fourth of July celebration or a county fair. It's not; it's half a world apart—or more. The parade, for instance, begins at 8 in the morning in the early-rising town of Papeete. Just one of the marching units is the French Foreign Legion. The Grand Ball takes place outdoors and is the one event of the year at which Tahitians wear semi-formal attire. Expect a kaleidoscopic Polynesian fashion show. This public ball, held on a specially constructed dance floor topped by strings of colored lights, lasts all night long.

Thatched roof booths called *Les Baraques* line the waterfront quais. Here you can buy anything from coconut milk to a glass of champagne; you can watch the action at the game booths and mobile dance halls, or you can join in.

Like the costumes, the events are kaleidoscopic. Watch a fruit carriers' race, in which participants carry close to 50 pounds on their shoulders as they run through Papeete streets. Follow outrigger canoe races, javelin throwing contests, bicycle races, and horse races. At the race track you'll see typically Polynesian jockeys riding bareback and wearing bright colored *pareus*.

Every night for at least a week there will be singing and dancing competitions. The sweet voiced choruses are a joy to listen to, the dancing of the super-fast *tamure* fascinating to watch. The participants who come from all over French Polynesia are a treat in themselves, and to the traveler, even the audience provides an entertaining show.

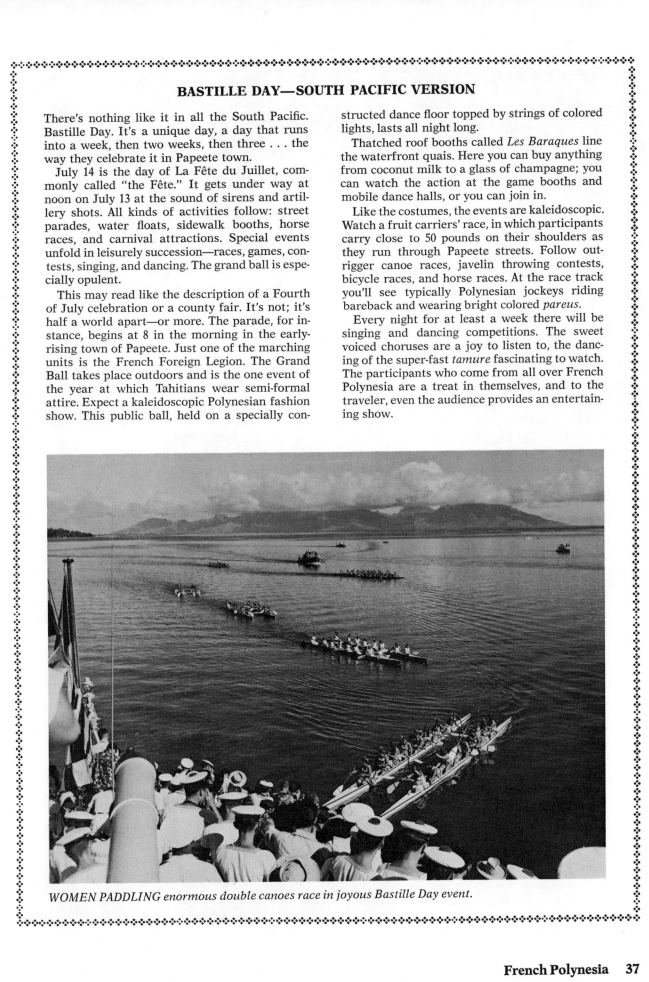

WOMEN PADDLING enormous double canoes race in joyous Bastille Day event.

IN MULTI-FACETED Fiji are villages such as this one, near Sigatoka, where pottery is made; towns where there's still a flavor of yesteryear—as on canal-lined Cumming Street in Suva (opposite page); and everywhere, smiling children.

Fiji... known as the happy islands

A FASCINATING BLEND OF MANY CULTURES AND MANY ISLANDS, BEGGING TO BE EXPLORED

You can't help liking Fiji. It's friendly. From the moment you enter by plane or ship, friendliness warms you like the waters of the South Seas. Dignified Fijians smile and say *ni sa bula* (hello)—not just once but time after time. There's a standing invitation for travelers to play or relax in modern towns or thatched-hut villages. Little wonder that visitors from all corners of the world consider Fiji one of the South Pacific's most hospitable areas.

Fiji takes pride in being known as the "happy islands." Here the beat of the *lali* drum calls you to *yaqona* (traditional drink of welcome), to feasting and ritual dancing. Laughter brightens the cricket fields, the lagoons, and the highlands. Listen for the sounds of Fiji: deep rhythmic vibrations (perhaps pounded out with bamboo lengths) of ancestral war chants, old-time hymns, or even Fiji "rock." Another type of rhythm—the pulsating jet roar of planes flown in and out of Fiji by 10 international airlines—has not dampened the jovial spirit of these islanders.

And the Fiji islands offer a fascinating blend of many cultures, of urban sophistication and rural simplicity, of a lifestyle that combines the primitive and the contemporary.

Viti Levu, the main island, will be your arrival point—Suva Harbor if you voyage by ship, Nadi (pronounced *Nan-dee)* International Airport if you travel by air.

These entry points, more than 100 miles apart on opposite ends of Viti Levu, are located along a 317-mile tourist road that encircles the island. Though this road leads you to many scenic contrasts and fine resorts, it is only a small sampling of what Fiji offers. In a week's time, you can extend your exploration inward to the highlands of Viti Levu or seaward to other islands. Fijians in these more isolated areas live almost as their ancestors

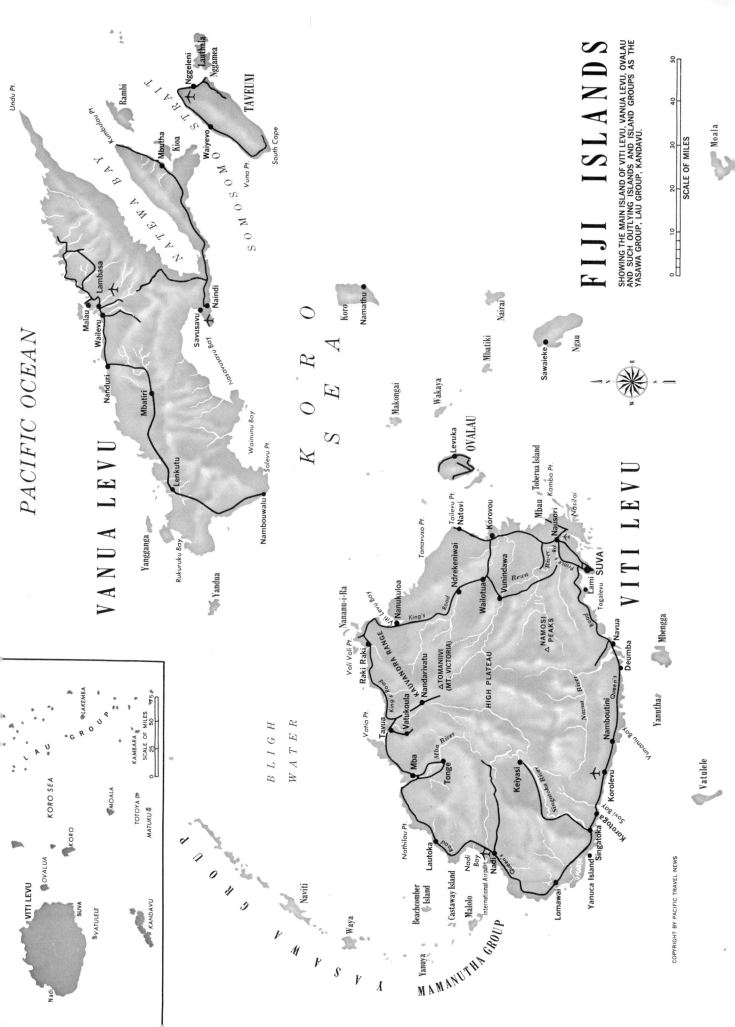

PACIFIC OCEAN

VANUA LEVU

Undu Pt.

Rambi

NATEWA BAY

Kumbulau Pt.

Malau
Wailevu
Nanduri
Mbatiri

Lambasa

Lenkutu

Nambouwalu

Yangganga

Yandua

Rukuruku Bay

Wainunu Bay

Solevu Pt.

Nasorusoru Bay

Savusavu

Naindi

S O M O S O M O   S T R A I T

Ngeleni
Lauthala
Nggamea

Mbutha
Kioa

Waiyevo

TAVEUNI

Vuna Pt.

South Cape

K O R O   S E A

Koro
Namathu

Makongai

Wakaya

Mbatiki

Nairai

Sawaieke

Ngau

OVALAU
Levuka

Toberua Island

Kamba Pt.

Nsilai

Mbau
Nausori

SUVA
Lami

Korovou
Ndrekeniwai

Natovi

Vunindawa

Wailotua

Taileu Pt.

Tanavuso Pt.

Nanukuloa

Nananu-i-Ra

Voli Voli Pt.

Raki Raki

Tavua

Vatukoula

Nandarivatu

K A U V A N D R A   R A N G E

King's   Road

King's Road

Vatia Pt.

Mba

Tonge

Keiyasi

Singatoka River

△TOMANIIVI
(MT. VICTORIA)

HIGH PLATEAU

△ NAMOSI
PEAKS

Rewa   River

Togalevu

Navua
Deumba

Namboutini

Nausori River

Queen's   Rd

Vunindi Bay

Yanutha

VITI LEVU

Mbengga

Vatulele

Korolevu
Korotonga
Singatoka

Sovi Bay

Yanuca Island

Lomawai

Nadi
International Airport

Nadi Bay

Castaway Island

Beachcomber Island

Malolo

Lautoka

Nathilau Pt.

Queen's   Road

Yanuya

Waya

Naviti

M A M A N U T H A   G R O U P

Y A S A W A   G R O U P

B L I G H
W A T E R

L A U   G R O U P

LAKEMBA
KAMBARA

MOALA
TOTOYA
MATUKU

KANDAVU

KORO SEA

OVALUA
KORO

VITI LEVU
SUVA
VATULELE

Nadi

SCALE OF MILES
0   25   50   75

FIJI ISLANDS

SHOWING THE MAIN ISLAND OF VITI LEVU, VANUA LEVU, OVALAU
AND SUCH OUTLYING ISLANDS AND ISLAND GROUPS AS THE
YASAWA GROUP, LAU GROUP, KANDAVU.

SCALE OF MILES
0   10   20   30   40   50

Moala

N   E   S   W

COPYRIGHT BY PACIFIC TRAVEL NEWS

did hundreds of years ago. Of the outer islands, some share Viti Levu's rugged and volcanic topography; others lie low and flat in atoll circlets. Many are rich in legend, beauty, and adventure.

Suva, Fiji's capital, is a fairly cosmopolitan city within the context of the South Pacific. Yet in some ways it seems not too far removed from the scenes of some yesteryear described by Somerset Maugham. Along Victoria Parade with its great Tahitian chestnuts arching over the street and its spreading flamboyant trees that drop a carpet of red at your feet, you pass turbanned Sikh and sari-clad Indian and coolie-coated Chinese. A uniformed sentry, resplendent in white skirt with deep-notched hem, guards the gate to Government House. Fiji's new flag with British emblem and Fijian shield ripples in the breeze.

Yet beyond the relative sophistication of Suva lie countless thatched-roof *bures* in countless villages that still cling to the old communal ways of life. (*Bure* is pronounced buray. The name originally meant bachelor quarters; today it means bungalow.) In the more isolated areas, Fijians live almost as their ancestors did hundreds of years ago. To village residents a time clock — even a kitchen clock—is unknown, for they live a sun-and-tides way of life geared to their fishing economy.

Geography

Depending on whether you count every little atoll or only the larger atolls and islands, anywhere from 300 to 500 islands make up the Fiji group. They straddle the 180th meridian just south of the equator, some 5,600 miles from the U. S. west coast —about 10 to 11 hours' flying time from San Francisco or Los Angeles by way of Honolulu.

As the major stopping point on north-south flights, Fiji has earned the distinction of being "the hub of the South Pacific." Suva's daily *Fiji Times* proclaims itself as "the first newspaper published in the world every day"—so it is, by virtue of Fiji's proximity to the International Date Line.

Fiji's largest island, Viti Levu, comprises some 4,000 square miles, more than half the total area of the Fiji Islands. Here are located the main centers of population: Suva, the capital; Lautoka, the center of sugar production; and Nadi with its international airport where the big jets come in.

Next in size is Vanua Levu. About half the size of Viti Levu, it lies north of its sister island and is reached by plane or boat from either Nadi or Suva. Several other islands and island groups — Tavenui, Kadavu, Ovalau, Vatulele, Yanuca, Beqa, Malololailai, Castaway, the Laus, the Mamanucas, and the Yasawas—all lie within visiting range from Nadi or Suva.

Mountain ranges of volcanic origin stretch along the larger Fiji Islands in a northeast-southwest line, creating marked differences between the windward and leeward sides. Heavy rainfall on the southeast, windward sides—up to 120 inches a year—creates dense tropical forests. On the northwest, leeward sides, rainfall is half as much, producing ideal conditions for growing sugar cane and the native reeds and grasses.

On Viti Levu alone there are 29 peaks with elevations of more than 3,000 feet. One of them, Mt. Victoria, reaches to more than 4,300 feet. Many rivers and small streams drain these ranges, the largest being the Rewa River, which flows down to the sea east of Suva and is navigable by punts and flat-bottomed launches for a distance of about 80 miles.

Fiji has its share of coral reefs, including the 350-mile Great Sea Reef west of Vanua Levu. Much of the coral elsewhere, however, lies in broken patches and fringing reefs along shore, rather than in long, lagoon-enclosing barriers.

History

Though it seems likely that Spanish navigators sailed through the Fiji Islands earlier than 1643, this is the year that history has awarded the honor of discovery to the Dutch navigator, Abel Tasman. Following Tasman, such well-known explorers as Captain James Cook and Captain William Bligh (of *Mutiny on the Bounty* fame) touched on these islands. But, other than the usual facts that are a part of recording a discovery, few details were known about the Fiji Islands until Christian missionaries came along after the turn of the 19th century.

Though everything the missionaries did can't be considered good, to them does go the credit for helping to abolish cannibalism. They also are responsible for being the first to reduce a Fijian dialect to writing. Their linguistic work eventually led to the publication of the New Testament in Bauan, a dialect later adopted as *lingua franca.*

Disturbed by inter-tribal wars for much of its early history, Fiji didn't become unified and somewhat peaceful until the mid-19th century, when a tribal chief of Bau, Ratu Cakobau, assumed leadership. After Cakobau found himself unable to resolve all the secular and religious problems, he tried in 1858 to give the islands to Great Britain. His offer was refused. Next he tried to give the islands to the United States. But because the United States was engaged in the Civil War, his offer was ignored. Britain, though, accepted a second offer; and under a Deed of Cession Fiji was annexed as a British Crown Colony on October 10, 1874.

FIJIAN LIFESTYLES reflect the traditional and the contemporary: bures (left) are built in villages; the police force includes both men and women; a drummer pounds on a lali drum (below); Sikhs among the Indian population wear traditional garb.

The islands prospered under the Crown for almost a century until October 10, 1970, when Fiji achieved full independence with Dominion status as a member of the British Commonwealth. It now has an elected House of Representatives, a Prime Minister, and a Governor General representing the British Queen.

Lifestyle

Fiji is a hodgepodge of racial strains, with two predominating. Its population numbers close to a half million. Of that number, more than 200,000 are Fijian, more than 240,000 are Indian, and the remainder are from other islands in the South Pacific, from Europe, from China, and a few from other parts of the world.

Predominantly Melanesian (with a strong influence of Polynesian strain noticeable in some), the Fijian people have a lively curiosity and intelligence, excellent manual dexterity, and a strong sense of rhythm. Whether they are walking along a road, serving guests in the hotel, or steering a cruise boat, they are conspicuously handsome— tall, muscular, and regal in their bearing.

For the most part, the Indian people of Fiji are island-born. Many of them are third generation and have never seen India. In the early years of Colonial rule, they were imported from India as indentured laborers for work in the sugar cane fields—a job that did not suit the Fijians' ocean-oriented way of life. Ambitious and hard-working, the Indians have prospered and increased in population to the point that they now outnumber the native Fijians. Many have become merchants, professional men, or farm and plantation operators. They live in separate communities, their homes easily identified because of their brightly-painted, multi-colored exteriors.

Though there may not be a word for "togetherness" in the Bauan dialect, there's certainly a reason for one. The basic principles of the native Fijian's social system are communal. Although there is a continuous breakaway by individuals, most of the 200,000 Fijians still live in small villages where obligations and rewards are shared equally. Each village is administered by a hereditary chief. Villagers divide the income, share in the cooking, help in the building of new bures, support their Western-style church, and share the responsibilities of caring for the orphaned and the aged. Even with some who leave the village, these obligations seem to remain a part of their life as evidenced by their contributions toward the village upkeep.

Fijians possess a strong sense of pride in their villages. They like to point out that Yadua, a village on Queen's Road, was awarded first place for neatness and cleanliness in a recent annual competition. Yadua, like many other small villages on the roads around Viti Levu, could be easily missed if it were not for the stretch of smooth road fronting it. This island-circling road, largely unsurfaced, is paved in front of villages to help keep the dust down.

In complete contrast to their ancestors who lived in a world of sorcerers, spirit houses, and cannibalism, Fijians are now virtually all Christians. Their sense of the past, however, is still very much a part of their present-day conversation. Strolling past a handsome old banyan tree with its branches towering above you—a Fijian at your side—you'll hear how his people still believe spirit gods live in banyan trees.

Because of the strong missionary influence over the years, the islands long have had a code of "blue laws" in effect. Bars and nightclubs close at midnight on Saturdays, remaining closed through Sunday along with all shops and places of business. A recent relaxation of these long-standing rules allows shops to remain open on the Sundays when a passenger liner comes into port.

One of the most colorful law enforcement units in the world, Fiji's 700-member police force is uniformed in black leather sandals, navy blue shirts, and crisp-looking bright white *sulus* (a skirt with notched hemline). The officers give downtown Suva the look of a pageant. And for a pageant with sound effects, the best show in town takes place at the

ROCKS AND RIVER are the laundry setting for Fijian women living in the highland region of the interior.

FIJIAN PRONOUNCING PRIMER ... MIND YOUR B'S AND Q'S

In the Fijian language, there's more to the printed word than meets the eye. Take, for instance, the town name—Nadi. It's pronounced Nan-dee. Or the town of Ba. It's pronounced Mba. Or the island of Beqa, where the firewalkers live. It's pronounced Mbengga. Sigatoka is pronounced Singatoka. Cakobau Road is pronounced Thakombau Road.

Keeping track of shifting consonants tends to boggle the mind of the visitor who'd like to pronounce his b's and q's and other consonants correctly while he's in the Fijian homeland. You even hestitate saying *Bula* (hello), wondering whether it shouldn't come out sounding something like *Mboula*. (It should.)

Actually there are just five consonants in the Fijian language that take special treatment. Fix in your mind the pronunciations of b, c, d, g, and q and you'll have an easier time with place names and you might even acquire a rudimentary vocabulary. As a starter, memorize the following pronunciations:

b—as mb (say Mba)
c—as th (say Thakombau)
d—as nd (say Nandi)
g—as ng (say Singatoka)
q—as ng-g (say Mbengga)

If you're interested in the structure of languages and want to know how these pronunciations evolved, get the paperback edition of *Spoken Fijian*, by Albert J. Schutz and Rusiate T. Komaitai, published in 1971 by University of Hawaii Press. And remember, as you drink a cup of *yaqona*, the Fijians' favorite drink, that some day you'll be telling a friend about something called *yanggona*.

Suva dock when the Fiji Police Band or the Fiji Military Forces Band serenades an incoming passenger liner.

The Fijian economy is self-supporting. Sugar, copra, bananas, and gold are the main exports—although tourism recently has become an important aspect of the economy.

EXPLORING VITI LEVU

Nadi-Lautoka ... sugar cane country

With the opening of the International Airport in 1960, Nadi changed from a collection of small shops on a short main street to a bustling little town of more than 3,000. Essentially still an unprepossessing, one-street town, Nadi is the first Fijian town the visitor comes to after leaving the airport. Flanking its main street are duty-free shops, their facades, signs, and displays doing their best to entice the shopper. More than a dozen hotels, located in and around Nadi and the airport, offer comfortable accommodations and a base from which you can begin your island exploration.

A twenty minute drive from Nadi will take you to her neighbor, Lautoka. Its population of about 11,000 makes it Fiji's second largest town. Like Nadi, Lautoka is geared to the in-transit tourist. It has several good hotels and is the departure point for cruises to the Yasawas, the Mamanucas, and other outer-island groups. Since it's about a

half-mile inland from the port, many Nadi-based tourists never see the town at all on the way to and from an offshore cruise.

Primarily a port and sugar mill town, Lautoka is considered one of the most attractive towns in the South Pacific. Wide streets and parks are shaded by a variety of island trees, a sugar cane train runs down one of the main streets, and the residential area sprawls over the low hills overlooking the sea. Large department stores and numerous duty free shops tempt the shopper. At Churchill Park the sports fan can watch local groups bowl or play cricket, rugby, football, and soccer in season. A yacht club and golf course are also on hand.

If you only have time for a brief visit to Lautoka, take the short walk up Vitogo Parade or Naviti Street or stroll through the public market at the top of the town. Here you'll see Chinese cabinet makers, Indians vending ice cream and hot foods in wheel barrows, and a market displaying a glorious array of spices along with the foodstuffs of the Fijian diet—taro root, yams, mangoes, potatoes, as well as a good many other edibles.

Visitors to Lautoka during sugar cane crushing season (May to December) can explore the South Pacific Sugar Mills on the outskirts of town. Guided tours on Tuesday, Wednesday, and Thursday between 2 and 4 p.m. are accompanied by a taped explanation. Every step of the mill processing is shown, from the crushing of cane and the forcing out of the juice to purifying and refining into the finished product.

The Nadi-Lautoka area is typical of the dry side of Viti Levu. It's the heart of the sugar cane country, which provides Fiji with its main source of income. Depending on the stage of growth, you're apt to see patches of sugar cane in varying shades of green. The first growth to appear is dark green; as it matures, it becomes lighter and lighter. No matter how small the plot (many are not more than 10 acres), each separate cane field is called a plantation. During the harvesting season, you'll come upon Indians loading cane onto the little cars of the sugar cane railroad, its narrow gauge tracks weaving in and out of the plantations for some 400 miles.

Oxen, with birds sitting jauntily on their backs, are still used to pull heavy loads of cane. Small Indian boys mind the oxen and perform other stock-tending duties. Indian women, wearing bright saris and preparing food in field kitchens, add visual spice to the scene.

Cane fields are cleared before harvesting by being set on fire. Visitors have been startled to see fields ablaze at night and to find smoke rising and hanging over the burned areas during the day. Only the charred cane stalks survive, and that is what is sent to the sugar mills.

Midway on the road between Nadi and Lautoka is the village of Viseisei. This is the site where ancient Fijians are said to have first landed. The chief (and leader) of that migration is considered to have been the legendary ancestor of the tribes of northwest Viti Levu. A visit to this small village on a Friday will be highlighted by a program of Fijian music and dance given by a group of Viseiseis, especially noted for their male choir.

In and around Suva ... between the green hills and the blue lagoon

Suva, capital of the Fiji Islands, is a colorful and cosmopolitan city of 85,000. As you might expect

SUGAR CANE country (upper right) surrounds the Nadi-Lautoka area. Nadi's main street (lower right) is lined with duty-free shops. Not far away is a Moslem mosque (above).

CHANGING OF THE GUARD takes place at Suva's Government House Gates (upper left); and a bit of bargaining ensues at the public market (lower left). Suva's superb setting is seen from Hospital Hill (upper right); and its wide Rodwell Road is graced by flamboyant trees (above).

atmosphere that seems to have been fixed in time several centuries ago.

Reflecting the island's British heritage, Suva has such place names as Victoria Parade, Albert Park, King's Wharf, Queen Elizabeth Drive, Prince's Landing, Gladstone Road. The changing of the guard at Government House—a ceremony not too far removed from the parade and pomp at Buckingham Palace—takes place every day at noon.

Along almost any downtown Suva street at any time of day, you'll see Fijians wearing *sulus* and sandals; Englishmen in white shirts and shorts and knee-high white socks; Indian women wearing elaborate saris; bearded Sikhs in turbans; Tongans in lava-lavas with plaited straw sashes; Chinese in traditional black mandarin suits; Samoans in bright flowered *lava-lavas;* and, of course, tourists in the inevitable drip-dries. As often as not, an umbrella is part of the costume.

Rain in Suva can be sudden and torrential—so take an umbrella or a light raincoat when you go out. If you do get caught downtown without one, you have several means of escape: the arcaded fronts of downtown buildings, in the doorway of one of Suva's many shops, or under the great green umbrellas created by the city's densely-foliaged old street trees.

This heavy green canopy of street trees helps make Suva's Victoria Parade one of the most pleasant downtown streets in the South Pacific. Along Victoria Parade and its extension, Queen Elizabeth Drive, are many of Suva's prime attractions. At its eastern end are the old government buildings, their backs to the harbor and their fronts to beautiful, well-manicured Albert Park. Opposite the park are the elegant old Grand Pacific Hotel (see page 57) and the new TraveLodge Hotel.

Farther east, at Queen Elizabeth Drive and Cakobau Road, are the Botanical Gardens (containing a remarkable collection of tropical plants) and the superb Fiji Museum. Probably the South Pacific's finest repository of Melanesian artifacts, of objects from Fiji's maritime era, of reminders of the cannibal days, and of bird and sea life specimens, the Museum is open weekdays, Saturday mornings, and Sunday afternoons. Beyond the Botanical Gardens is Government House, sitting on a hill and surrounded by its own lovely gardens.

Another of Suva's biggest attractions is City Market. On Prince's Street, near the heart of wharf and port activity, the market dazzles the senses with its kaleidoscopic array of fruits and vegetables, fish, flowers, tobacco, handicrafts, and souvenirs (tapa, woven mats, baskets, shells, jewelry). Business begins at 8 a.m. daily (except Sundays).

From Prince's Street, a short walk takes you to Prince's Wharves. Here the big cruise liners tie

of a crossroads of the Pacific where ships from all over the world drop anchor, it is both gracious and gaudy. Backed by low, dark, and lush green hills of the Suva-Rewa Range, much of Suva's waterfront is built on land reclaimed from tangled mangrove swamps (like those you see along the road into town). Downtown Suva is rather a hodgepodge of Colonial-style, two-story wooden structures, their second floor porches overhanging the sidewalks. These are joined by utilitarian commercial houses of more recent origin, a scattering of pleasant, new, well-designed buildings with contemporary lines, and some faintly Victorian buildings with grey and moldy faces.

Turn off on any side street, and you will probably find it lined with sign-burdened, "duty-free" shops-of-all-wares: a boutique selling Waikiki-inspired resort wear; air-conditioned tour and airline offices; a jewelry shop selling Mikimoto pearls and French perfumes; a chemist shop; an Indian shoe store with pointed-toe stock direct from Hong Kong; camera, radio, and stereo dealers beyond count; a fan-cooled ice cream and refreshment fountain; an Indian repair shop for clocks, irons, and toasters. On the main streets, department stores run by solid, old-time South Seas trading companies sell Dior cosmetics, along with frozen foods. A few blocks away, the public market offers vegetables, fruit, fish and fowl in a commercial up, depositing passengers very close to downtown activity. Docked here also are visiting naval vessels, Japanese freighters discharging their latest electronic cargo, work-worn inter-island cargo boats unloading copra, local boats being filled to the gunnels with Fijians commuting to some nearby island, and glass-bottom cruise boats taking on eager tourists.

Look into these other attractions:

Cumming Street, near Nubukalou Creek, between Thompson Street and Renwick Road. A block-long maze of offbeat shops.

Harbor Lights Aquarium, on the corner of Niagara and Matua streets. Rainbow displays of tropical fish, shells, marine life. Open to the public Monday through Friday, Saturday mornings, and Sunday afternoons.

Marau Model Village, in Tamavua, 3 miles from town. An authentic replica of an early Fijian native village showing the way of life and handicrafts. Open Monday through Saturday.

Polynesian Craft Center, directly across from Tradewinds Hotel, 4½ miles from Suva. Contains an assortment of craft objects from Fiji, Samoa, and Tonga islands, and other islands as far away as Niue, the Tokelaus, the Cooks, and the Gilberts. Open to the public Monday through Saturday and evenings until 10 on days when passenger ships arrive.

Inland and around the island

A visit to Viti Levu will really blossom into a memorable experience if you leave your base in the Suva, Nadi, or Coral Coast area and explore the rest of the island.

The circle tour. Offering generous samples of Fiji's simple and unspoiled areas, a coastal road stretches some 330 miles around Viti Levu. Along the south coast the road from Suva to the Nadi-Lautoka area is called Queen's Road; along the north coast it's called King's Road. Because rough and winding road conditions limit your speed, the trip in either direction makes it advisable to stay overnight along the way. Graded but unpaved, the road is dusty in dry weather, muddy when it's raining.

Sprinkled along Queen's Road, a number of well-known hotels and resorts offer refuge. Although the Fijian, the Korolevu Beach, and the Reef are the best known, all hotels have enough shore and offshore resort-type facilities to easily persuade the visitor to stay for several days. Whether you settle for skin diving, sailing, bicycling, horseback riding, touring, or cruising, or simply relaxing by a swimming pool or on your private deck, you're sure to enjoy your stay. For specific details on hotels, see page 57.

To tap a more primitive part of the island, take the drive between Suva and Nadi by way of King's Road. Traversing the north side of Viti Levu, it's

SUVA'S COLOR emerges in these scenes: buildings such as the one at left—Suva's oldest; and bands serenading passenger liners in port.

SHOPPING IN FIJI ... CAMERAS TO KEROSENE LAMPS

Suva has often been called the shopping center of the South Pacific. It's a justifiable label, and one that could be stretched to include—on a smaller scale—Nadi.

Let's stick to Suva shopping for the moment. Even though you won't for a moment be reminded of a shopping center at home, Suva's varied shops have some obvious attributes. For one thing, the shopping area is compact. You can cover it all on foot. And the range of merchandise is incredible. You can buy a bottle of Chanel No. 5 in one store, a Nikon camera next door—or a transistor radio, treadle sewing machine, scuba tank, kerosene lamp, Indian sari, or piece of *masi* (Fijian tapa). Sometimes you will find such unlikely combinations all in the same store.

Free port prices on certain categories of goods are the main attractions of Fiji shopping. This includes all types of watches; radios, record players, tape recorders, television sets; electric razors; still and movie cameras (except movie cameras larger than 16 mm), photographic accessories, projectors for 35 mm slides and 8 mm movies; portable typewriters; telescopes, binoculars, monoculars; furs, perfumes, and jewelry with precious and semi-precious stones.

Because goods are imported into Fiji duty-free, prices on free port goods are lower than on the same merchandise in the United States. This happy arrangement brings the price of merchandise down to 30 or 40 per cent of the usual U. S. price. Occasionally it's closer to 50 per cent.

Visitors interested in purchasing a major piece of equipment should shop at one of the larger trading companies known for its solid reputation. If you're familiar with how U. S. prices run for the particular model or brand you're shopping for, so much the better. Bargaining is an accepted practice in many stores.

You'll also find free port prices for the same goods in Nadi and Lautoka. But in Nadi, you won't see as many stores—fewer still in Lautoka. And the advantage that comes from competitive pricing is less.

Nadi International Airport has several shops where departing visitors or travelers in transit can buy duty-free liquor.

Two shopping suggestions: spices and British woolens. You don't have to be a gourmet chef to appreciate the wondrous assortment of spices sold in the public markets. The condiments that go into curries and other exotic Indian dishes usually cost no more than a few cents. British woolens are also good buys, and tailors will make a suit or topcoat for you in a day (although allowing a few more days may result in a better-finished product).

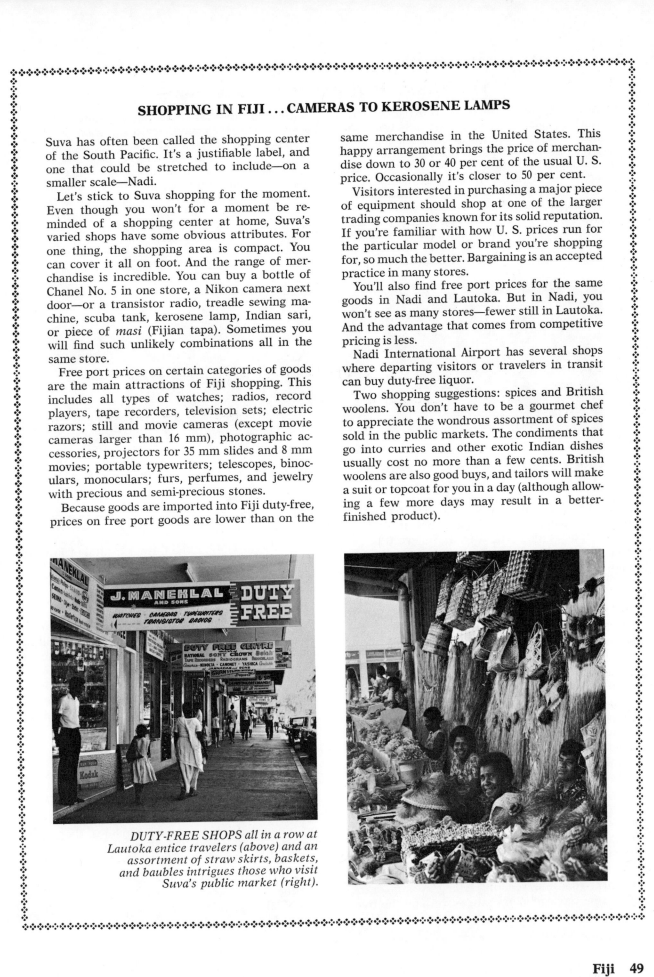

DUTY-FREE SHOPS all in a row at Lautoka entice travelers (above) and an assortment of straw skirts, baskets, and baubles intrigues those who visit Suva's public market (right).

TAKE THE SUGAR TRAIN . . . IT'S A FREE RIDE

Not many sugar trains still exist around the world, let alone those that carry passengers. But in the northwest corner of Viti Levu you'll find a real, honest-to-goodness sugar train running in and around the sugar cane plantations, picking up bundles of cane, and carrying them away to the refinery. Pulled by a small but distinguished looking locomotive, British-built, circa 1915, the little open-air cars run on narrow gauge tracks. The fact that it's a free ride adds to the charm.

Owned by South Pacific Sugar Mills Ltd., the Sugar Train operates out of Lautoka during the sugar crushing season from May to October. For a short ride (4½ hours), board the train on a Monday or a Thursday at 7 a.m. at Lautoka. You'll arrive in Ba at 11:30 a.m. Arrange to have someone meet you there unless you want to make the round trip that gets you back to Lautoka about 4 p.m. For a longer ride (10 hours), board the train in Lautoka on a Tuesday or Friday at 7 a.m. and you'll arrive at Kavanagasua (Sigatoka) around 5 p.m. It's best to arrange for someone to meet you there; the train doesn't go back to Lautoka until the next day.

RAILROAD warning sign, Sigatoka.

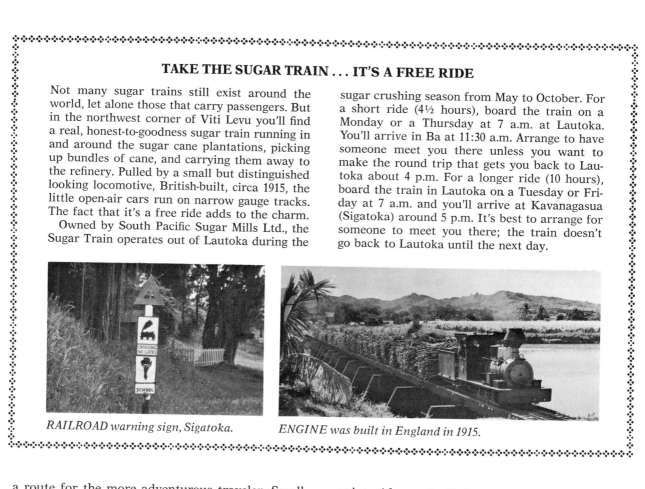

ENGINE was built in England in 1915.

a route for the more adventurous traveler. Small hotels, adequate for an overnight stay, are located at four villages along the way: at Tailevu (the five room Tailevu Hotel), at Raki Raki (the 48-room Raki Raki Hotel), at Tavua (the 11-room Tavua Hotel), and at Ba (the 11-room New Ba Hotel). If you can spend an extra day at Raki Raki, the cruise that goes to Nananu-i-ra Island is worth taking. It leaves every morning from the jetty behind the hotel and includes coral viewing, a barbecue lunch, and time for swimming.

Traveling on either the King's or Queen's roads, you'll see contrasts in landscape—brown, dry highlands on the Nadi-Lautoka side, lush rain forests in the Suva area. At times the roads climb high enough for sweeping views of the deep blue sea pounding the reef and palm-fringed lagoons.

Popping into view every little while are small villages where you can stop, unannounced and unexpected. Simple, genuinely friendly people pop out to greet you. If you aren't in too much of a hurry, chances are that you'll be invited to sit down in the shade of a *bure* for a cup of *yaqona* or just to pass the time of day.

Along the way you'll pass fishermen and farmers at work, roadside vendors selling swamp crabs right from the lagoon or oranges fresh off the tree, smiling children selling coconuts for a nickel apiece (they cut off the top so you can enjoy the cool refreshing milk).

The side roads. Bau, the former capital of Fiji, can be reached from King's Road or by launch from Suva. Once the village of "King" Cakobau and his royal tribesmen and now the home of the highest chiefs of Fiji, Bau is located on a 20-acre islet connected to the east coast by a narrow coral causeway. Flanked by a village of craftsmen and a village of fishermen, Bau's major sights are the Cakobau Memorial Church, a council house, and an ancient tree, peppered with notches—each notch said to be a record of a villager who met his fate in the oven of an old-time cannibal chief. Arrangements for visiting Bau must be made through the Fiji Visitors Bureau.

Heading inland from Tavua, another interesting side trip off the King's Road is the seven mile trip to Vatukoula. Built, owned, and run by the gold mining interests which operate there, Vatukoula is Fiji's third largest town. "Downtown" includes a Chinese bakery, two taxi companies, shops, grocery stores, and a theater. If you're interested in visiting the mining operations, inquire at the offices of the Emperor Gold Mining Company, Ltd.

Other side roads stab into the interior. One, in the Nadi area, takes you up to the Nausori Highlands. You can go by private car or take the 3 to

*LOOK AND LINGER as you drive around the island
—at palm-fringed beaches; outriggers cutting through
the lagoon; mountain ramparts rearing up beyond
plantations; and sea shells for sale near a hotel.*

FIJIANS LIVE in villages along the shores of the spectacular Navua River (above) where fishermen stop for lunch. In most villages, the church is the community center.

3½ hour tour. Departing from Nadi hotels twice a day, the tour is by a *buremobile*—a vehicle that is powered by a four-wheel drive land cruiser, but looks like a *bure*. The road slices through sugar cane country as far as the foothills, then heads upward in a winding pattern, and finally emerges on the rolling grasslands of a plateau. Here you pick up a narrow lumber mill road, once a foot and horse trail. At the end of the line is a panoramic view of farmlands, the mountains of the Sabeto Range, island-studded Nadi Bay, and the international airport.

Before returning to Nadi, the *buremobile* stops at the village of Nausori. Here you can meet the village chief, Tugara Ni Koro, who permits tourists to take photographs of village life. You'll probably be invited to try beating the huge *lali* (drum) that he uses to call villagers to meetings. (Villagers are accustomed to hearing the erratic rhythms pounded out by the practicing tourists; and they don't, for a moment, mistake any of these thumpings as a call-to-meeting.) Small children follow you about, some of them posing for you on their favorite horses.

Taking only about two hours, another inland trip out of Nadi goes into the lush green Sabeto Valley. The road follows the course of the meandering Rippling River.

For those who like more rugged sightseeing, a five-day horseback and hiking trip takes you to the village of Nabutautau. After leaving Suva by automobile, you change to mountain pony for a ramble up into the hill country by way of an isolated jungle track. Although you trek through tangled undergrowth and rolling grasslands, moist green glades and semi-tropical forests, you do so without fear of snakes or dangerous animals—Fiji has neither. Village *tuis* (chiefs) will welcome you to take your meals and stay overnight in native villages.

EXPLORING THE OTHER ISLANDS

By sea

No trip to Fiji is really complete without some island hopping, Fijian fashion. From either Suva or Lautoka, you can reach an almost deserted isle by mid-day and still have time for a barbecue lunch, swimming and sunning, and possibly a shelling prowl before nightfall. If you can spend several days instead of one, you can taste the pleasure of having your boat tie up every night at a different island or atoll.

As a general rule, any of the following boat trips (including meals) will cost about $10 per day:

Out of Lautoka. Two popular cruise destinations are the Mamanuca Islands and the Yasawa Islands. You can visit the Mamanucas in a two-day cruise and the somewhat more distant Yasawas on a three-day cruise. The Mamanucas are a group of 13 small volcanic islands that lie to the west of Viti Levu. All but two are uninhabited. Golden beaches, calm lagoons, and sunny weather (more sun per year, it is claimed, than anywhere else in the South Pacific) make the islands ideal stopping places for swimming, snorkeling, searching for sea wrack and shells, or toasting in the sun.

The Yasawas, north of the Mamanucas, are made up of a chain of islands that starts about 25 miles out of Lautoka and stretches for some 50 miles. Approximately 20 islands make up the group. The largest, Naviti, covers 13 square miles.

You need not be an indefatigable adventurer or sailor to explore the Yasawas. Well-appointed cruise

vessels, ranging in size from 40-foot sailing vessels to 125-foot diesel-powered ships, provide all the necessary comforts and conveniences. Passenger capacities range from 5 to 40 persons. Trips vary in length from one to three days; some boats are available for charter.

Several of the one-day trips offer overnight options. Visitors to Matacawalevu on Yasawa Island can use the accommodations in the Yasawa

FIREWALKING: THE MYSTIFYING RITUAL

Fiji is one of the few places in the world where you can still observe a firewalking ceremony. Before your first exposure, you may have some doubts: do the firewalkers of Beqa Island really walk on hot stones, or is there some sleight of hand (or foot) involved?

An inspection of the fire pit just before the ceremony begins is enough to convince—and impress—you. The immense heat of the hot stones hitting you in the face will push you back a step or two. You'll see for yourself that the Beqa Islanders' feet are bare and unprotected. After the ceremony, the performers will sit with their feet upturned for inspection. The skin seems a little tougher than usual—nothing more.

According to the Beqa Islanders, the ritual of firewalking has been going on for a long time. It came about one day when one of their warriors, Tui-na-lviqa-lita, promised a famous storyteller that he would give him whatever he caught while fishing. He caught an eel. After he landed the eel, it was transformed into a spirit god. Pleading to

be set free, the spirit god offered in exchange the gift of immunity to fire. Then he built a fire pit, leapt onto the white-hot stones, and commanded Tui to follow. Tui did so and was unharmed. The ceremony growing out of this legend is one of the more thrilling tourist experiences.

Today the Bete (leaders of the firewalkers) are said to be direct descendants of Tui-na-lviqa-lita, having inherited his ability to walk on fire and to lead others onto it.

Performances of this unusual ceremony take place at the Korolevu Beach Hotel twice a month —on the first and third Fridays—at 6:30 p.m. At the relatively new Fisherman's Lodge, 11 miles from Suva on the Coral Coast, this ceremony is also performed twice a month—on the second and fourth Wednesdays of the month.

The South Indians who have settled on Fiji also have a custom of firewalking. Traditionally a once-a-year ritual during a religious festival, it is based on different concepts and is conspicuously different from that of the Beqa Islanders.

WHITE-HOT STONES are a fierce carpet for unprotected feet. After walking on these stones, the firewalkers display their feet—and you see that they are not burned.

Lodge, which has five double rooms; occupants share the one bathroom. Plan on taking along a food supply, replenishing it as necessary from stock aboard the daily boat service. The day trip to Tai Island (also called Beachcomber Island) gives you the chance of spending five hours ashore and returning to Lautoka or of staying overnight in one of the self-contained Beachcomber *bures*. Another excursion goes to the island of Malololailai in the Mamanucas every morning for a visit to the Castaway Island Resort and Plantation Village. You have a choice of making the trip by hydrofoil, launch, an 83-foot topsail schooner or by daily scheduled air flights. All modes of travel allow time ashore for lunch and a brief look around, but you can also opt to stay overnight at either Castaway Island Resort or Plantation Village, where the atmosphere is relaxed, the setting languorous. Slightly closer to Lautoka, Castaway Island Resort has 31 *bures* (each sleeping up to three persons), a dining room for meal service, and hotel-organized excursions for coral viewing and deep sea fishing. Plantation Village has 25 *bures*, each sleeping up to six persons. Although meals are served in a dining room, each *bure* has a kitchen. Sports facilities and organized excursions are also available.

For those on limited time, two to three hour glass-bottom boat cruises offer both coral viewing and a bit of shore exploring at one of the islands not too far beyond Lautoka. They're scheduled every morning and afternoon out of Lautoka.

Out of Suva. Suva Harbor is dotted with a number of small islands—destinations for half-day or full-day cruises. You have any number of choices, ranging from a 3½-hour twilight cruise around the Harbor to a 7 or 8-hour glass-bottom boat cruise.

Many other idyllic cruises are possible if you charter a boat. Doing this is a perfect way to visit such historical islands as Ovalau, Wakaya and Koro, Vanua Levu, and Taveuni, as well as some of the islands in the Lau group. To add to the fun, you can choose the kind of craft you want to transport you there: a twin-screw diesel yacht or a ferroconcrete houseboat outfitted like a camper.

For longer cruises—three days or more—look into the possibilities of chartering a boat out of Suva and sailing as far south as the Astrolabe Lagoon and Kadavu, one of Fiji's lustrous islands. Known for its beautiful stretch of clear waters, the lagoon lies in the mile-wide channel between Great Astrolabe Reef and North Astrolabe Reef. Within the Great Astrolabe Reef is Kadavu Island, its Galoa Harbor once a thriving 19th century whaling and timber port.

For a list of boats available for charter, write to the Fiji Visitors Bureau, P.O. Box 92, Suva, Fiji Islands.

By air

To add an extra dimension to your sightseeing on Viti Levu, take one of the many flights offered by Fiji Air Services for an aerial view of the land and water. If you're in Suva on a Sunday and the weather is clear, go out to Nausori Airport anytime between 9:30 a.m. and 4:30 p.m. and board one of the flights leaving every half hour. You'll wing over the surrounding islands and reefs, as well as the countryside around the capital city.

Fiji Air Services also provides the fastest and easiest access to three other important islands in the Fiji group—Vanua Levu, Taveuni, and Ovalau.

Vanua Levu. It may seem to the casual visitor that Viti Levu, the largest island, *is* Fiji. There's reason enough for such an assumption. Here you'll find the largest communities, the capital city, the jet runway, the major ports, the developed resorts and hotels, the headquarters of major cruise and tour organizations. Vanua Levu, the second largest island in the Fiji group, is, by comparison, virtually undeveloped. But it's not to be overlooked. Along with its get-away-from-it-all quality, it offers all the comforts of home at several small resorts, including a new 48-room TraveLodge.

From Suva, you can fly to SavuSavu, one of the main towns, in 45 minutes. Two round trips a day (Monday through Saturday, and one on Sunday) are scheduled.

Taveuni. A smaller island just east of Vanua Levu, Taveuni is another mini-paradise. Just as a reminder of the pressing 20th century, though, the recently built Taveuni TraveLodge at Waiyevo has 33 very comfortable and modern rooms and is located right on the beach. The flight from Suva to the airport at Matei takes an hour; a flight that stops in Labasa on Vanua Levu takes close to two hours. Two round trips a week are scheduled for the direct flight; the one-stop flight departs five times a week.

Ovalau. A volcanic island, Ovalau has great crags, deep gorges, and a mountain mass that slopes right down to the sea. Of all the outer islands, none has a richer historical background. During the reign of Cakobau and up until 1882, its port town of Levuka was the capital of Fiji. Now it is a picturesque little town drowsing on a narrow shelf of land with little or no room to expand—even if it wanted to.

Levuka boasts three places to stay: the Royal Hotel, with 14 rooms; the Ovalau Guest House, with 4 single rooms; and the Rukuruku Resort, with several cottages. All three are simple and unpretentious but perfectly satisfactory for a brief stay.

No scheduled flights go to Ovalau, but charter

ONE DAY you're going ashore for lunch on a deserted islet. The next, you're watching native women stencilling masi—a type of tapa—in Somosomo; or walking down a village lane on Vanna Levu; or visiting a village huddled at the edge of a lagoon.

flights can be arranged through Fiji Air Services, Ltd. You land at Bureta, just to the south of Levuka. Levuka is one of Fiji's three official ports of entry, and it may be reached by regular launch service out of Natovi (just north of Suva). Numerous charter cruise itineraries also include it in their ports of call.

PRACTICAL INFORMATION

Entry regulations

To visit Fiji for a period of four months or less, a United States citizen needs only a valid passport. Upon landing you are issued a visitor's permit good for four months; you need not have applied for this before leaving home. For a longer stay, special permission must be obtained from the Fiji Immigration Department.

Customs regulations (on entry)

Admitted duty free are your personal effects (including 200 cigarettes or 50 cigars or 8 ounces of tobacco and 1 quart of liquor per person) and up to $17 worth of new merchandise for personal use.

Climate

Fiji's climate is considered cool for the tropics. Moderated by the prevailing trade winds, temperatures seldom go higher than 90°. But between December and March when the humidity is at its peak, 90° can seem steaming hot. Coolest months are May through October, although temperatures seldom fall below 60°. On Viti Levu, rainfall reaches 120 inches on the wet windward (Suva) side and up to 80 inches on the drier leeward (Nadi-Lautoka) side. Though rainfall extends over the whole year, the driest months are June through September.

Communications

To help you keep in touch with desk-bound friends left behind or with what's happening around the world, Fiji has several means of communication. Airmail service to North America, Australia, and New Zealand is on a daily basis. International telephone service is available from Suva; cable and telex services are available at the Post Office in Suva 24 hours a day. All the main centers of Fijian population are linked by telephone. Separate newspapers are published in English, Fijian, and Hindi. Every day the Fiji Broadcasting Commission relays several overseas news bulletins. If a respite from late night horror movies appeals to you, you will be happy to learn that Fiji has no television.

Currency and banking

Fiji adopted the decimal system of dollars and cents (100 cents to the dollar) in January, 1969. Linked with the pound sterling, the monetary unit, the Fiji dollar, is worth approximately $1.19 in United States currency. In Fiji one U. S. dollar is worth about 84 cents. This rate is subject to small variations.

The many banks in Fiji (Suva has five) are open for business from 10 a.m. to 3 p.m. on weekdays and 9:30 to 11 a.m. on Saturdays. Because the banks' rate of exchange is more advantageous than that given at hotels and other places of business, activity can be brisk and you may find yourself practicing a common United States' custom—standing in line.

Health and medical

You can leave your medical anxieties behind: the islands are considered quite healthful. Safe water supplies and strictly controlled sanitary conditions in restaurants eliminate some of the usual tropical health hazards. The pesky mosquito is liable to be active at night—especially during the hot season—so it's wise to have mosquito repellent within easy reach. If you're going to take any cruises to offshore islands, another handy item is a supply of motion sickness pills. But if the unexpected occurs and your carefully toted supply of medicines from home just doesn't fill the bill, you'll find hospitals, doctors, and dentists, as well as pharmacies (called chemists), in the main cities.

Public holidays

Fiji recognizes 10 public holidays a year: New Year's Day, Good Friday, Easter Saturday and Easter Monday, Queen Elizabeth's Birthday on June 14, Bank Holiday on August 2, Dominion Day on October 11, Prince Charles' Birthday on November 14, Christmas Day, and Boxing Day on December 26.

Tipping

Tipping in Fiji is not essential; it should be measured by the service given. Under normal circumstances, large tips are not expected.

For information

The Fiji Visitors Bureau maintains headquarters at the corner of Victoria Parade and MacArthur Street in Suva. It also has an office at the Nadi airport that is open during arrival and departure

WHERE TO STAY in Fiji? Among many hotels are the venerable Grand Pacific Hotel in Suva (above), the Korolevu Beach Hotel betweeen Suva and Nadi (upper right), and the Tradewinds Hotel outside Suva (lower right).

of all commercial overseas flights. During the visits of large passenger ships, the bureau also maintains a wharf office in Suva, in which you'll find banking and post office facilities. From these offices you can get up-to-date maps, pamphlets, and information about shopping, sightseeing, and other subjects of tourist interest.

Where to stay

Fiji's hotels cluster around Suva and the Nadi-Lautoka area, though a few dot the circle-island road and outer islands. Suva's twenty or more hotels run the gamut from resort hotels like the Tradewinds, Isa Lei, and the relatively new Suva TraveLodge to the islands' elegant veteran, the Grand Pacific Hotel.

Equipped with all the modern-day amenities, the 139-room TraveLodge fits its contemporary design into the Fijian scene without taking on the air of a brash newcomer. A few hundred yards away is the 72-room Grand Pacific Hotel, built sixty years ago and affectionately known as the GPH. Even though it has been modernized and enlarged in recent years, the GPH still evokes the atmosphere found in a Somerset Maugham story. Big mosquito blade fans still hang from the ceiling—generous cooling insurance in a building that is fully air conditioned. The latest hotel to open its doors in Suva is the 30-room Southern Cross. A five-story building, it is located on Gordon Street.

More than a dozen hotels use Nadi International Airport as their address. Some are within sight of the airport, others a few miles away in Nadi or on the beach. Offering the best accommodations are the Sunlover, Fiji Gateway, Fiji Mocambo, Hibiscus, Nadi Airport TraveLodge, Skylodge, Coconut Palms, and Hotel Tanoa. A half-dozen more hotels are located in the Lautoka area, the principal ones being the Cathay and the Lautoka.

Major hotels along the Coral Coast—the Fijian, the Korolevu, the Flagship Beachcomber, and the

Reef—operate largely on a resort basis. Several days of each calendar week are ringed with special events. On Wednesday and Saturday evenings, all three hotels offer Fijian entertainment; the Reef schedules it on Monday evenings as well. Always a heart-stopping tourist attraction, the fire-walking ceremony is held on the first and third Fridays of every month at the Korolevu Beach and on the second and fourth Wednesdays at Fisherman's Lodge, also on the Coral Coast. Performed by the Beqa Islanders at sites close to the hotels, the fire walking is one of those electric performances that may exceed your expectations (see page 53).

Some of these hotels offer a full day tour into the Sigatoka Valley—a lush, rich notch in the mountains cut by the Sigatoka River. Another day-long excursion organized by the Korolevu Beach Hotel takes you by boat to Vatulele Island, famed for its red prawns and tapa makers' handiwork.

Unique to Fiji are several resort hotels that are located on their own islands. The Toberua Resort Hotel nestles all by itself on a four-acre hideaway island three miles off the mouth of the Rewa River near Suva. The Fijian sits on 100-acre Yanuca Island and is reached by causeway from Queen's Road about 45 miles out of Nadi. The Barefoot Village Hotel on Bekana Island is a mile offshore from

AWAY-FROM-IT-ALL resorts, some occupying an entire offshore island, such as Toberua Resort Hotel (upper left) and Fijian Hotel (lower left). The interior of a housekeeping Beachcomber bure on Tai Island (middle left); and Castaway Island Resort (above).

Lautoka, and the Mana Island Resort on the island of the same name is 22 miles offshore from Lautoka.

Conveniently located off the well-traveled routes are a number of small guest houses, cottages, and *bures*. For more detailed information, check with your travel agent or write to the Fiji Visitors Bureau, Box 92, Suva, Fiji Islands.

As they do all over the world, Fijian hotel rates vary and are always subject to change. For the latest hotel rates, check with your travel agent.

How to get around

By taxi. Taxis are plentiful in the main centers of population on the island of Viti Levu, and some operate on Vanua Levu and Taveuni. Drivers are well informed and rates are low. For trips of any distance (especially to places outside city limits), it's wise to settle on the amount before departure. Other excursions to various points on the island have fixed rates determined by the Fiji Taxi Union.

By rental cars. Because taxis are inexpensive and plentiful and distances within Nadi and Suva are short, a rental car isn't as practical on Viti Levu as it is in other parts of the South Pacific. Many travelers find it more advantageous to get around the island by other means—air, bus, or taxi—largely because many of the roads out of town are narrow, winding, dusty, and subject to flash floods during storms. Following the British tradition, drivers use the left side of the road—a practice that is guaranteed to keep you on your toes. Those who prefer to do their own driving will need a valid United States driver's license.

Half a dozen car rental agencies (including Avis, Hertz, and Mutual) operate in Suva; half a dozen in Lautoka and four in Nadi (two at the International Airport). On Vanua Levu, agencies are located at SavuSavu and Labasa. Even though the island of Taveuni has scarcely 50 miles of roads, it also has an agency.

Rates range from a low of under $5 per day and 8 cents a mile to a high of around $11 per day and 14 cents a mile.

A lower-priced option for run-about transportation in Nadi is the *fijip*. Better known as the mini-moke, it's a very small car with striped canopy. In Nadi, the United Touring Company rents a *fijip* for $2.50 a day, plus insurance and mileage.

By bus. Two companies operate daily bus service between Suva and Nadi by way of Queen's Road. Coaches are air-conditioned and have comfortable seats and wide windows for sightseeing. Time schedules and stops en route differ slightly, as do the fares. Operating between Suva and Nadi Airport, the Chieftain Coach Lines Limited leaves Suva at 9 a.m. After picking up passengers at the main hotels, another Chieftain bus leaves Nadi at 9:15 a.m. on its way to Suva. Going in either direction, stops en route are made at three hotels: the Korolevu Beach, the Reef, and the Fijian. Including a stop for lunch, the trip takes about eight hours. Along the way, a hostess describes points of interest. The fare including stop-over privileges is under $6 one way.

Another bus company, the Pacific Transport Limited, operates daily express coach service between Suva and Lautoka. Stops are made en route at Nadi International Airport and other places. Leaving Suva at 10 a.m., the bus arrives at Lautoka at about 5 in the afternoon. In the opposite direction, a bus leaves Lautoka at 9:15 a.m. and arrives in Suva at about 4:30. One-way fare is under $5.

Going the other way around the island (commonly referred to as "east-about") via King's Road, daily bus service is operated by Sunbeam Transport Limited. Stops are scheduled at eight villages en route. The eight-hour trip is not the most comfortable way of traveling: buses are not air-conditioned and windows have to be kept closed because of the dusty roads. It's a travel bargain, however, with its one-way fare of a little over $2; this averages out to be only a little more than a penny a mile.

For sightseeing in Suva, you might take a local commuter bus. This costs pennies and gives you a taste of how the Fijians live and work. The circular route through the city takes 45 minutes. Buses leave from the bus station, located next to Suva's busy public market.

By boat. For an idea of the large and varied assortment of cruises operating from Fiji ports to offshore islands, see page 52. In addition to these popular excursions is a cruise of a different order: on board a small cargo vessel operating in and out of island ports. Various ships sail from Suva to the inhabited islands of the Fiji group, leaving supplies, picking up copra, and taking on board an occasional passenger. If you have leeway in your itinerary and don't demand a luxuriously appointed ship, sailing on one of these vessels is a recommended way to see some of the real Fiji that lies beyond the shores of Viti Levu.

Because weather, cargo loading, and related conditions affect departure times, your schedule has to be flexible.

By air. To see as much of Fiji as you can within a reasonable time, you'll have to do some of your traveling by air. Numerous flights run between Suva and Nadi daily, the flight taking only 20 minutes on Air Pacific's new BAC 1-11. Air Pacific and Fiji Air Services provide frequent service to other popular destinations within the Fiji islands: be-

YAQONA . . . IT'S A DRINK AND A CEREMONY

In Fiji and other islands of the South Pacific, the ceremonial drinking of *yaqona* is a symbol of welcome, proclaiming hospitality and friendship. On some of the other South Pacific Islands, you'll find the same drink called *kava*.

A non-alcoholic beverage, *yaqona* is made by mixing a powder obtained from huge pepper tree roots (or roots themselves) with water. In appearance, it's about as muddy looking as the Colorado River, and the taste is similar. Those with a discriminating palate may tell you *yaqona* has a dash of spice in it. If you were to drink several bowls of *yaqona*—an unlikely circumstance—the after-effects might be a slight numbing of the tongue and lips.

The preparation and drinking of *yaqona*, accompanied by chants and the sounding of the *lali* (wooden drum), follow a stylized ritual which demands silence on the part of the honored guests. You sit cross-legged in front of a *tanoa* (wooden bowl with legs) and clap twice. Your portion is served in a coconut shell *bilo* (cup). Grasping the cup with both hands, you must drain the liquid at a single draught. Your hosts then cry *maca* (pronounced *maathaa*—meaning "it is drained") and clap. At various hotels, the *yaqona* ceremony precedes an evening of native dancing and feasting and is also held before a firewalking demonstration.

A shortened version of the *yaqona* ceremony is called *sevusevu*.

PREPARING YAQONA is a ceremonial ritual.

tween Nadi and Korolevu, Nadi and Malololailai; between Suva and the following places—Korolevu, SavuSavu and Labasa, both on Vanua Levu, Levuka on Ovalau Island, Matei on Taveuni Island, and to Lakeba Island in the remote Lau Group. From time to time the frequency of flights to the foregoing destinations is stepped up, and new routes are added to the airlines' schedules.

Eating and drinking

Foods in Fiji are enough to activate your taste buds just thinking about them. Native feasts with stone-roasted suckling pig, Indian curries, and cooked-to-order Chinese dinners add zest to the menu. Gastronomical oases, though, are for the most part limited to the main resort and tourist hotels. Few restaurants outside the hotels serve the kind of food that could by any stretch of the imagination be called "gourmet."

Local foods include a variety of fish, fresh and well-prepared. Fruits and melons—mangoes, oranges, *paws paws* (papayas), bananas, pineapples, coconuts—are plentiful. Tapioca (grown locally), British-type puddings, and ice cream (served in lavish scoops) serve as desserts to finish the meal.

Lolo, a coconut milk obtained from grating and straining the meat of a fresh coconut, is used to prepare much of the Fijian cookery, flavoring everything from a turtle specialty to the lowly *dale* (taro root). A favorite meal opener is called *ika lolo:* chopped raw fish or sea urchins, onions, and coconut marinated in lime juice.

The Fijian *magiti* is a feast of multitudinous proportions usually held in connection with a *meke*, a Fijian night of songs and dances. Foods are prepared in a *lovo* (earth oven). Main dishes are chicken in banana leaves, crabs, shrimps, oysters, stone-roasted suckling pig, New Zealand ham, plantains, *kumala* (sweet potato), and yams of various hues. Most of the foods are wrapped in leaves and steamed in slanted earthen ovens for several hours. The *magiti* is featured along with the *meke* (Fijian dance) at a number of the major hotels.

In Fiji the traditional drink is *yaqona* (made from pepper tree roots), but the most popular libation is Fijian beer. All wines and liquors are imported. As a rule, mixed drinks are served British-style (without ice) unless you specify otherwise.

Liquor may be served from 11 a.m. to 2 p.m. and 4 to 9 p.m. On Sundays a local prohibition goes into effect but does not apply to tourist hotels. You can order drinks at any time room service is available. Public bars in Fiji are open to men only. Other bars—saloon bars, lounge bars, and house bars—admit both sexes.

INTER-ISLAND FERRY makes regular sailings to Ovalau Island. Fijian-style feasts are a regular attraction on cruise boat excursions.

Night life

Night clubs in Fiji are spotty. But the major tourist resorts and hotels often provide combos for dinner dancing, and some kind of Fijian entertainment is scheduled at least one or two nights a week. During the evening, Fijian groups present a program of music and dancing, along with the traditional *yaqona* ceremony. When cruise ships are in port, a *magiti* (Fijian feast) is staged at Loki's Fijian Bure at Tamavua Village on the outskirts of Suva.

Sports . . . golf to game fishing

Arousing fervent enthusiasm in Fiji are a number of action-packed spectator sports: rugby, soccer, hockey, cricket, track, boxing, and wrestling. Competitions in polo, skin diving, deep sea and river fishing, swimming, bowling, bicycling, yachting, and power boating are also popular.

For golfing devotees, Fiji has a total of 10 golf courses, 9 on Viti Levu and 1 on Vanua Levu. Fairly flat with tree-lined fairways, the Fiji Golf Club's layout at Suva is the only 18-hole course. Visitors are welcome daily except on Tuesday afternoons when the course is reserved for ladies. Saturday afternoons are reserved for men's competitions, and visitors may play in the draw by arrangement. Rental clubs are available, green fees about $2.50.

The toughest golf course (the neighboring jet stream is not one of its hazards) is the 9-hole one at Nadi Airport. Other courses on Viti Levu are located at Lautoka, Nausori (within 2 miles of Nausori Airport), Ba, Vatukoula, Penang (near Raki Raki), Korolevu, and Yanuca Island (on the grounds of the Fijian Hotel). On Vanua Levu there is a course at Labasa.

For archers, the Fiji Archery Club hosts a shoot every Saturday and Sunday at the Nadi Airport Club. The man to call for details is Mr. Arnie Anfinson in Nadi, telephone 72-500. In Suva, members of the Suva Archery Club welcome visitors to their weekly shoots. Contact Mr. Don Welsh, telephone 23-031.

Tennis lovers will enjoy playing on the lawn courts at any of the 12 tennis clubs. The season runs from May to late November (before the rains start). Have your hotel or local travel agent arrange an introduction to a club official. The only requirement is that you must wear white, including white tennis shoes. Best facilities are provided at the Nadi Sports Club: three grass courts and one of concrete. Offering the only night playing in Fiji, the Club also has changing rooms, showers, and a bar. Courts of the Suva Lawn Tennis Club are in Albert Park, just across from the Grand Pacific Hotel. In the same park are the Municipal Courts. An attendant is on duty at these hard courts every day from 6 a.m. to 6 p.m.

For avid shell collectors, several easily accessible areas just off Viti Levu offer a great variety of specimens. The Coral Coast is noted for golden cowries, the area off Queen's Road between Navua and Suva for cowries and mitres. Be wary of cone shells in these areas; they can be poisonous. The area around Suva is also a shell collector's paradise. And you'll want to stop at the Fiji Museum in the capital city to see their wide-ranging collection. On Vanua Levu, another area worth a visit is the one around Natewa Bay. Here you'll find helmets and tritons.

Skin divers won't be disappointed in Fiji. Major reefs provide a wide range of waters — shallow areas inside the lagoons for snorkelers and spear fishermen, deep waters on the outside of the reefs for scuba divers. On the island of Viti Levu, you'll find good diving waters off Queen's Road between Suva and Nadi. Other good spots include the Astrolabe Lagoon, one of the most captivating areas and one that is infrequently dived; the Qelelevu Lagoon, about 36 hours by boat from Suva; and the Argo Reef in the Lau Islands.

Around the larger islands, waters are the clearest during the cool and dry months of June to October. During the rainy season, rivers discharge great streams of muddy waters, clouding the coastal waters for miles around. On the outer reefs, good visibility is considered to be 150 feet the year around. Water temperatures range between 74 and 80 degrees most of the year, but during July and August plan on slipping into a wet suit.

Masks, snorkels, flippers, and spear guns can be rented at most of the beach hotels, or you can buy Japanese or Australian-made diving products in Suva, Nadi, and Lautoka. To take you out to the best diving areas, charter boats are available in Suva, Lautoka, Korolevu, and Yanuca Island.

Using spear guns fired with cartridges is prohibited in Fiji unless you are a member of a spear fishing group and have received special permission from the Fiji Police. (Police will only exempt equipment brought in for temporary use.)

Fishermen will revel in Fiji's year-round fishing season. Despite having produced several world records over the years, Fijian waters remain virtually untapped — even with the fast-spreading publicity that is part of such events. Billfish are hooked the year around. Most black marlin and sailfish strike between October and April, the height of the season occurring in January and February. Yellow fin tuna are plentiful from December to June. Dolphin, barracuda, bonito, walu, and wahoo are in abundant supply throughout the year. Game fishing boats can be chartered at Lautoka, Yanuca Island, Sigatoka, Korolevu, and Suva.

A Fijian's fishing guidebook would include the following prime locations: *off Korolevu:* Beqa Passage and Lagoon; Cakualekaleka, between Beqa and Vatulele; Vatulele Island; the Coral coastline. *Off Lautoka:* the Mamanucas and the Yasawas. *Off Suva:* Astrolabe Lagoon and Kadavu Island.

For the indefatigable fisherman, the rivers of Fiji offer the chance to pull in an *Ika droka* (jungle perch). To find this unusual species, head for the Navua River, a bountiful stream about 30 miles southwest of Suva. When you reach Calia, drive up the river valley about four miles. At the site of an old sawmill, stop and leave your car. You can fish downstream from here, or, plying your way cautiously, ford the river and fish the other side (the Navua runs waist deep in places, so avoid crossing it if the current is running swiftly). On the far side, the water is deeper, and near the banks you'll find the *Ika droka* lurking below grass roots.

For the most current fishing reports, drop by Bob Wright's tackle shop in Suva.

Yachtsmen who are accredited members of overseas yacht and power boat clubs will be welcomed by the Royal Suva Yacht Club. Visitors who are in Suva for any length of time can arrange for honorary membership privileges and may join in the club's activities.

SIX-FOOT-LONG SAILFISH is the trophy of the morning on a deep sea fishing excursion in Fijian waters.

A CALENDAR OF EVENTS...FROM FIJIAN FIREWORKS TO INDIAN FIREWALKING

If you want to see a Fijian's face light up, just ask him about the Hibiscus Festival . . . or the Dominion Day celebration . . . or the cricket matches at Easter. If you're in Fiji when these or some of the following events come up on the calendar, you will add immensely to your Fiji experience.

January. "Vakatawase," or welcoming of the New Year. The first Monday of the month. Fireworks, floral decorations, festivities.

Easter weekend. In Suva, annual Easter Cricket Tournament; the Friday before Easter through Easter Monday. In Levuka, the old capital of Fiji on Ovalau Island, annual Easter Sports Meeting; professional track events with participants from all over Fiji; Good Friday through Easter Monday.

Easter Monday. At Sawa-i-Lau Island, in the Yasawas, swimming and diving competitions for young people at swimming caves.

Early April. In Suva, rugby season opens. Matches held every Saturday at Albert and Buckhurst parks.

Early June. Queen Elizabeth's official birthday. Celebrated the Monday closest to June 14. In Suva, South Pacific Bowling Carnival. Lawn bowlers from Fiji, Australia, and New Zealand compete in a 10-day event.

Mid-July. In Lautoka, a three-day Adi Salusalu Festival celebration. Floats, bands, bazaars, beauty contests, displays, singing and dancing competitions.

Mid-July. In Nadi, the Bula Festival. A week-long event with floats, processions, and the crowning of a Bula Queen.

Late July or early August. At Ba, the Bougainvillea Carnival.

Mid-August. At Sigatoka, the Coral Festival and Nadroga-Navosa Young Farmers Show. A three-day event with decorated floats, Fijian and Indian dance performances, sporting events with a variety of competitions.

Late August. In Suva, the Hibiscus Festival. During the last week of the month. Fiji's biggest celebration of the year includes processions and floats; entertainment by Fijian, Indian, Chinese, and Polynesian groups; flower shows; sporting events, including a full program of sports from rugby and soccer to bowls and bicycling, as well as a regatta and a gymkhana. The final event is the Hibiscus Queen's Ball.

Late August. In Suva and elsewhere on Viti Levu, exhibitions of Indian firewalking performed by the Madrasi sect in honor of the goddess Maha Devi.

Early September. In Suva, the annual Orchid and Horticultural Circle Flower Show. Display of tropical plants, flowers, and spectacular floral arrangements.

Mid-September. In Suva, Fiji Show and Trade Fair. Exhibition of products and handicrafts at Buckhurst Park.

Early October. Opening of the cricket season.

Early October. In Lautoka, the Sugar Festival. A week-long program of dance performances, sports competitions, and parades with gaily decorated floats.

Early October. Dominion Day. On the Monday closest to October 10. This day celebrates independence from Great Britain (and commemorates a previous historic event, on October 10, 1874, when a Deed of Cession was signed and Fiji was proclaimed a British Crown Colony). Celebrations take place in all principal towns throughout the Fiji group.

Mid-November. Prince Charles' Birthday. November 14.

November. The Diwali Festival, observed throughout Fiji, marking the beginning of the Hindu New Year. Indian houses are decorated with colored lights.

December. Christmas Day, celebrated in Fiji with feasts and special church services.

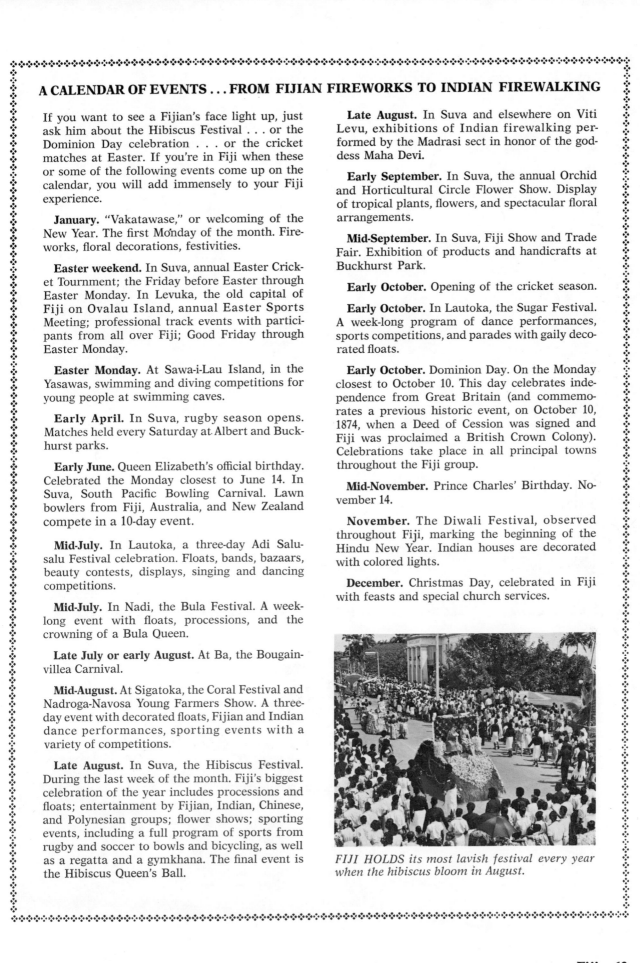

FIJI HOLDS its most lavish festival every year when the hibiscus bloom in August.

PAPER-WHITE BEACHES, the quiet street during the noontime siesta, and an armful of long loaves are typically New Caledonian.

New Caledonia...
the island of light

PINE-CLAD HEIGHTS, SNOW-WHITE BEACHES, OFFSHORE REEFS, PART MELANESIAN, PART FRENCH

New Caledonia remains in the mind's eye long after you have taken a last look at the Grande Terre and its small offshore island dependencies. You remember the haunting beauty of the Isle of Pines, its remarkably short-branched pine trees, incredible beaches, and abundance of wild orchids; Amédée Island, a mere sand spit in the sea where a lighthouse built in the time of Napoleon III soars; Nouméa, with its overlay of *la vie française*, its excellent restaurants and shops; and the vast, remote reaches making up the rest of New Caledonia, where Melanesians live in neat, well-tended villages.

The last land discovered by Europeans, New Caledonia is an Overseas Territory of the French Republic. In French it is referred to as *L'Ile de Lumière*, the Island of Light. When you catch your first glimpse of the gleaming white beaches, the luminous blue mountains, and the sparkling Coral Sea surrounding the island, you'll nod in agreement.

Despite many special attractions, New Caledonia over the past years has not been a popular tourist destination. This has been largely due to the nickel mining boom, which has affected almost every aspect of the island's economy—including the pre-empting of hotel rooms by businessmen and technicians. Too often there just wasn't a place for the tourist to stay, let alone a seat on an airplane going in or out of Nouméa. Little by little this situation has lessened. You'll find new hotels (more are slated for construction) and a larger number of flights to and from Nouméa. Though the nickel boom continues, the days of sparse tourism seem to be a thing of the past. For the time being, however, the result is pleasant: New Caledonia is not yet crowded with visitors.

Geography

Shaped like a cigar (250 miles long and 30 miles wide), New Caledonia lies 7,000 miles southwest of

S O U T H

P A C I F I C   O C E A N

TIGA

MARE

Tadine •

VAUVILLIERS

OUA

Baie de Chateaubriand

We •
• Baie du Sandal

Chepenehe •

LIFOU

Baie de Chateaubriand

ILES LOYALTY

NOUVELLE CALEDONIE

ILE DES PINS

Kuto •

Passe de la Sarcelle

Canal de la Havannah

Baie Du Prony

Yate •

OUEN

TURTLE CLUB HOTEL •

Baie Boulari

Amedee •

Recif Kue

La Dumbea •
Mt. Dore •
NOUMEA •

Baie Ouinne

Recif Aboré

Passe de St. Vincent

NOU

Paita •

Recif de l'Annibal

MATHIEU

Tomo •

Recif Esterieur

Bouloupari •

HUGON

DUCOS

LEPREDOUR

Grand Recif Esterieur

Thio •

TOUPETI

Nakety •

Baie de Nakety

LEBRIS

La Foa •

Kouaoua • Cap Dumoulin

Baie de Canala

Canala •

Baie Moari

Baie d'Ugail

Fonwari •

Moindou •

Nessadiou •

Houailou •

Ba • Cap Bocage

Cap Koua

Ponerihouen •

Gouaro •

Bourail •

Baie de Bourail

Poindimie • Cap Baye

Poya •

Cap
Goulvain

Touho •

Mueo •

Hienghene •

Pouembout •

Tipindje

Kone •

Tao

Voh •
Temala

Oubatche

Platean de
Koniene

Pouebo •

Baie Splendide

Grand Recif de Cofarte

Grand Recij de Gatofe

Balade •

Koligoh •

Grand Recif Mathieu

Ouaco •

Gomen •

Cap Deverd

Arama •
Pam •

Koumac •

BALABIO

Baie de Harcourt

Paagoumene •

Baie d'Nehoue

Baie Banare

BABA

Poum •

YANDE

Baie des

Grand Recij

de Koumac

ILES BELEP

Recifs de
l'Astrolabe

Grand Recif Mengalia

Recif de
Cook

C O R A L   S E A

Beautemps-Beaupre

OUVEA

Baie
Fayaoue

Fayaoue •

MOULI

Logon d'Ouvea

Relais de Fayaoue •

St. Joseph •

Pleiades Du Nord

Pleiades Du Sud

NEW CALEDONIA
A N D   D E P E N D E N C I E S

LEGEND

PRINCIPAL ROADS ————
MINOR ROADS ————

0   25   50   75

San Francisco; 1,150 miles northeast of Sydney, Australia; 1,135 miles northwest of Auckland, New Zealand. By air, it's about eight hours from Honolulu, less than three hours from Sydney.

Compared with other South Pacific islands, New Caledonia is second in size only to New Zealand. The island is believed to be part of an ancient land mass that was once linked with Australia.

New Caledonia's dependencies include the three Loyalty Islands (Ouvéa, Lifou, and Maré) lying off the east coast, the Isle of Pines to the south, and other uninhabited islands, islets, and reefs. Included are the Chesterfield Islands north of the mainland, a habitat of rare sea birds.

Running the length of the island and dividing it into two distinct regions, is the mountainous Chaîne Centrale. The east side is lush and wet, vegetation is dense, and large rivers cut a path to the sea. A drier climate on the west side makes the land more pastoral, with much of it given over to cattle raising. Two of the major peaks, Mt. Panie to the north and Mt. Humbolt to the south, rise to elevations of more than 5,000 feet.

Enormously rich in nickel resources, New Caledonia has as its economic mainstay the business of extracting and refining ore. In the production of nickel, the island ranks third in the world, after Canada and the Soviet Union. Flying over the mountains behind the city of Nouméa, you see great gashes in the red earth below that vividly testify to the magnitude of nickel mining—a startling contrast to the surrounding tropical setting.

New Caledonia's mainland is surrounded by a thousand miles of barrier reef—second in size to Australia's Great Barrier Reef. At Nouméa, the reef is about 11 miles offshore and protects a calm lagoon that offers nearly ideal conditions for swimming, fishing, and sailing.

History

Happy anonymity was the lot of New Caledonia until 1768, when it was first noted in the ship's log by Bougainville as he sailed south from the New Hebrides. But is was not until six years later—in 1774—that Captain James Cook actually discovered the island. Because its pine-clad ridges reminded Cook of Scotland, he named his discovery New Caledonia. From a landfall at Balade on the northeast coast, Cook eventually sailed south to discover the Isle of Pines. During the next 50 years and more, a variety of navigators, explorers, missionaries, traders, and runaway seamen flocked to the island.

Not until 1853 did France officially claim New Caledonia in order to protect French missionaries on the island who occasionally had been attacked by cannibalistic natives.

SHY BUT SMILING, a Melanesian woman wears a Mother Hubbard and tucks flowers in her hair.

From 1864 until around the turn of the century, New Caledonia was a penal colony to which some 40,000 prisoners—most of them long-term political prisoners from France—were exiled.

Lifestyle

Of New Caledonia's population of some 115,000, about 50,000 are Melanesians. Some live in Nouméa, but by far the greater number live in very small villages scattered throughout the island.

Outside of Nouméa, Melanesians still live according to long established traditions and are governed by tribal law. Each tribe is ruled by a Great Chief, a Little Chief, and a Council of Elders. In their villages, thatched roof dwellings are clustered around a large square carpeted with well-kept lawn. Residents exist on a subsistence economy, largely based on fishing, coffee, and copra.

In Nouméa, where at least half of all New Caledonians live, the population is predominantly French, with smaller numbers of Tahitians, Indonesians, Vietnamese, New Hebrideans, as well as Melanesians. Living accommodations range from old French Colonial cottages and contemporary one-family dwellings to units in huge, government-built housing projects.

The reigning economic force in Nouméa is Société le Nickel—the French nickel mining company that provides thousands of jobs, influences the cost of living index, and affects wages and salaries. The nickel company has a marked effect on New Caledonia's whole way of life. Because the cost of living

THE LOOK of Nouméa: the old post office building with wrought iron trim; the public market where a customer carries home a fish; a church on a hillside eminence; the new museum, handsome in the simplicity of its design.

in Nouméa is high, almost everyone—wife as well as husband—works. In summer, during school vacation, child-care "clubs" take over: you'll see groups of small children at the beach doing calisthenics, taking swimming lessons, or observing the quiet time of a mid-morning nap.

One common characteristic of Nouméans, no matter what their income: they eat well. Enjoyed everywhere—from the smallest home to the finest hotel dining room—is the custom of a large noon-time meal of many courses.

NOUMÉA, THE CAPITAL

La vie française permeates almost every facet of Nouméa: the good French restaurants, the boutiques (more than 20), the narrow streets with sidewalk cafes, the economic domination by the French-controlled nickel industry, the predominance of the French language throughout the city. Often labeled "the Paris of the Pacific" (and not without some justification), Nouméa is a city touched with a light-hearted zestful quality—one that stimulates you to join in the fun as you stroll the streets. Fortunately situated on a hilly peninsula, Nouméa overlooks a succession of lovely, curving bays and a magnificent, almost land-locked harbor.

Two square towers of St. Joseph's Cathedral, built in 1893, dominate Nouméa's downtown skyline. From the cathedral's statue-filled hillside courtyard, you can see the town's business section—a view that is changing rapidly as a result of a boom in new construction.

To get your bearings from the cathedral, look down to the large Place de Cocotiers, or Central Square (almost immediately below you on the left), crisscrossed by paths and bordered by flamboyant trees (in bloom November and December). The Square is actually two squares, the center of one marked by a turn-of-the-century bandstand, the other by a fountain. In between the two is the focal point of Place de Cocotiers, Fontaine Monumentale. Along one side of the square, at the intersection of Rue d'Austerlitz and Rue Anatole France, are the town's principal bus and taxi stations. This is the older section of Nouméa. Faded brick buildings and vine-covered wooden structures of French Colonial style lend a distinctly mellow quality to this part of the city. Overall, the city is somewhat of an architectural hodge-podge, the old mixed with an assortment of contemporary buildings.

Befitting a city which offers many shopping-and-browsing possibilities, much of Nouméa is a good walkabout place. However, to see the greater part, including the residential areas, suburbs, beaches, and bays, you can take a city tour for a comprehensive over-view in two or three hours. Another approach is to hire a driver-guide or a well-informed taxi driver.

Nouméa is an early-rising town where a 2½ to 3-hour lunch break is the rule. The day begins some time before 7 a.m. This is the hour housewives are returning home from their daily round of shopping at the market (it opens at 5 a.m.). Most shops and stores are open by 7:15, but at 11 commerce adjourns for 2½ hours to 3 hours; then the shops come to life again until 6 p.m. Exceptions to the mid-day closing custom are the restaurants. They stay open throughout the day, and you sit down to what routinely becomes a two-hour lunch.

Sightseeing around the city

For an overall view of Nouméa, you might head for Mount Ravel or one of the other good lookout points. Stretching out before you will be a broad sampling of the island's topography: the peninsula's jagged coastline with its deep-notching bays, and the distant Grande Récif, where a foaming line of the Coral Sea marks the encircling barrier reef. Cradled within its protecting arm you'll see Baie des Citrons and Anse Vata Bay, cerulean blue on a sunny day, with the white sands of two fine public beaches, flanked with hotels and restaurants. Spicing this colorful show are yachts setting sail for a race; fishing vessels with heavy catches, riding low in the water; and barges loaded with nickel ore being towed toward the tip of Doniambo Peninsula, where a cover of billowing smoke marks the site of the smelter. Back in the city, here are just a few of the places to visit:

The Aquarium of Nouméa is world-renowned. The aquarium is open from 1:30 to 5 p.m. every day except Monday and Friday. Its fluorescent display of deepwater coral formations takes place between 2:30 and 3:30 p.m. Note: Special arrangements may be made with the aquarium for groups to visit on a Monday or Friday.

The Mineralogical Museum, located in the office buildings of the Service des Mines, Valle du Tir, offers an interesting display of New Caledonia's many minerals. Open to the public from Monday to Friday from 7:30 to 11 a.m. and from 2 to 5 p.m., the exhibit also features a large relief map of New Caledonia showing the various mining areas.

The Market Place is Nouméa come to life. Housewives and chefs haggle over the best buys in everything from breadfruit and coconuts to squawking poultry and live fish. Because Nouméa has a law forbidding the sale of dead fish (unless cooked), fishermen keep their catches in tanks that ride on wheels to the market, where fish are lifted out alive

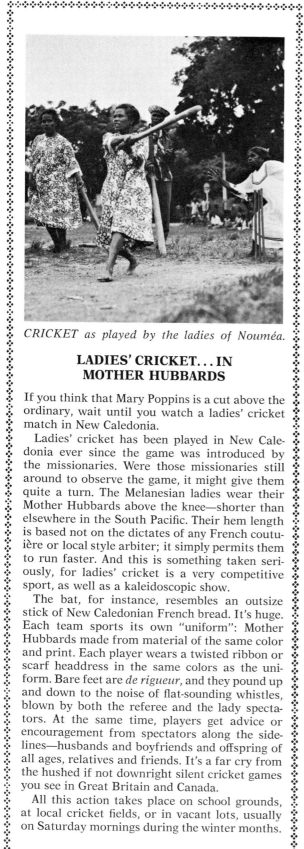

CRICKET as played by the ladies of Nouméa.

LADIES' CRICKET... IN MOTHER HUBBARDS

If you think that Mary Poppins is a cut above the ordinary, wait until you watch a ladies' cricket match in New Caledonia.

Ladies' cricket has been played in New Caledonia ever since the game was introduced by the missionaries. Were those missionaries still around to observe the game, it might give them quite a turn. The Melanesian ladies wear their Mother Hubbards above the knee—shorter than elsewhere in the South Pacific. Their hem length is based not on the dictates of any French coutuière or local style arbiter; it simply permits them to run faster. And this is something taken seriously, for ladies' cricket is a very competitive sport, as well as a kaleidoscopic show.

The bat, for instance, resembles an outsize stick of New Caledonian French bread. It's huge. Each team sports its own "uniform": Mother Hubbards made from material of the same color and print. Each player wears a twisted ribbon or scarf headdress in the same colors as the uniform. Bare feet are *de rigueur*, and they pound up and down to the noise of flat-sounding whistles, blown by both the referee and the lady spectators. At the same time, players get advice or encouragement from spectators along the sidelines—husbands and boyfriends and offspring of all ages, relatives and friends. It's a far cry from the hushed if not downright silent cricket games you see in Great Britain and Canada.

All this action takes place on school grounds, at local cricket fields, or in vacant lots, usually on Saturday mornings during the winter months.

for the customers. Opening every day at 5 a.m., the market is located near the Place de Cocotiers, at the corner of Rue Anatole France and Rue Georges Clemenceau.

The Museum of Nouméa. There's nothing musty about this handsome museum and its excellent exhibits. The building, covering a whole city block, was opened in 1971. It's a huge open rectangle with an inner courtyard containing a garden and a stream. A botanical treasure-trove, the garden contains some 180 varieties of plants collected from the Plaine des Lacs, an area near Yaté about 40 miles from Nouméa.

Even the rich red soil and the stones over which the stream trickles were hauled in from the Plaine des Lacs. Opening onto the garden are other courts containing artifacts from the New Hebrides and the Loyalty Islands, as well as New Caledonia. These displays trace the history and way of life that were typical to the tribes of this region. Another court, housing a painting exhibit of local as well as overseas artists, opens out onto a lawn, a full-size native *case* or hut sitting in the center.

Located on Avenue du Maréchal Foch between Rue August Brun and Rue Tourville, the museum is open to the public Monday through Friday, from 7:30 to 11 a.m. and from 2 to 5 p.m.

Nickel smelter tours can be arranged for groups interested in seeing crude nickel ore converted into ingots ready for shipping. The Société le Nickel plant at Nouméa refines some 70,000 tons of ore per year. Requests for this tour must be made to the Office du Tourisme at 27 Rue de Sébastopol in Nouméa, and should be made well in advance so that protective gear and coveralls will be ready for your arrival.

South Pacific Commission Headquarters, on Route de L'Anse Vata, is housed in the former World War II headquarters of Admiral William F. "Bull" Halsey. In these white colonial buildings, a small museum displays typical artifacts and styles of architecture of the 14 South Pacific island groups with which the commission is concerned.

Formed in 1947, the commission is an advisory body involved in the islands' agriculture, communications, transport, fisheries, forestry, labor, marketing, production, trade and finance, public works, education, health, and housing. Activities range from research to technical assistance.

Shopping

Wandering around Nouméa, you'll find boutiques here and there—almost anywhere. But if you haven't the time to hunt and seek, try Rue de l'Alma,

NOUMÉA'S SPLENDID aquarium, world famed for its fluorescent displays of deepwater coral formations; Rue de l'Alma, one of Nouméa's main streets; and the smoke-belching nickel smelter, the city's economic lifeline.

where you'll find numerous shops in the vicinity of Place de Cocotiers. Other streets worth exploring in this general area are Rue de Sébastopol, Rue Georges Clemenceau, and Rue Anatole France. Some of the newer shops (a good many have opened in recent years) are farther from the center of town. In the vicinity of the new post office (in the Baie de la Moselle area), try shopping on Rue de Sébastopol and Avenue Maréchal Foch in the three blocks between Rue Frederic Surleau and Rue Eugene Porcheron.

Some tips for best buys among the shops' French collections: bikinis, shoes, shifts, costume jewelry; men's shirts, ties and sweaters; French culinary utensils. In addition, examine the wide selection of perfumes from Paris; colorful hand-blocked scarves, sundresses and bikinis designed and made in Nouméa; sun togs from Australia; swimsuits, bags, and sandals from Italy; casual sportswear from London. The variety is more than enough to deplete your carefully planned budget.

And for a peek at the latest high-fashion clothes and accessories, don't miss a visit to Bettina, Claude-France, Dorothe Bis, Françoise, Frou-Frou, Maurice Boutique, Piccolo Boutique, Rozanne, Truc Much, and other Nouméa shops.

Some of the New Caledonian-made jewelry is beguiling. Take a close look at the cagou (the national bird) and fish brooches, made in gold and silver, and the gold tikis, mounted on mother of pearl pendants. You'll find displays at Bijouteries Gaspard and at Hesnault.

Perhaps the most conspicuous forms of the New Caledonian natives' artistic expression are their wood carvings and handicrafts made from pandanus bark, and the shell necklaces and tapa cloth (the latter, an art the Melanesians acquired from the Polynesians). Most of the shops are stocked with various kinds of handicrafts, but for the largest assortment of all, try the department stores.

WORK AND PLAY: a cattleman rounds up his herd on the west coast; soccer teams compete on a playing field in Nouméa.

You'll find sculptured wood figures of totemic and religious significance, model canoes in many sizes, carved clubs and spears, Ouvéa mats in varying degrees of fineness, rectangular shopping baskets, handbags, and dancing skirts. Nouméa's two largest department stores are Ballande, on Rue de l'Alma, and Barrau, on Rue Anatole France.

Shops are open Monday through Saturday from 7:15 to 11 a.m. and from 1:30 to 5:30 p.m. There is no bargaining.

Sports

One of the major sports centers in a sports-minded South Pacific, New Caledonia had the honor of hosting the South Pacific Games in 1966. Especially built for this event were a new Olympic swimming pool, tennis courts, and playfields where island groups now compete in football, track and field events, basketball, rugby, cricket, cycling, boxing, weight lifting, tennis, and swimming.

With the barrier reef offshore from Nouméa and the crystal clear waters surrounding its outlying islands, New Caledonia is considered one of the best areas in the world for skin diving and snorkeling. The lagoons are ideal spots for sailing, motorboat racing, swimming, and water skiing. The sporty deep outer waters and protected bays attract yachtsmen and deep sea fishing enthusiasts from all parts of the world.

Nouméa's race course holds two-day meets two or three times a year, drawing enthusiastic response from residents. But locals and visitors give their noisiest support to the Melanesian teams that play

English cricket. Matches are held at local playfields and on the vacant lots near the nickel factory every Saturday.

Visiting sportsmen wishing to use local club facilities — horseback riding, tennis, yachting, bowling, soccer, flying, cycling, basketball, rugby, and spear fishing—can get visitors' cards from the Office du Tourisme.

AROUND THE ISLAND

Once out of Nouméa, your chances of bumping into other tourists grow slim. The hinterlands are an unexpectedly silent world of gentle, sometimes spectacular, beauty. Spaced at intervals throughout the parts of the island reached by roads, there are small and unpretentious (but adequate) hotels.

Travel on practically all of the island roads is time-consuming. It's worth it if you *have* the time; but bear in mind that only about 125 miles of New Caledonian roads are sealed (hard-surfaced); the remaining 2,700 miles of road are dusty and fairly rough. Traffic on several sections of major roads is controlled, with one-way stretches of 10 miles and more. These sections include the two crossmountain routes (one between Boulouparis and Thio and the other between La Foa and Koh), and the short stretch between Yaté Dam and Yaté, on the southern end of the island.

Along the west coast. From Nouméa, the road rambles nearly 300 miles up the coast to Poum, its northernmost point. Side roads branch off the main road, leading to villages and native reserves. Some trickle off to fine beaches: at Tiaré (turn off at Port Laguerre); at Ouano (turn off at Qua Tom); at Poé (turn off at Bourail).

Much of the route along this west side crosses broad savannahs punctuated with stands of the lovely tree called *niaouli*. It winds through lush pasture lands, grazing areas for race horses and cattle—a harmonious landscape, and lightly settled.

Taking a one-day trip to Bourail (about 106 miles from Nouméa) you'll see some of New Caledonia's small towns, Melanesian villages, cattle ranches, and mining districts. On Col Boghen, stop for a panoramic view (over native beehive huts) of the ocean and barrier reef. Just a few miles from Bourail is Pierced Rock, where the sea has cut a tunnel about 150 feet long at beach level from the open ocean straight through a towering cliff. You can enjoy a picnic on Roche Percée Beach or lunch at the Hotel Niaouli; both can be easily arranged through your guide or driver. On the return drive,

THE MELANESIAN HUT... IT'S LIKE A BEEHIVE

The traditional Melanesian hut was a round structure with low walls and a steep-pitched conical roof that had the look of a beehive. A doorway, low and narrow, was the only opening. Inside was a single room without so much as a chimney.

Walls of these huts were either of bark from the niaouli (a species of eucalyptus) or of bamboo. The roof was thatched with grass, sometimes laden with stones to prevent wind damage.

The largest and finest hut in the village was the ceremonial residence of the supreme chief. It bore several distinguishing features: it occupied a prominent location in the village; its approach was usually bordered by stately pines; its rooftop was marked with a carved spire. This latter totem (or *flèche tetière*) rose from the peak of the conical roof and displayed the coat of arms of the royal born chief. The residence was also marked by carved door posts and rafters representing ancestral guardians of the ruling family and tribe (the Melanesians excelled at wood carving). The huts of other members of the tribe were smaller, located in less prominent sites, and without the rooftop totem.

You still see Melanesian huts that fit this description in villages on the east and west coasts and on the island of Ouvéa. But, for the most part, the round houses you see today are ones that have been rebuilt in the style of the ancient dwellings. The Melanesian of our time lives in a hut influenced by European architecture: it is rectangular rather than round; the walls are higher; the openings include windows as well as a door. Building materials are also different these days; the structure is made either of niaouli poles covered with mud and whitewashed, or of straw latticed with small rods.

A ROOFTOP SPIRE, the flèche tetière, (left) once crowned Melanesian hut occupied by supreme chief.

you can visit the New Zealand War Cemetery and stop at Boulouparis for refreshments and a close-up view of the famous cagou, New Caledonia's national bird (a running bird similiar to New Zealand's kiwi).

On the east coast. Yaté, known as the Paradis Botanic, is about 40 miles from Nouméa in the Plaine des Lacs area. The area contains more than 2,000 different kinds of plants, many found nowhere else in the world. It's not surprising that botanists consider this one of their most rewarding workshops. Especially showy along the road to Yaté are the multi-color bush flowers, thriving in rather barren country and in very acidic moist soil. At Yaté you'll find a small Melanesian village and a huge hydro-electric power plant and dam.

Outside of Yaté and Thio, the east coast is most easily seen if you fly from Nouméa to either Houaïlou or Touho and then travel by road along the coast. At Houaïlou the modest Hôtel Bel Air has 12 good rooms and a restaurant; at Touho the small Hôtel de Touho has six thatched bungalows and a restaurant.

About 25 miles from Touho (an hour's drive over a rough road) is The Relais de Koulnoué at Hienghène, a small village boasting spectacular surroundings and two fine small hotels. The Koulnoué has 15 bungalows in attractive grounds, and the 11-room Chez Maître Pierre is situated on the river. At

SCENIC CONTRASTS of New Caledonia's east coast range from rocks that rear up from the sea to little churches beyond tree-lined lanes, from river crossings by cable-guided ferries to coffee beans drying in the sun.

either hotel, an overwhelming feeling of having left the world behind you quickly takes hold. On the drive from Touho to Hienghène, you'll pass little villages tucked into the dense green tropical foliage. In these Melanesian reserves, the natives still live and are ruled according to their ancestral tribal customs. All along the road, Melanesian children are waiting to wave as you pass by. It's customary for you to wave, and they return your greeting.

Along the way you can watch the friendly Melanesians picking coffee, preparing copra for market, and working in the fields. You can taste tart wild cherries, handle the drying coffee beans, and drink water from a coconut freshly cut by a native boy. In the tropical jungle, you can hear flying foxes (fruit bats) at night, and, in the daytime, parrots (black, green, and red), who will typically squawk an answer to your car horn. Teasing your senses is the smell of fragrant ginger, lemon, or coffee blossoms. At the Melanesian village of Poyes, an elderly chief demonstrates his lethal throwing sling and his accuracy with a javelin. Native women invite you to visit their kitchens and watch while they work on their handicrafts. And, you won't have to wonder if picture taking is considered an insult—most villagers are more than willing to pose for you, some of them even hamming it up. Between the native village and Hienghène, you'll have your fill of spectacular scenery. Naturally sculptured limestone rocks tower 250 feet above the Bay of Hienghène, and massive grottoes take you through mountains of limestone from one small valley to another.

A dramatic landscape, the east coast has bold escarpments, with rocky outcrops punctuating the shoreline and wide rivers pouring into the sea. You will soon cross the Tipindic River over a new concrete bridge—a landmark on this coast where crossings are commonly made using punts running along a cable to ferry cars to the other side.

For an outing that gives you a sample of the west coast as well as the interior mountains and the east coast, try this 200 mile loop: go up the coast to Boulouparis, then up and over the mountain spine of Chaîne Centrale and down to Thio, a nickel mining town on the east side of the island. Then drive on to Canala and La Crouen. Stay overnight at the Hotel La Crouen (nine rooms and a restaurant) before heading back over the mountains to La Foa. Here the Relais Melanesien has 10 rooms and a restaurant—a good place to stop for the night. It's another 75 miles back to Nouméa by way of Boulouparis. This loop is no trip to do in a day unless you go virtually non-stop from dawn to after dusk on the rough island roads.

Road conditions, as well as the language barrier (French and many Melanesian dialects), discourage many travelers from touring the island on their own. If this is the case with you, look into the two alternatives offered: take a tour arranged through a local travel agent, or use the fly-drive service of Air Calédonie (they provide ground taxi service for short distances at all the points this airline serves).

THE ISLE OF PINES AND OTHER OFFSHORE ISLANDS

Several of New Caledonia's satellite islands can be easily reached by plane or boat. They offer enough attractions to deserve a visit if your time permits. Perhaps the best known of these smaller islands is the Isle of Pines. It's one of those places you dream about—hauntingly beautiful and serene. Its low hills and rocky shores are rimmed with the majestic *Araucaria cooki*, a species of pine that prompted Captain Cook to give the island its name. The sand on its paperwhite beaches is almost powdery in texture. Inland, wild orchids bloom in the forests, and the natives and their small villages remain hospitable and unspoiled.

Silhouetting themselves against the sky, the island's trees are 200-foot columns, a sharp contrast to their 6-foot-long bristling branches. In some lights and from some vantage points, they appear so unreal that it's no wonder early explorers reported sighting columns of basalt.

An area of about 50 square miles, the Isle of Pines is a Melanesian reserve, land held in perpetuity for the people. If you're lucky enough to visit one of the villages on the right day, you'll enjoy seeing a Melanesian wedding and feast. Activities usually start before dawn; and the feasting, singing, and dancing go on until all the food, presented as wedding gifts, has been consumed. Holding true to the reigning religious belief, all wedding ceremonies are Roman Catholic. The food—taro root, suckling pig, breadfruit—is typically Melanesian, but the service is strictly French. Volunteer Melanesian waiters line up (white napkins draped over their arms) to serve the wedding guests scattered around a table set in the shade of a thatched roof. A royal wedding couldn't have much more fanfare.

The Isle of Pines is situated some 70 miles southeast of Nouméa, 30 miles off the mainland. Its climate is dry—with temperatures consistently lower than on the main island. By air, it takes about 35 minutes to reach the island from Magenta Airport in Nouméa. Approaching the airstrip, don't be frightened when your plane buzzes over the bungalows of Relais de Kanuméra, the island's only hotel. This is the signal for the bus driver to start up the narrow, winding road leading to the open-field airstrip to pick up passengers.

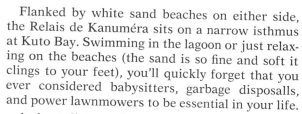

THE ISLE OF PINES offers an idyllic, isolated atmosphere. Beaches and rock-rimmed lagoons and streams that can be crossed on horseback are a small part of the island's charm.

Flanked by white sand beaches on either side, the Relais de Kanuméra sits on a narrow isthmus at Kuto Bay. Swimming in the lagoon or just relaxing on the beaches (the sand is so fine and soft it clings to your feet), you'll quickly forget that you ever considered babysitters, garbage disposalls, and power lawnmowers to be essential in your life.

A short distance from your bungalow, 12 other beaches as well as offshore atolls and other coral formations, shoals, and cays invite you to explore. Canoes, paddle boats, water skis, and ping pong equipment are available for your use; just ask at the hotel desk. Spear fishing equipment may be rented. A must for visitors is a hotel-arranged trip around the island to visit the caves, the bay of Oupi, the mission, the famous *tumuli* (mounds) where you can gather wild, multicolored orchids by the armload. The hotel also arranges fishing trips, climaxed by fish and lobster being cooked for you on the beach.

Three other offshore islands with special attractions are Amedée, Ouen and Ouvéa:

Amedée Island is less than one square mile in area. It has sandy beaches and shade trees, all dominated by the towering lighthouse dating back to 1862 and the time of Napoleon III.

Originally built on the hills of La Villette in Paris, the lighthouse was dismantled and shipped to Nouméa, to be reassembled rivet by rivet, piece by piece. It was officially inaugurated and put to work as an aid to navigation on November 15, 1865, the birthday of the Empress. Now automatically controlled, it's a fine sight—even though you can't get inside to climb the spiral stairs to the top of the tower.

From Nouméa several boats make the day-cruise to Amedée Island every day except Monday. Cruises include a barbecue lunch on the beach and time for swimming and snorkeling in the lagoon.

Ouen Island has truly a get-away-from-it-all atmosphere. About 15 minutes by air from Nouméa, the small island has one small resort—the 10-bungalow Turtle Club, situated about 50 yards from the airstrip. You'll find equipment for boating and fishing, water skiing and snorkeling. Visitors seeing sea turtles languidly swimming about in offshore waters quickly understand how the hotel came to be named.

Ouvéa, smallest of the three main Loyalty Islands, is northernmost in a chain that lies 50 miles east off the coast of Grande Terre. The only one of the Loyalties with tourist accommodations, it has 10 bungalows at the Relais de Fayaoué, with restaurant and bar.

Low, sandy, and crescent-shaped, Ouvéa is about 30 miles long and 4½ miles across. It encloses a large lagoon, which most of the island's villages face. Although the terrain is flat, Ouvéa is well-wooded. The island population is about 2,100.

Not many tourists manage to visit Ouvéa—it's an hour's flight from Nouméa's Magenta Airport—but those who do can convince you that your trip to New Caledonia is incomplete without seeing Ouvéa.

Part of the island's charm comes from its very remoteness, part from the topography that puts you in an intimate relationship to the sea, and part from the indefinable quality that you find in places not yet catering to many tourists. You're a novelty in Ouvéa, and you receive a spontaneous welcome.

PRACTICAL INFORMATION

Entry regulations

To visit New Caledonia, you'll need a valid passport and an international smallpox vaccination certificate. Without a visa, an American citizen may stay up to 30 days. For longer visits a visa can be obtained from your nearest French consulate.

Customs regulations

In addition to your personal effects, you are permitted to bring in duty-free 200 cigarettes (or a half-pound of tobacco or cigars) and one bottle of liquor. Customs officers may ask you to register any items of high value such as jewelry, transistors, tape recorders, portable radios, and cameras; and you may be required to show these certificates of registration on departure.

Climate

New Caledonia has a semi-tropical climate. Average daytime temperatures range from 73° in July to 85° in February. Its cool season is from June through September, its hot season from December through March. During the warm summer months, an occasional hurricane or thunderstorm will pummel the island.

Like Fiji, the island of New Caledonia has a wet and a dry side. Rainfall is more abundant—up to 90 inches a year—on the fertile east coast. As an example of the west coast's dryness, Nouméa's rainfall averages only 40 inches a year. The heaviest rainfall comes during the months from January through May; the lightest, from September through November.

Communications

International telephone service is available from Nouméa. Cables can be sent from the post office in Nouméa, and airmail is dispatched five times a week. Two French-language daily newspapers as well as a bi-weekly and two weeklies are printed in the capital city.

Currency and banking

New Caledonia's monetary unit is the Cours du Franc Pacifique, usually written CFP or just frs. The fluctuating rate of exchange is approximately 92 frs. to the US dollar.

Nouméa has branch offices of Banque de l'Indochine, Banque Nationale de Paris, Banque de Paris et des Pays Bas, and Société Générale. Banking hours are 8 to 11 a.m. and 2 to 4 p.m.

Health and medical

You'll find doctors, dentists, a government hospital, private medical clinics, and pharmacies in Nouméa. Outside the city 17 medical centers and 18 dispensaries are located in villages throughout New Caledonia and on its outlying islands. Water in hotels and restaurants is safe to drink, but it's wise to be careful in other places.

For information

Branches of the Office du Tourisme are located at Tontouta Airport and on the wharf at Nouméa; the main office is at 27 Rue de Sébastopol. Maps and brochures are available here. A second source of information is the office of the Syndicat d'Initiative on Rue Jean Jaures at Rue d'Austerlitz.

Public holidays

Legal holidays in New Caledonia include the following: January 1; Easter Monday; May 1; Ascension Day (40 days after Easter); Whit Monday (the day after Pentecost, or the Monday following the sixth Sunday after Easter); July 14; August 15; September 24; November 1; November 11; and December 25.

Tipping

Visitors arriving at the Tontouta Airport outside Nouméa will be pleasantly surprised to see a sign reading "No tipping, please. Help preserve the custom and don't cause embarrassment." This advice is applicable not only at the airport but also at other places where you might ordinarily tip. The only exceptions to this custom might be for special services that are clearly beyond the call of duty.

Language

French—New Caledonia's official language—is spoken everywhere. Although a knowledge of the language is helpful, you can get along quite easily with English in Nouméa and the resort areas. However, a small French dictionary is very handy to have along. The peoples of the Melanesian population speak 25 or 30 different dialects, with no one dialect predominating. Men from different tribes communicate in French. If you do not speak French and plan to travel into the hinterlands, it's wise to hire an interpreter-guide.

Where to stay

Although Nouméa has at least a dozen hotels (none with more than 85 rooms), it's well to make reservations well in advance of your visit.

Located on Anse Vata Beach, the Château Royal is Nouméa's most lavish and luxuriously appointed hotel. Its Louis XV appointments (although somewhat incongruous) lend a particular elegance. The Château boasts a nightclub, a French restaurant on the terrace, three bars, and has a variety of gear available for water sports. By mid-1973, the hotel will have an additional 230 rooms.

Located across the road from Anse Vata Beach and set in five acres of tropical gardens, Le Nouvata is also classed as a luxury hotel. Three of the relatively newer hotels, close to the water, are the Isle de France at Anse Vata; the Lagon, also at Anse Vata; and the Mocambo, overlooking the yacht harbor at Baie des Citrons. In Nouméa you'll discover a number of small, comfortable hotels with more modest accommodations. They don't have as many resort-type facilities and in some cases no air-conditioning (or if they do, there's an extra charge for it), but their rates are considerably lower than those of the luxury-class hotels.

Rates for two in air-conditioned rooms range from a high of almost $45 a day down to less than $20 a day.

Outside Nouméa. At towns and villages on the east and west coasts of the island (and on several offshore islands, as well) are small hotels and a *relais* or two (*relais*, literally translated, means relay or shift). They make comfortable overnight stopping points for anyone exploring the vast, lightly inhabited parts of New Caledonia and its island dependencies. Few of these hotels offer many of the amenities that travelers come to expect at larger establishments, but their very smallness helps to create a unique wayside inn atmosphere.

The Relais de Koulnoué at Hienghène on the east coast is a perfect example. It's an hour drive from the airstrip at Touho. Except for the car that delivers you to the door of the *relais* and transports you back to the airstrip, the sound of an automobile is unheard. In mid-afternoon you can usually have the whole *relais*—swimming pool and all—to yourself because everyone else will be taking a siesta. You might also have the beach to yourself and—for your headquarters—a Melanesian cottage with thatched roof and open, shuttered windows providing cross-ventilation. At nightfall the only light will be by a kerosene lamp. It's a lovely place to relax, watch the sea, stroll the beach, swim in the

SEA BIRDS swoop low over the water at the edge of a reef-protected strand. Passengers walk from an airstrip to the Isle Ouen resort around the bend. Amedée Lighthouse rises majestically from a sand spit in the sea, its entrance testifying to its age.

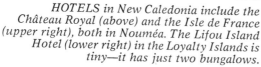
HOTELS in New Caledonia include the Château Royal (above) and the Isle de France (upper right), both in Nouméa. The Lifou Island Hotel (lower right) in the Loyalty Islands is tiny—it has just two bungalows.

pool, and nap in the afternoon. And after several laps in that pool, your conscience won't flash a red light when those fine French meals are set before you. All of this may sound *too* relaxed — but it probably won't seem so, not after you've driven the rugged up-island roads or spent the last few days climbing in and out of airplanes.

On the east coast, small hotels (none with more than 15 rooms) are located at Thio, La Crouen, Houaïlou, Poindimié, Touho, and Hienghène. On the west coast, similar hotels are located at Boulouparis, La Foa, Bourail, Koné, and Koumac.

Hotels on the three outer-island dependencies of New Caledonia are the Turtle Club (10 rooms), on Isle Ouen; Relais de Kanuméra (35 rooms) on the Isle of Pines; and Relais de Fayaoué (10 rooms) on Ouvéa, in the Loyalty Islands.

For the latest, up-to-date list of hotels, including their rates and facilities, write to the Office du Tourisme, 27 Rue de Sébastopol, Nouméa, New Caledonia, or check with your travel agent.

How to get around

If you arrive in New Caledonia by ship you'll anchor at the new wharf facilities in Nouméa's magnificent natural harbor.

If you arrive by plane, you land at Tontouta International Airport, about 30 miles north of Nouméa. It's a ride of 45 minutes or an hour to your hotel. By taxi, the ride costs over $20; by airport bus, the fare is under $5. Taxis in Nouméa are also costly: over $1 for every two miles. With several persons, the cost is whittled down—four can ride for the price of one. But from 7 p.m. to 5 a.m. and all day on Sundays and public holidays, the fare goes up 50 per cent. In Nouméa a bus is called a "baby car"—the original vehicles resembled prams—and baby cars provide efficient and

VARY YOUR TRAVEL by sightseeing in New Caledonia by launch, by airplane, and by Nouméa's public transportation—buses that are called "baby cars."

inexpensive service. Every few minutes these blue minibuses (each with space for 18 passengers) leave from Place de Cocotiers, the main square, on their routes throughout the city and into the suburbs. Each vehicle is individually owned, but the municipality of Nouméa licenses and inspects them. Altogether, the baby cars form Transport en Commun, considered the best public transportation in the South Pacific Islands.

To rent a car and drive in New Caledonia, you need a valid driver's license, either international or domestic. Driving is on the right side of the road. Traffic is ordinarily quite heavy in Nouméa, where there are more cars per person than in many of the world's large cities. One rule to remember: don't honk your horn. It's illegal—except for wedding parties. Outside the Nouméa city limits and the road leading to Tontouta Airport, little more than 100 miles of the 2,700 miles of roads on the island are sealed. Traffic in the hinterlands is exceedingly light, but you should keep a sharp eye out for pedestrians, animals, and the other driver

who may not be expecting an oncoming vehicle.

Rental cars can be arranged through your hotel. Popular makes are Volkswagen, Renault, Fiat, and Peugeot. Rental charges range from about $5 a day plus 10 cents per kilometer for the smallest car to more than $9 a day plus 14 cents per kilometer for larger vehicles.

By air. The local Air Calédonie provides frequent air service from Nouméa to outlying places in New Caledonia and to the offshore Isle of Pines, Isle Ouen, and the Loyalty Islands. All flights leave from Magenta Airfield, a small airport located within the Nouméa city limits. These local airline flights fit especially well into an itinerary with limited time—particularly because land travel tends to be slow and sometimes rugged and regular boat service to the "outliers" is limited. Among the possibilities:

To the Isle of Pines: 30 miles offshore, a half-hour flight, with one round trip a day, and fare under $30, round trip.

THE PLEASURES of travel: dinner at Nouméa's Dolce Vita, and a sojourn at Touho's Hotel Touho on the east coast.

To Isle Ouen: 10 miles offshore, a 20-minute flight, with five round trips a week, and fare under $18.

To Ouvéa in the Loyalty Islands: a one-hour flight with seven round trips a week, and fare under $50. (Flights also go to Maré, Lifou, and Tiga in the Loyalty Islands; no accommodations are available.)

To Koumac, on the west coast near the north end of the island: a 1¾-hour flight, with eight round trips a week, and fare under $65, round trip.

To Touho, on the east coast: a 1½-hour flight, with nine round trips a week; fare under $50.

By boat. A new service out of Nouméa offers fishing and diving excursions, along with one and three-day tours. Charters are available for groups.

Eating and drinking and night life

New Caledonians eat well and, by the same token, so do visitors. In Nouméa's small restaurants and hotel dining rooms, the French way with food is very much apparent. Everyday eating becomes a gastronomic adventure. You'll be tempted to try mangrove oysters, a local delicacy, and other concoctions on the menu: perhaps *poulet Beaulieu* (chicken with garlic and black olives), *champignons Provençale* (mushrooms with garlic and parsley), *porc aux marrons* (pork with chestnuts), *salade Tahitienne* (raw fish marinated in lemon and the

oil of a freshly squeezed coconut), *salade de coeur de cocotier* (hearts of palm salad), or one of many entrees made with local crayfish, crab, and shrimp. And you'll want to try some of the specialties served at restaurants featuring Cantonese, Vietnamese, and Polynesian cuisine.

A list of the top restaurants in and around Nouméa would include the following: Dolce Vita, considered the city's best restaurant (its chef once cooked for the French ambassador to Moscow); La Potinière, Nouméa's oldest restaurant; the Rotonde, recently opened; Coq Hardi, another new one; and the Esquinade, the Santa Monica, the Biarritz, the Cercle Civil, as well as all of the hotel restaurants. Outside of Nouméa, the Auberge at Mount Koghi (a 25-minute drive) serves excellent food and has a magnificent view. The Gentilhommerie in Bourail is as good as any in Nouméa. And outside the range of French restaurants are the Deux Dragon and the Mandarin, both of which serve topnotch Chinese food.

If you're interested in attending a *bougna* or Melanesian feast, make arrangements through a local travel agent. Fruit and vegetables, pig, fish, and chicken, cooked in coconut milk and banana leaves, are prepared on hot stones in a sand or earth oven at a beach.

Drinking is pretty much an around-the-clock activity. Most hotel cocktail lounges and bars throughout the city stay open as long as there are customers, even though 11 p.m. is the official closing hour. And some bars open as early as 4 a.m. to accommodate the public market goers.

Night clubs are small, lively, and usually very crowded. The dancing—whether the super-fast Tahitian *tamure* or the latest dance on deck—gets more earthy as the night wears on. For night life, try these clubs: Santa Monica, Capa Club, Club 7, Le Dancing, Pacha, and Tahitian Ticki Tapu.

Calendar of events

Every year on Bastille Day and Anniversary Day, the most colorful celebrations take place. Some of the smaller events, held on a weekly basis throughout the year, are also of special interest to tourists. Weekly calendars of these events are available from the Office du Tourisme.

Following are some of the gala celebrations:

Almost every Sunday. Charity fete at Hôtel de Ville (city hall). Some of these fetes include a buffet luncheon with homemade Indonesian, Chinese, French, and Indian dishes, as well as lotteries and drawings.

February or early March. Mardi Gras. Children in costume parade to the Central Square and the Hôtel de Ville, where prizes are given for the most original costumes.

July 14. Bastille Day. Beginning on the night of July 13, Nouméa celebrates a week. A torchlight procession, a fireworks display, and a public ball at the Town Hall are among the highlights. The program is filled out with walking and bicycle races, native dances by children, and a military parade.

September 24. Anniversary Day, commemorating the raising of the French flag on September 24, 1853. The celebration lasts a week, with horse races, a queen contest, international soccer matches, boat races, a torchlight procession, and a public ball on the program.

November 2. "Fête des Morts" or All Saints' Day. Nouméa's cemetery is painted, and residents from the environs bring armloads of flowers to leave at the graves.

Third Sunday of November. Melanesian Fête Day. Singing and dancing groups in native dress come to Nouméa from all over New Caledonia to assemble in the municipal stadium and compete for prizes. A brilliant day-long spectacle of color, movement and sound.

Early December. Annual Public School Week. Highlights include recitals of French folk dancing and singing by participants wearing provincial costumes as well as displays of school art and handicraft. Held at the College Theatre in Nouméa.

December 24. Père Noël arrives in Nouméa each year by means of a different, unusual means of transport. Previously he has arrived by such conveyances as a submarine, a "satellite," and a rocket. After his arrival, a parade winds through the streets and terminates at a major department store, where candies are given to the children.

NATIVES PREPARE for pilou pilou, *a dance, (left), and children celebrate Mardi Gras.*

BLOWHOLES STUD the shore of American Samoa; every village has its church (here, in Western Samoa); and villagers decorate themselves for feasts and other special occasions.

The Samoas...
cradle of the race

PUREST POLYNESIA, HOME OF HIGH CHIEFS, TALKING CHIEFS, AND A PLETHORA OF CHURCHES

The Samoas—American and Western—are considered the heart of Polynesia, the cradle of the race. And once you have been there, visited their villages, laughed with their people, you will understand why: *fa'a Samoa* (the Samoan way) seeps into your consciousness.

In open *fales* (native dwellings), you see high chiefs, talking chiefs, and all manner of other chiefs sitting cross-legged on their woven grass mats, solving problems and living out their lives unhurriedly and with great dignity. Women sit placidly, hour after hour, at their work: stringing shells on fishline for a *ulasisi* (shell lei), weaving baskets made of *pandanus* (leaves), bleaching the fiber of hibiscus bark for dancing skirts. Children dive into deep pools in front of their *fales*. When you stop at their villages, they come running; and suddenly you see a whole crowd of happy bronze faces in the ground glass viewer of your camera.

The sixteen islands in the Samoan group lie about 2,300 miles southwest of Hawaii—about half-way between Hawaii and Sydney, Australia. By air, it's about 5½ hours from Honolulu to Pago Pago, American Samoa. Apia, in Western Samoa, is about a half-hour flight from there. Seven of the islands make up American Samoa; nine of them comprise the independent state of Western Samoa. American Samoa has a population of about 28,000, Western Samoa about 145,000.

History

The first European to visit the Samoas is thought to have been Jacob Roggeveen, a Dutchman in command of an expedition around the world in 1721 and 1722. More than 40 years later, Bougainville visited the Samoas. Next came La Perouse in 1787. Not until 1830, however, when John Williams of the London Missionary Society reached Samoa, did much information circulate about the island group.

In the years that followed, missionaries reduced the Samoan language to print.

Until about 1860, the islands (American as well as Western Samoa) were ruled by tribal chiefs. From 1860 until 1899, the Samoas were still ruled by chiefs, but the chiefs were directed by British, American, and German consuls. Around the turn of the century, the Samoan Islands east of the 171st degree of west longitude became an American Territory—the United States having had a naval station on the islands since 1872—and the islands of Western Samoa became a German colony.

As a Territory, American Samoa was administered by the U. S. Navy for the first half of the 20th century. When the naval base was closed in 1951, the administration of American Samoa was transferred to the U.S. Department of the Interior, under which it is governed by an appointed governor and a bicameral legislature, called the *Fono*.

After World War I, the League of Nations mandated Western Samoa to New Zealand, and following World War II, Western Samoa became a Trusteeship Territory, still administered by New Zealand. Then came a period of self-government in the 1950s. Finally on January 1, 1962, Western Samoa achieved independence—the first Polynesian state of modern times to do so.

Western Samoa's constitution is the supreme law. It provides for a head of state, a prime minister, a legislature, and a judiciary. The first head of state holds office for life, and thereafter the office is to be filled by a vote of the legislative assembly.

Lifestyle

Closely related to the Hawaiians, the Tahitians, and the Maoris of New Zealand in their Polynesian heritage, the Samoans are friendly, generous, modest, and fun-loving. They are well known for their splendid physiques as well as for their fondness of ceremonies and flowery speeches.

The *aiga* (family) still persists as the basic unit of the village community. Family units are ruled by a *matai* (elected head of a family), and beyond that by a hierarchy of chiefs, high chiefs, and talking chiefs (or orator chiefs). Chiefs and high chiefs are similar to head of state and premier. Titles are hereditary only to a degree; every energetic and capable young man can aspire to the possibility of holding a title some time. At present, about one-fourth of the adult males hold titles and participate in village, county, and district councils. In return for service rendered (and money contributed) by family members, the *matai* represents them in vil-

A CLUSTER of open-sided fales *in a typical Samoan village; and a nearby stream, used for laundry and bathing.*

lage affairs, takes responsibility for their protection and well being, and acts as trustee for family lands and property.

Typically the Samoan family lives in a neat village, of which there are hundreds. Their houses are *fales* (pronounced follis): elliptical, open-sided structures that are set in a semi-circle around a grassy village green. Each *fale* supports a thatched or corrugated metal roof. It has no walls; open-mat blinds are lowered for protection from rain and wind. Its open sides make the *fale* conspicuously different from other native dwellings in the South Pacific. Recently, the Samoan *fale* has begun to display a characteristic common elsewhere in the South Pacific: the tin roof, less expensive and more easily replaced than thatch. (A modern touch: some of the remaining thatched-roof *fales* are crowned with a circle of used automobile tires to help secure the roof against gusty winds.)

Homemakers do their washing by hand, sitting by an outdoor water spout or a running stream. Cold water, often from mountain springs, is used for most purposes; a hot water supply is not commonplace. *Umus* (Samoan ovens), made of rocks and covered with leaves and burlap sacks, are used for cooking.

Samoans have large families, and the children

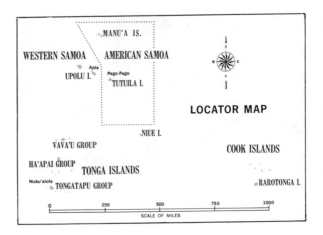

are trained to accept familial responsibilities. Their place is to serve the parents or anyone older than they are. Considered children until they are 19 years old, they are reared under strict discipline, taking care of younger children and assuming many other household chores. They build the fires, do much of the cooking, haul the water, catch fish, and clean beaches and village grounds.

In both American and Western Samoa, Sunday is a day of rest. That Samoans take their Christianity seriously is shown by the plethora of im-

ETIQUETTE, SAMOAN-STYLE

If you take part in a feast or a Sunday *toagai* (type of breakfast) where chiefs and village *matais* are present, you may need some tips on what the Samoans consider to be good manners. Here are a few:

• Don't drink a cup of *ava*, the traditional Samoan beverage, without first tipping a little out of the cup onto the ground immediately in front of you, at the same time saying *Manuia* (good fortune).

• Don't walk across the mats in the *fale;* instead, circle around the edge of them when you approach your host.

• When you sit, cross your legs in front of you, or fold them in back of you. It is considered rude to stretch out your legs and feet in front of you.

• Always address a chief from a sitting position.

• Before eating, wait for grace to be said.

• Note the serving of food: you as a guest, will be served first, followed by the chiefs in order of rank. The children usually sit outside the *fale* with an *aiiga* (a basket that is a basic utensil of the Samoan culture, used to take extra food back home when the diners have left).

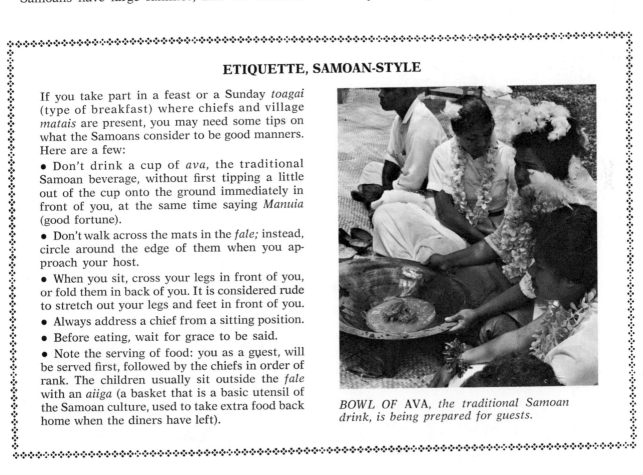

BOWL OF AVA, *the traditional Samoan drink, is being prepared for guests.*

SAMOANS in their Sunday clothes—barefooted women take pride in wearing fancy hats.

posing churches you see, as well as the many Samoans filing to services every Sunday, walking to vespers at dusk, or gathering in their homes to hold family prayers.

Climate

Temperatures are moderate—from 70° to 90°—and excessive humidity is rare. Winds are near constant but seldom violent. November through March is both the hottest and the wettest season, bringing downpours in January, February, and March that can be downright torrential, going on for days without letup. Some rain falls the year around (August has the least); the pattern tends to be one of brief downpours alternating with stretches of sunshine. American Samoa is somewhat wetter than its sister nation: rainfall averages about 200 inches a year at Pago Pago, about 118 inches in Apia.

AMERICAN SAMOA

What makes American Samoa so unusual? Cloud-topped mountains rise steep-sloped above placid lagoons. Thatched-roof huts look out to sea through a freize of waving palms and breadfruit trees. Little boys amble along the road leading toward the copra plant, carrying gunny sacks bulging with coconut. You look inland to plantations of coconut trees, row upon straight row as far as you can see.

But you pay your bills in U. S. dollars, use U. S. postage stamps (and zip code 96920), read the English-language *Samoa Times*, stay in the luxury of an international resort hotel, and have no trouble whatsoever communicating with the people. New paved roads reach into the jungle-grown areas; parks and beaches are being created; an extensive and impressive system of educational television is in effect.

Gradually, American ways have filtered into these islands. But beneath the thin overlay of a few institutions and features of modern America, Samoa is still very Samoan.

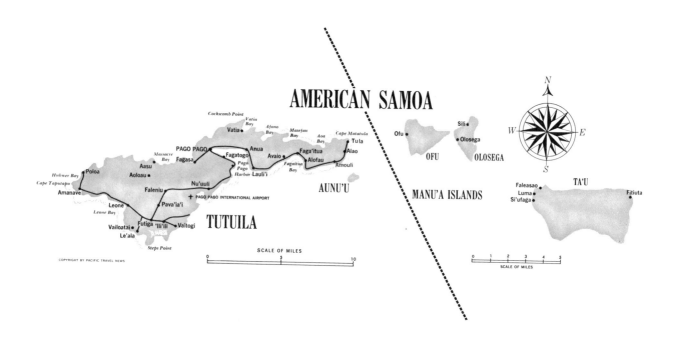

PASSENGER SHIP noses into port at
Pago Pago, American Samoa. Lee Auditorium
(upper right) was built to resemble the form of
a turtle. Class (lower right) receives lessons
by television.

Geography

The islands of American Samoa cover an area of
76 square miles. Five of the islands—Tutuila, Tau,
Aunuu, Olesega, and Ofu—are high islands of volcanic origin. The two others—Swains and Rose—
are coral atolls.

Tutuila, the largest island (52 square miles) and
the only one developed for tourists, is nearly bi-
sected by Pago Pago Bay. One of the most spectacular tropical island harbors in the world, it was
formed when the seaward wall of a great crater fell
away many centuries ago. The effect of arriving by
ship in Pago Pago is that of sailing into the water-
filled cone of a great, lushly green volcano—one of
the most thrilling travel experiences imaginable.

Pago Pago

Pago Pago (pronounced Pango Pango) is the name
of one of several small villages situated at the head
of Pago Pago Bay. The Inter-Continental Hotel,

shops, ship docks, and business and government
buildings are located in two adjacent villages.
These are Fagatogo (pronounced Fangatongo) and
Utulei. But the fame of Pago Pago is such that it is
now used collectively to refer to the several villages.
Locals always refer to Pago Pago as simply Pago.
And residents of outlying areas still call Pago Pago
"the Station," even though the U. S. Navy closed
its base here more than two decades ago. Strictly
speaking, the village of Fagatogo is the capital of
the Territory.

On the north shore, directly across the harbor
from the Pago Pago area, is the village of Anua. Its
fales nestle beneath the towering green Mount Pioa,
rising abruptly to 1,718 feet. The Samoans call it
"The Rainmaker," and its massive bulk fully justi-
fies the title: it drains the moisture from the clouds
that touch its peak, giving Pago Pago more than its
fair share of rain.

Pago Pago has a scruffy, ramshackle, haphazard
look to its small shopping center that spreads out
along two or three short streets. Most shops are of

YOU CAN RIDE across Pago Pago Bay in a
cable car; and you can visit the small museum in
Government House (above) in Fagatogo.

the general store type; a little patience sometimes
rewards you with a minor shopping discovery.
Cotton cloth splashed with gaudy South Seas colors
is an especially good buy. The main stores are
Burns Philp, B. F. Kneubuhl and Company, Max
Haleck, and G. H. C. Reid.

The village residential section sprawls up the
hills, footpaths continuing from dead-end roads to
the entrances of homes. Almost every block has its
place of worship. Sundays in Samoa provide the
visitor with a never-to-be-forgotten experience: villages and churches filled with Samoans in their
best bib and tucker—usually white, immaculate,
almost uniformlike in their sameness. In the
churches, you'll thrill to the rich rolling tones of
sermon and *himene* (hymns).

These are some places of interest in the Pago
Pago area:

Market Place. The *malae* (or village green) is where
Samoan handicrafts are displayed on the ground
and in a typical Samoan *fale*. Occasionally contests
—such as setting fire without matches, basket
weaving, dancing, and singing—are held on the
malae. Photographers are welcome.

Lee Auditorium. Designed in the traditional *fale*
style but made of modern materials, the community
hall was named by the local chiefs in honor of
former Governor H. Rex Lee. In its general shape,

the building suggests a turtle, a reptile that figures
prominently in a traditional Samoan story, "The
Shark and the Turtle." The hall is about five minutes by taxi from the Inter-Continental Hotel.

Tramway ride. The mile-long aerial tramway between Pago Pago and 1,600-foot Mount Alava carries you across Pago Pago Harbor in about six
spectacular minutes. At the Mount Alava tramway
terminal, you'll enjoy exploring the television
transmitting tower. From the snack *fale* on the
mountaintop, there are wide views of both sides of
Tutuila. You'll have great opportunities from this
breathtaking site for photos of the island's coastline and of Pago Pago Bay. On days when passenger
ships depart the harbor, flower petals are showered
down from the tram cars to say a Samoan *tofa*
(goodby). The tram operates between 8 a.m. and
4 p.m daily, including holidays.

Government House Museum. Relatively new, this
museum contains an impressive assortment of artifacts of historical interest. Among them: a muzzle-
loading cannon that belonged to King Kalakaua's
Hawaiian "fleet" of just one vessel; a 20-foot canoe
that the American explorer William Willis carried
on his balsa raft from Callao, Peru, to Pago Pago.
Government House, in which the museum is located, is of some historical interest itself. Built in
1903, it has been the home of the Territory's chief
executives for almost 70 years. The museum is open

to visitors from 2 to 4 p.m. on Thursdays and Fridays and from 10 a.m. to noon on Saturdays.

Television Center. Visitors may tour the Michael J. Kirwan Educational Television Center in the village of Utulei. Heart of the pioneering educational television system established by former Governor Lee, the center produces lessons in 25 elementary schools and four secondary ones. An interesting fact about this educational television system is that, rather than being used as an instructional supplement in the classroom, it virtually replaces instruction. Teachers supplement the TV lessons, covering all grade levels and practically all subject areas. Instituted to upgrade in a brief time the educational level of Samoan schools, the TV system has created on this remote Pacific island one of the most modern school systems in the world.

Two of KVZK-TV's six channels are used for nighttime entertainment and educational broadcasts. Adult TV viewing at schools in the evening is controlled by the village chiefs. To visit the television studio, make arrangements ahead of time with the Station Manager, KVZK-TV.

Sadie Thompson territory. Of interest to visitors familiar with Somerset Maugham's story, "Rain," is the site of the Sadie Thompson Inn, where Maugham is said to have gathered material for his famous story. The former inn is now the Max Haleck Store #3, located on the highway.

Tuna canneries. The Star-Kist and Van Camp tuna canneries, across the bay from Fagatogo in Atu'u, are open to those visitors who are not put off by the rather pungent odor that hangs in the air near these buildings. Telephone in advance to make sure that packing operations are scheduled (Van Camp, 2312; Star-Kist, 3646).

Sightseeing outside of Pago Pago

Wherever you are in American Samoa, magnificent scenery and interesting village life are always close at hand. The practical way to experience as much of the Samoan scene as you can is to make arrangements with a local travel service for guided tours to outlying villages and to specially arranged feasts. Here are a few suggestions:

Around the island. Owned and operated by the government, the launch *MV Manusina* leaves its dock by the customs building in Pago Pago at 9 a.m. on Monday, Wednesday, and Friday and returns in mid-afternoon. The first stop is made at the small offshore island of Aunu'u, the launch then proceeding to the north shore of Tutuila for stops at Afono, Vatia, Aasu, and Fagamalo villages. Air-conditioned

and comfortably appointed, the launch has ample space on deck for camera fans.

Among the many interesting villages on Tutuila: *Amanave*, situated on an azure blue bay, on the western side of the island; *Leone*, landing place of the first Christian missionaries, with nearby flatlands that were battlefields dating from the Samoan-Tongan wars; *Vaitogi*, where by advance arrangement with the village chief you can visit the place where the legend says the singing voices of grandmothers and young children can bring a shark and a turtle swimming together to the surface of the sea; *Anua*, where much of the local woodcarving is done.

The Manu'a Group, about 80 miles north of Tutuila, is a relatively isolated part of American Samoa. Its three tiny islands (Taù, Olosega, and Ofu) may be reached by an occasional cargo vessel or by a charter flight aboard a float plane which takes off from Pago Pago.

Believed to have been the mythical home of the old Samoan sea gods, the Manu'as are also thought to have been a dispersal point from which early Polynesian voyagers sailed in search of Havaiki. It was on the island of Tau that Margaret Mead lived in 1926 when she was gathering material for her anthropological classic, *Coming of Age in Samoa.*

Shopping

Samoa offers a great array of tapa cloth, carvings, *lauhala* mats, baskets, and woven purses. Look for

EVENING PRAYERS, not just on Sunday but every evening, are announced by the ringing of a bell.

A CRICKET GAME is in progress, and on the sidelines, a little interference. At Fagatogo, the sidewalk is a shopper's bazaar.

good buys (and bargain before you buy) in Samoan carved wood fish bells, carved models of outrigger canoes, and island totems. Other interesting souvenirs: *ulas* (bead and seed leis); *ulasisis* (necklaces) made of *pippipi* (white shell), and *piccaci* (yellow shell); double woven floor mats; plaited place mats; *tonoa* bowls for the preparation and serving of *ava*, the ceremonial drink. A short stroll toward the ship dock from the Inter-Continental Hotel will take you to Boutique Samoa, popular with visitors for its imaginative clothing, Samoan jewelry, and unusual souvenirs. The duty-free shop at the International Airport at Tafuna has the usual assortment of liquor, jewelry and perfumes. When a ship is in port, a duty-free liquor store adjoining the dock is open (check times) during the day.

Sports

Obviously, opportunities for water sports abound around Samoa. Surfing and lagoon swimming are quite good at Carter Beach, near the airport, and at Alofau and Leone bays. Reef snorkeling gives you a chance to see (and spear if you like) a vivid assortment of fish. Since some areas are dangerous, swimmers should check with the Office of Tourism for safe diving spots.

Fishermen hook impressive catches of marlin, broadbill, dolphin, yellow fin tuna, and white tuna. Still fishing and spin casting for other varieties—such as bass—are best in the bay and from the reefs. Fishing for all species is open all year. Charter boats are available, fully supplied with equipment.

A tip for shell collectors: large *faisua* oyster and clam shells clutter the beach at Vaitogi and Nuuuli Lagoon. Samoan *paopaos* (dugouts) can be rented in some areas for exploring the lagoons.

Numerous primitive trails challenge a hiker's skills. Tennis courts are available, and a golf course is under construction.

For spectators there are various boat races—yachts, *paopaos*, and 50-man longboats—as well as softball, rugby, and cricket contests. The Samoan cricket season lasts from January to April. Samoan cricket is somewhat less restrained than the English variety; here some 50 to 100 barefoot contestants play, while cheering sections sing and dance to the rhythm of music beaten on a kerosene tin.

PRACTICAL INFORMATION

Entry requirements

To enter American Samoa, you must have a ticket for onward transportation or return trip. You also need an international smallpox vaccination certificate. United States citizens do not need a passport or visa but should have proof of citizenship. A passport is required of persons who are not United States citizens. For a stay of more than 30 days, you need permission from the island governor.

Customs regulations

Tourists are allowed to bring two fifths of alcoholic beverages, for personal consumption, into the Territory. United States residents returning home from American Samoa are allowed $200 in duty-free merchandise, if at least $100 worth was acquired in American Samoa (or other United States Territory). United States residents returning home are allowed to take one gallon of alcoholic beverages with them duty free.

Where to stay

American Samoa has only one large hotel—the 100 room, air-conditioned Hotel Pago Pago Inter-Continental. Unlike many of the new tourist hotels that are high-rise blocks of concrete, it was designed to look like a traditional Samoan village by the sea; the effect is quite captivating. The hotel, which replaced the fabled Rainmaker, occupies the site of the old navy Goat Island Club on a peninsula reaching into Pago Pago Bay. All rooms and public facilities have views of the bay or of Rainmaker Mountain.

The hotel consists of 24 separate Samoan *fales* (thatched-roof bungalows) and three two-story long houses (with private lanai for each room), resembling traditional resident *fales*. In addition to two bars, a restaurant, and a snack bar, the hotel complex includes a sandy beach, an Olympic-sized swimming pool, and a duty-free shop.

A smaller hotel, the Malaeimi, located two miles from the airport, has 20 rooms, and additional units are planned for the immediate future.

Eating, drinking and night life

Center of most of the social activity that takes place outside of native villages is the Pago Pago Inter-Continental Hotel. At the hotel's Rainmaker Restaurant and the Laumei Lounge, you can order European cuisine or American specialties, as well as cocktails and wines of your choice. Hotel entertainment includes Samoan floor shows, dancing, and a weekly cocktail party. Traditional entertainment ranges from choir singing to the *siva siva* (ceremonial dance) and *o le afi* (fire dance), a feat of courage performed on special occasions only. In Pago Pago and along the road to Fagasa, you will find several beer taverns offering night club acts in rustic surroundings. The airport terminal has a small restaurant.

Fiafias. Villages regularly present *fiafias* (entertainment for tourist groups), and island feasts can be arranged through local tour agencies. At the feasts, you either sit outside or on floor mats placed in a circle in an open *fale*. Various families participate and furnish the food, which is wrapped in leaves and cooked over hot stones in an earthen oven. The feast usually consists of New Zealand ham, roast beef, lobster, roast pork, taro, breadfruit, and vegetables flavored with coconut milk.

How to get around

If you arrive in American Samoa by ship, you will disembark virtually downtown at the main dock in the central part of busy Fagatogo, just southeast of Pago Pago. If you arrive by air, you land at Pago Pago International Airport, about eight miles southwest of Pago Pago.

Getting around the island is easy:

Taxis come in all shapes, sizes, and colors, but they can be recognized by the letter T preceding the license number. Rates are based on the length of the trip or the time involved; up to four passengers can ride for the same fare as one. Sample fares: from the International Airport to the hotel in Pago Pago, about $3; for sightseeing trips, about $5 an hour.

Rental cars are available in the Pago Pago area. You need your domestic driver's license for rentals. Cars may be picked up at shipside, at the airport, or in Pago Pago, and can be turned in at any of these points. On Tutuila there are about 30 miles of paved primary roads, 8 miles of paved secondary roads, and about 20 miles of unimproved roads.

Buses are a bargain with a bit of adventure thrown in. You can travel from one end of Tutuila Island to the other for less than a dollar, all by open-air bus whose seats are benches that have been built

DESIGNED to resemble a Samoan village, the Hotel Inter-Continental in Pago Pago succeeds in blending into its surroundings.

onto the bed of a long truck. Buses run frequently to the villages east and west of Pago Pago but not on a precise time table or along a prescribed route. If a passenger has copra to deliver to a ship, that's where the bus will go. Don't expect any specified bus stops; you merely signal the driver when you want to board, letting him know when or where you want to get off.

Boats make the 80-mile trip between Pago Pago and Apia, Western Samoa, several times a week. The trip involves cruising along the south coast of Tutuila, crossing a 15-mile channel, and sailing along the north coast of Upolu Island. Along with inter-island cargo, the small vessels carry 12 to 15 passengers.

By air. Polynesian Airlines offers scheduled service and special charters to Apia, Western Samoa, and return. The flight takes about 45 minutes.

Tipping

Tipping is not widely prevalent in American Samoa. At the Pago Pago Inter-Continental Hotel, a 10 per cent service charge is added to the bill to take care of tipping. At restaurants, it's normal to tip about 10 per cent of the bill.

For information

You'll find an information desk in the lobby of the Hotel Pago Pago Inter-Continental where a clerk can answer most of your travel questions. Another source of information is the Office of Tourism, Government of Samoa, on the Fagatogo *malae*.

WESTERN SAMOA

Western Samoa is undeveloped—a condition responsible for much of its charm and beauty. With its jungle-clad mountains, luxuriant greenness, reef-enclosed lagoons, and benign atmosphere, it avoids having that well-trammeled look. Because its efforts to attract tourists are limited, it draws relatively few of them. The fact that there is no international airport for big jets and no lavishly developed resort area is not just an accident of geography and economics. Until 1965, Western Samoa actively discouraged tourism; only in recent years has economic necessity changed this policy. The Western Samoan people, gentle and friendly by nature, were concerned that their way of life might be radically altered if they were to seek the tourist trade. They were—and they still are—intent on retaining the elements of *fa'a Samoa*.

How long Western Samoa's delightfully primitive islands will remain as unspoiled as they are today remains an open question. But for now, those who visit this fully independent Polynesian nation will find, in the words of Somerset Maugham, "a scented languor which seemed to melt the heart."

Of Western Samoa's population of 145,000, all but approximately 15,000 are Samoan Polynesian. Western Samoa, in fact, shelters the largest population of full-blooded Polynesians in the world. Others in the population, technically classified as foreigners and known as "local Europeans," include Europeans, part Europeans, and Chinese.

About 20 per cent of the population lives in Apia, the remaining 115,000 in villages along the shores of the islands and scattered inland.

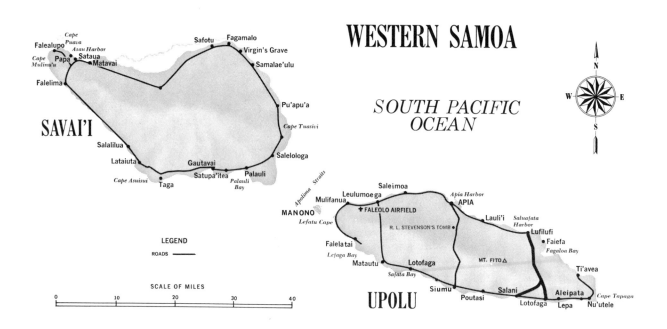

SIDEWALK VENDORS on the main street of Apia, Western Samoa, display their wares in the arcade; natives saunter along in the rain; a policeman directs a trickle of traffic.

Geography

Situated about 80 miles northwest of American Samoa, Western Samoa lies approximately 450 miles northeast of Fiji and 1,800 miles northwest of New Zealand. By air, it's approximately 45 minutes from Pago Pago. Its nine islands of volcanic origin comprise slightly more than 1,000 square miles, an area about 14 times larger than American Samoa.

Its two main islands are Upolu and Savai'i—the latter bearing peaks that rise 6,000 feet above the sea. A 10-mile wide strait separates Upolu from Savai'i, the westernmost island and the largest one of the group. Within this strait are two almost uninhabited islands—Manono and Apolima. The five remaining islands of Western Samoa, all of them uninhabited, are within or near the reef surrounding Upolu.

Apia, the capital

Apia, the capital and only town in all of Western Samoa, is a perfect picture of a South Seas port of the pre-jet era. Perched on the north coast of Upolu, it's attractive in a ramshackle way. And it's easy to explore. The main street curves around the harbor; the bordering sidewalks are uncrowded; the streets are almost empty.

Although there is very little traffic, Apia has at least three intersections where policemen in *lavalavas* stand on mid-street platforms. Two automobiles going in opposite directions stop at the intersection, and a policeman majestically directs each vehicle to proceed in turn.

Nor are words needed to direct you to the conspicuous line of large general stores along the length of Beach Road: S. V. MacKensie & Company, Burns Philp, O. F. Nelson & Co., I. H. Car-

THE ENTRANCE to Robert Louis Stevenson's
Road of Loving Hearts leads to his former home.
The island of Savai'i (above) is home
to these happy children.

ruthers, H. J. Retzlaff Ltd., and Morris Hedstrom. Varied street-vendor displays, neatly laid out, are on view in front of the buildings in the main business section of town—everything from woodcarvings and woven mats to plaited baskets, tapa cloth, hand-printed fabrics, and accessories made of shells. Bargaining is in order outdoors but not in the gift shop next door to Aggie Grey's Hotel. The shop has a very good selection, at prices about as low as you can find anywhere on the island.

Sightseeing out of Apia

Any trip on the island of Upolu passes mile after mile of pristine landscape. The sole point of departure for excursions is Apia, and perhaps the easiest way to see the major points of interest on Upolu is to take one of the tours offered by one of Apia's travel agencies. You can go around the island and cross it, visiting villages and plantations (coconut, cocoa, and coffee), stop at waterfalls (Tiavi, Falefa, Fuipisia, and Foga'afu), and Robert Louis Stevenson's home.

Here are some of the points of interest:

Vailima, home of Stevenson and now the residence of the Head of State, is three miles from Apia. This gracious, serene looking house with yellow oleander lacing its porte-cochere is approached by the famous Road of Loving Hearts. Flanked on both

sides by handsome old teak trees, the road was built by the Samoan people for their beloved "Tusitala," (teller of tales). You can't go inside, but it's worth the visit to see it from the road.

Directly above Vailima is Mount Vaea. At its summit is Stevenson's tomb, the words of his immortal "Requiem" carved on it. A trail to the top (a series of switchbacks) ascends 500 feet and is best taken in the early morning before the day gets too hot.

Tiafau drive. Tiafau, commonly called Mulinu'u, is the ancient capital of Western Samoa and the location of *fono fale* (Parliament House), Land and Titles Courts, and other buildings. On this drive you also see the Apia Observatory and the tomb mounds of the ancestors of Samoan chiefs. It brings to mind the words of Robert Louis Stevenson: "The western horn (of Apia) is Mulinu'u, the eastern Matautu; and from one to the other I ask the reader to walk. He will find more of the history of Samoa spread before his eyes in that excursion, than has been collected in the blue books or the white books of the world."

To Savai'i. Having about a third the population of Upolu, the big island of Savai'i is even less Westernized. Although there are no hotels, a few guest houses will take tourists. Savai'i does have once-a-week air service on Air Samoa from Apia to Asau.

A one-day "package" tour out of Apia, including transportation, sightseeing, lunch, and swimming, is available through Apia tour operators. For the more adventurous, a motor launch speeds to Savai'i. Leaving Mulifanua Wharf, about 25 miles from Apia, the 12-mile crossing takes about 1½ hours.

Sports

Western Samoans are as enthusiastic about sports as their cousins in American Samoa. Villagers compete in cricket, rugby, volleyball, lawn bowling, boxing, horse racing, track and field events, tennis, and longboat racing. Longboat competition is the most colorful for the spectator.

Held offshore from Apia during the Flag Day celebration every year, longboat races involve boats that are 100 feet long and manned by as many as 46 crewmen. The event is an exciting and noisy one: coxswains beat the rhythm of the strokes on biscuit-tin drums, and crowds on the beach yell their support. For this all-important event, village crewmen train the whole year long.

Cricket season lasts from January to April. Rugby season, at Apia Park, runs from March to May. Boxing tournaments take place at the Apia Tivoli Theatre from August to October.

Water sports are plentiful for active sportsmen:

Swimming and surfing. Two popular spots are Vaiala and Mulinu'u beaches, both a short distance out of Apia. Another, 30 miles southwest of Apia, is Lefaga Beach, the 1952 movie location of James Michener's *Return to Paradise* which starred Gary Cooper (a fact that locals vividly remember). Two black sand beaches, Solosolo and Lauli'i, are within easy reach of Apia.

Plum Pudding Rock, about eight miles east of Apia, is another popular spot, adjoining a lovely white sand beach (which, however, is too rocky for surfing or skin diving). Many lagoons and fresh water pools in the rivers add to the variety of swimming possibilities.

Skin Diving. Scuba divers report excellent visibility at depths down to 200 and 250 feet in the lagoons at Lauli'i and Luatuanu'u. You can rent snorkeling and scuba equipment at Aggie Grey's Hotel or at Seafari Samoa, Ltd.

Deep-sea fishing. Arrangements can be made through Aggie Grey's for equipment and boats for reef fishing or trolling in the lagoons or ocean. Fishing prospects are topnotch.

Other sports facilities:

Golf. The Royal Samoan Country Club, about three miles from Apia, has a well-maintained nine-hole course. Visitors may arrange for games and caddies through the secretary at the club.

Tennis. Games can be arranged and courts reserved by the clerk at your hotel.

Bowling. Lawn bowls, that genteel game they play so avidly in New Zealand, can be watched at the Apia Bowling Club. Visitors can also make arrangements through the club to play.

PRACTICAL INFORMATION

Entry regulations

Visitors may remain up to three days (72 hours) without a visa, provided that they have confirmed hotel reservations, as well as onward transportation reservations to a country which they are permitted to enter. For a stay of longer than three days, a visa must be obtained through the nearest New Zealand consular offices. Send a cable fee along with your application (the transaction by mail takes about a month). A smallpox vaccination certificate is required.

Customs

The bringing in of firearms, ammunition, and explosives of any kind is prohibited. Only one bottle of alcoholic beverage per person is allowed, and cigarettes must not exceed 200.

Where to stay

Aggie Grey's Hotel, a South Pacific landmark made famous by its energetic owner-founder, Aggie Grey,

AGGIE GREY'S HOTEL, one of the famous hostelries of the South Pacific, is on main street of Apia.

easily qualifies as the social center of Western Samoa. It has 90 rooms, all air-conditioned, some in *fales* and some in wings of the main building. In the hotel's large, hibiscus-filled garden, situated beside a river, are a swimming pool and facilities for lawn bowls. The open-air bar is a gathering place for travelers from all over the world. Arrangements can be made through the hotel for Samoan feasts with music and dancing, deep-sea fishing parties, canoeing, picnics, and sightseeing. Rates, based on the American plan, include meals served family style in the open-sided dining areas, as well as morning and afternoon tea. Aggie Grey's started out as a boarding house a good many years ago; now it is a large, comfortable hotel. Despite its expansion, it is a friendly place that has never lost its very personal quality.

Western Samoa has three other small hotels: the Apian Way Inn, in downtown Apia; the Samoan Hideaway Hotel, about an hour's drive from Apia; and the Savai'ian Guest Fales, located in Lalomalava village on the island of Savai'i (accessible by launch or a 10-minute flight from Apia). The latter, which is managed and hosted by Parliament member and village chief Luamanuvae Eti and his wife, is a real Samoan experience. Its *fales* are equipped with mattresses placed around the floor of the circular open dwellings—with no partitions between sleeping quarters. Private dressing rooms adjoining bathing facilities are available outside, however, for men and women. Meals are served Samoan-style on banana leaves or platters; guests sit on the floor in a circle or an oval, depending on how many there are. The Savai'ian has accommodations for 50.

Food, drink and night life

Two of Western Samoa's night clubs, the Tanoa and the Surfside, and Aggie Grey's offer simple, unsophisticated entertainment, music, dancing, and food. All have cocktail terraces and facilities for *fiafias*.

All liquor and beer is sold under government control on a point system. The Apia area has about 15 pubs, known as "clubs," where visitors are permitted as guests of members. The most popular are the RSA Club, the Pearl of the Pacific, Mount Vaea, Sunset, Five Stars, and Manaia.

Communications

Apia has two bilingual weekly newspapers and a government-owned radio and television transmitter station that receives TV broadcasts from American Samoa. The government newspaper, *Savali*, is printed in Samoan and published monthly. Apia radio, the main connecting link for overseas messages, provides overseas radio-telephone service.

Currency and banking

United States currency is acceptable in Western Samoa. The Samoan units of currency are the *tala* and the *sene*. One *tala* equals 100 *sene*. Converted to United States currency, the US dollar is equal to about 68 *sene*; one *tala* equals about US$1.47. The Bank of Western Samoa, located on Beach Road at Post Office Road, offers banking services.

How to get around

If you arrive in Western Samoa by sea, your ship will dock in Apia, directly across the waterfront road from Aggie Grey's Hotel. If you arrive by plane, you will land at Faleolo airstrip, about 25 miles from Apia. From the airport to Apia, it costs about $7 by taxi, $1 by airline bus.

Taxis are plentiful in Apia, and fares in town are moderate. For longer trips, the charge is about $7 an hour.

Rental cars are available at a number of different firms in Apia. In addition to your domestic driver's license you will be required to pass a local driving test and obtain a local license.

Bus service. Though you can also get around the island by bus, the service is sporadic—no timetable, no exact departure schedule. Consult the policeman on duty at the Market Bus stand for information about when the next bus may leave and the route it may take.

Guide-driven cars are available through Aggie Grey's or local travel agents; bicycles and motor scooters can be obtained through Aggie Grey's or Nelson's Hardware.

Tipping

This advice, printed in a Western Samoan brochure, sums up the subject of tipping: "Samoan authorities want to avoid commercialism of tourism in their islands, and practices such as tipping are unnecessary. While you are in Samoa, you are regarded as the guest of every Samoan..."

For information

Western Samoa's Department of Economic Development in Apia (P.O. Box 862) is in charge of tourist promotion. Visit them for brochures and information, or consult the desk clerk at Aggie Grey's.

The Kingdom of Tonga... where time begins

ON A BENIGN SET OF ISLANDS: GENTLE PEOPLE, A TOWERING KING, AN INTRIGUING ANTIQUITY

THE ROYAL TOMBS in Tonga, the last remaining Polynesian kingdom. Men—and women, too—wear woven mats about the waist. Called a ta'ovala, *it is a symbol of respect.*

Tonga sits on the international date line, the first country in the world to greet each new day. And what a splendid place for the day to begin: a luminous, sea-girt realm that Captain Cook named "The Friendly Islands."

At first glance, Tonga may seem to be like most of the other South Pacific island groups, but it is an island group with a difference. For one thing, it's a constitutional monarchy, the last remaining Polynesian Kingdom. Towering King Taufa'ahau Tupou IV rules from a Royal Palace that is splendidly Victorian, a 100-year-old, two-story structure with red roof, wide verandas, and stately cupola. It is also the most thoroughly Christian group of islands in the South Pacific.

Considering its isolation and background, Tonga is a remarkably progressive kingdom. Some years ago, its leaders decided to supplement its coconut and banana economy by providing facilities for tourists and then encouraging them to come.

Its attractions are the usual for the South Pacific: coral reefs, clear blue skies, inviting atolls, and a benign landscape. The pluses are its gentle people who maintain a traditional way of life that has changed little in more than 10 centuries.

Geography

An agglomeration of more than 150 islands—some of volcanic origin, some of coral—Tonga has a land area that totals only 269 square miles (about half the size of Los Angeles). The islands lie southeast of Fiji, south of the Samoas. By air, it's a 2-hour flight from Suva, Fiji, to Nuku'alofa, on the island of Tongatapu; from Apia in Western Samoa, it's about a 2½-hour flight.

Tonga is divided into three island groups: Tongatapu, Vava'u, and Ha'apai. Tongatapu, the main island, covers 99 square miles and contains about three-fourths of the Tongan population. Tonga's main port and capital city, Nuku'alofa, lies on the north side of triangular-shaped Tongatapu.

History

Two Dutch navigators, Schouten and Lemaire, were the first Europeans to visit Tonga, arriving in 1616. The next European to reach Tonga was Abel Tasman who came across the islands in 1643. Others came later: Captain Wallis in 1767, Captain Cook in 1773 and again in 1777, and Captain Bligh in 1789 (the mutiny occurred in the Tonga area).

Missionaries came to Tonga in the 1820's, and by mid-century they had converted all Tongans to Christianity. Civil wars that had wracked the country for half a century came to an end about this time, the victor being King George Tupou I. It was this king who introduced a constitutional form of government; established parliament, privy council, and cabinet; and instituted land reform policies that are in effect today. Political and social stability exist largely because of his influence.

Today the Kingdom of Tonga is ruled by a direct descendant of King George, King Taufa'ahau Tupou IV, who became king following the death in 1965 of Queen Salote Tupou. The royal family traces its descent from ancient ruling chiefs whose names have been preserved in Tongan art and legends.

Until June 4, 1970, Tonga was under the protection of Great Britain, with the status of a British Protected State. It is now fully independent and a member of the British Commonwealth.

Lifestyle

In Tonga, all land is the property of the Crown, and the system of its disposition is unique: every male Tongan, when he reaches age 16, is entitled to an 8¼-acre parcel of farming land (called an 'api), and a 2/5-acre village site on which to build a house. For the farm land, he pays an annual rental of a few dollars; his home site is rent free. According to the land grant laws, every 'api holder is required to plant 200 coconuts within 12 months after acquisition and to maintain them in a weed-free condition. In actual practice, young Tongans for some time have had to wait years before receiving their land grant; since this policy was inaugurated in the middle of the nineteenth century, a land shortage has developed.

The basis of Tongan economy is agriculture: crops include coconuts, bananas, plantains, taro, sweet potatoes, yams, and on Vava'u, vanilla beans. Tongans raise cattle, a large number of pigs, and some poultry. On festive occasions, as many as 8,000 pigs have been roasted for a single feast attended by thousands of persons.

Education, compulsory from age 6 to 14, is carried on at more than 150 government and denominational schools on the islands. Instruction in primary schools is in Tongan; English is taught as a second language. Children and teachers welcome visitors to the classroom.

Most of the 86,000 Tongans live in thatched-roof villages scattered throughout the island. Usually bare-footed, they seem to glide about soundlessly, dressed in the traditional wrap-around *vala* (skirt): the women's long, the men's short. Around the waist they wear a *ta'ovala* or soft mat as a sign of respect, the mat held by a *kafa* (or belt) made of woven coconut fiber. The men of Tonga are skilled

VAVA'U ISLAND
Neiafu • Ene'lo Beach
KAPA I.
VAVA'U GROUP
LATE I.

KAO I.   HA'ANO I.
TOFUA I.   FOA I.
           Pangai • LIFUKA I.
HA'APAI   GROUP

NOMUKA I.

Kolovai
Nukunuku Nuku'alofa
Pea   Terraced Tombs
Blowholes Mu'a
TONGATAPU   Airport
ISLAND   Oholei Beach
TONGATAPU   GROUP
      EUA ISLAND

TONGA
SCALE OF MILES
10 5 0   10   20   30

A VILLAGER holds completed tapa in front
of his thatched cottage. A smile comes easily to
two Tongan women performing native dance.
Uniformed bandsmen play at state ceremonies.

A VILLAGER holds completed tapa in front of his thatched cottage. A smile comes easily to two Tongan women performing native dance. Uniformed bandsmen play at state ceremonies.

navigators and fishermen; the women are noted for
their gentle beauty and handicraft expertise.

Many Tongans belong to the State Church (a
Tongan version of the Wesleyan Methodist), although virtually every Christian denomination is
represented. Sunday observance of the Sabbath is
written into Tonga's Constitution: "The Sabbath
Day shall be sacred in Tonga for ever, and it shall
not be lawful to do work or play games or trade
on the Sabbath. Any agreement made or documents
witnessed on this day shall be counted void and not
recognized by the Government."

NUKU'ALOFA, THE CAPITAL

Nuku'alofa, small and somnolent, sprawls along
the sea with a lagoon to its back. It has the look of
a 19th century New England town of white frame
houses and contains a scattering of commercial
establishments. Vuna Road, a wide thoroughfare
that runs along the waterfront, is known as "The
Beach." It is the center of activity—at one end is
the King's Palace, at the other, the Yacht Club's
box-like building. Midway along The Beach, the
town wharf protrudes; on either side of it are the
Royal Chapel, the public market place, the town
malae (meeting place), the residences of Tonga's
royal family, and the hotels. Running at a right

RED-ROOFED CUPOLA towers above the Royal Palace in Tongatapu. Downtown, a three-wheeled ve'etolu carries passengers past building with Victorian trim. A typical grave is marked with bottles. At public market, sellers display produce in the shade of big old trees.

angle to The Beach is Taufa'ahau Road (the main business street), busy with markets, small shops, general stores, pool rooms, cinemas, transportation offices, government buildings, and churches.

The population of Nuku'alofa (approximately 20,000) is predominantly Tongan, with a few Europeans and a scattering of peoples from other Pacific islands.

Sightseeing in Nuku'alofa

The King's Palace. Although the Royal Palace, surrounded by a wall of coral, is not open to visitors, you can view the palace over the low wall that surrounds it. With a view to the sea and the Nuku'alofa waterfront, the palace stands in immaculately kept grounds which are planted with tropical flowers and shrubs and an encircling stand of massive Norfolk Island pines. Built in 1867, it has remained unchanged except for the addition of a second-story veranda in 1882.

At the Royal Palace, Her Majesty Queen Elizabeth II and His Royal Highness The Duke of Edinburgh stayed overnight during their visit to Tonga in 1953. On this occasion, more than 100 Tongan men and women with flaming torches kept a nightlong vigil outside the palace in accordance with ancient Tongan custom. To help the distinguished visitors greet the new day, four Tongans played bamboo nose-flutes as dawn broke.

The Royal Chapel. In this chapel, located next to the palace, the royal family worships and the coronations of King George Tupou II, Queen Salote, and Tonga's present king have taken place. All weddings and baptisms of royalty also occur here. Visitors may attend church services on Sunday evenings. The chapel was prefabricated in New Zealand and assembled here in 1882.

The Royal Tombs. Elevated above the ground in Tongan fashion, the Royal Tombs are situated on the estate of Tonga's first king, George Tupou I. He was entombed on these grounds (named *Mala'ekula*) in 1893, and Queen Salote Tupou was entombed in 1965. On her grave you will see small round black stones, known as *kilikili*. Placed there by her son, King Taufa'ahau Tupou IV, they form part of a tradition that dates back hundreds of years.

Talamahu Market. Farmers bring their produce in great abundance to Talamahu, Tonga's major fruit and vegetable market. The market is open every day except Sunday.

Fa'onelua Tropical Gardens. Here you can see a model Tongan village surrounded by more than 100

MOBY DICK...REVISITED

Tonga is one of the few places in the world where men still hunt the humpback whale using small boats and harpoons. For Tongans, it's a matter of economic necessity: almost every morsel of whale—including the skin and blubber—is sold for food. The profit for the whaler can run into hundreds of dollars.

If you see two boats sail up to the Nuku'alofa beach flying black flags during whale hunting season from June through October, they have a whale in tow. This doesn't happen often (only four whales were caught last year); but when it does happen, excitement runs high, and people from all over the island converge on the beach.

Tongan whalers, equipped with hand harpoons, lances, and whale line, set out to hunt their prey in gaff-rigged wooden boats, 30 to 35 feet long. Two boats, each carrying up to a dozen men, usually hunt together.

When a whale is sighted, the boats keep upwind of it. They eventually catch up with it, sometimes with the help of a good wind, sometimes when the whale pauses to bask in the sun. Once within range, they cast hand harpoons. The harpoons, which have steel heads that open out when lodged in the whale, are attached by whale lines to the boat. After the harpoon has lodged in the whale, it's only the beginning of the chase. The whale may drag the boat for half a day or more. All the while, the men will keep pulling the line, trying to draw closer to the whale. When the prey is a grown whale (usually measuring more than 50 feet in length), this can be extremely dangerous. But even a baby whale (measuring up to 20 feet long) can test a whaler's mettle.

Eventually the whale gets tired or the boat manages to close in on it; then lances are thrust, killing the whale. Two or three men jump overboard into what is now a bloody and shark-infested sea to sew up the whale's mouth so that it won't fill up with water.

Once the whale has been towed in and landed, it is immediately chopped up and sold. If it is a large whale, the heart—the most succulent part —is presented to the royal household. If it is a baby whale, the carcass is presented to the king.

varieties of hibiscus, as well as a large variety of other flora indigenous to the South Pacific.

Shopping

Tonga ranks as one of the best market places in the South Pacific for fine examples of traditional handicrafts. Among the specialties are tapa cloth, handbags, and finely woven mats and baskets. Tongan baskets are a welcome find for many a traveler with over-crowded luggage; they are handsome, durable, and inexpensive. Other goods of excellent quality include trays, fans, turtle shell ornaments, and wood carvings.

If you have a philatelist in the family, put the Post Office on your list of shopping places. Tonga's uniquely-shaped stamps are among the more elaborate in the world these days, rivaling the equally unusual stamps of Sierra Leone.

In addition to small shops throughout Nuku'alofa, handicrafts are also displayed and sold at the Langafonua Women's Institute on the main street. A duty-free shop sells cameras, radios, perfumes, and other goods at the International Dateline Hotel.

On ship days and other special occasions, handicrafts are spread out for sale on the open green near Nuku'alofa's main pier. You can expect vendors to call at your hotel, as well.

Sports

Tongans have a practically unbounded enthusiasm for sports—so much so, in fact, that at one time when cricket was riding high in popularity, the government put a curb on it by issuing a regulation that prohibited play except at certain hours on designated days. Rugby union and soccer matches also generate a lot of enthusiasm. Since soccer is one of the King's favorites, you might just happen to rub shoulders with His Majesty at one of the soccer games. Other popular spectator sports are basketball (the English version, played outside by both men and women on seven-man teams), tennis, track and field events, yacht races, and boxing. Major sports events are held at the sports ground in Nuku'alofa—rugby during their winter months (our summer), cricket and athletics during their summer.

Because of an abundance of white sand beaches, swimming and snorkeling opportunities abound. The best beaches on Tongatapu are 'Oholei, Ha'atafu, Monotapu, Ha'amalo, Laulea, 'Utukehe, Fahefa, and Fua'amotu.

For deep sea fishing, you can throw in a line from one of the small inter-island shipping vessels and probably pull out a marlin while en route between islands. Or you can charter a launch at the dock for a fishing trip, or make arrangements through Ma'afu Enterprises in Nuku'alofa, or at your hotel, or through local tour operators.

No golf courses have been built, but you can sharpen your putting on the nine-hole putting green at Ha'amalo.

Outside Nuku'alofa

Along the east and west coast roads on Tongatapu, you drive through many typical Tongan villages, travel deep into banana and coconut plantations, and pass white sand beaches and the lagoon where Captain Cook landed.

On the east coast are two major points of historical interest: the Ha'amonga Trilithon and the terraced tombs known as Langi. The Ha'amonga Trilithon, erected around A.D. 1200, consists of two great uprights—16-foot-high slabs of coral—topped by a horizontal connecting stone or lintel 19 feet long and mortised into the tops of the uprights. Each of the three stones is estimated to weigh 40 or more tons. For years the trilithon was thought to have been a gateway to a royal compound. In recent years, however, observations made by the King have led to the theory that the trilithon was probably used as a seasonal calendar, a kind of South Pacific Stonehenge. Notches carved in the lintel point directly to the rising sun on the longest and shortest days of the year.

Six miles from the Ha'amonga are the Langi (ancient kings rest in these terraced tombs), the first of which were built around A.D. 1200. Forming quadrilateral mounds, the tombs are faced by huge blocks of coral stone 12 feet high.

Hufangalupe, "The Pigeons' Doorway," is one of Tongatapu's most scenic areas. About 12 miles from Nuku'alofa, it has three dramatic features: the sea churns through a natural bridge, cliffs tower above the shore, a beguiling beach lies at the base. You can reach the beach along a steep trail in the cliff.

'Oholei Beach, a rewarding little resort on the east coast, is a favorite with visitors for an evening of feasting and dancing. The feast is sumptuous: roast suckling pig, crayfish, and locally grown vegetables, all cooked over open fires. The entertainment takes place in Hina's Cave, a superb natural theatre. Arrangements can be made through the International Dateline Hotel.

On the west coast of Tongatapu within 12 miles of Nuku'alofa are three points of interest: the Desiccated Coconut Factory (name of the year!) at Havelu, the Blow Holes of Houma, and the Flying Foxes at Kolovai. At the Desiccated Coconut Factory, the Tonga Copra Board takes visitors on tours through the modern factory that processes coconut to be shipped from Tonga to users around the world.

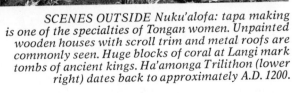

*SCENES OUTSIDE Nuku'alofa: tapa making
is one of the specialties of Tongan women. Unpainted
wooden houses with scroll trim and metal roofs are
commonly seen. Huge blocks of coral at Langi mark
tombs of ancient kings. Ha'amonga Trilithon (lower
right) dates back to approximately A.D. 1200.*

THE BLOW HOLES of Houma where the sea spurts through vents in coral reef. One of the flying foxes of Kolovai—a huge bat with a fox-like head. Picnic on a motu or islet offshore from Nuku'alofa. Port of Vava'u from ship's bridge.

At high tide on days with rough seas and a strong wind from the southeast or southwest, the Blow Holes of Houma are a spectacular sight. Great waves come thundering in to crash against the coast; the sea spurts through holes in the coral limestone reef in great geysers of 50 feet and more.

The Flying Foxes of Kolovai are a type of bat (*Pteropus tonganus*) with a foxlike head and a wingspan that measures up to three feet. You can see them by the hundreds, hanging heads downward in the casuarina trees—chattering during the day, flying out at night to forage for fruit, homing to the trees at dawn. Sacred to the Tongans and protected by custom, they may only be hunted by members of the Royal Family.

Eua Island, offshore from Tongatapu, is just 25 miles from Nuku'alofa. A delightful contrast to the big island, this small (approximately 34 square miles) island of rolling hills, dense forests, and high cliffs is just the right distance and the right size to fit a day cruise out of Nuku'alofa. And the launch leaves every day except Saturday and Sunday.

Eua's attractions are many. You'll want to visit

Hafu Pool: surrounded by hibiscus and other tropical plants, it's a small pond of crystal clear water fed by a mountain stream. Matalanga 'a Maui, on the southern end of the island, is a natural bridge through which the sea surges. Less than a half-mile away are the cliffs of Lakufa'anga, dropping 350 sheer feet to the shore. You can usually see turtles playing in the sea at the base of these cliffs. Hikers will want to walk through Eua's forests with their chattering, screeching, blue-crowned lories and red-breasted musk parrots.

The Vava'u Group, 170 miles north of Tongatapu, consists of 34 islands with a land area of approximately 45 square miles. Largest island is Vava'u (approximately 35 square miles), with a population of 11,800. Vava'u's port at Neiafu is one of the most beautiful in all the South Pacific—a landlocked harbor reached by sailing up an eight-mile passage to the fiord-like entrance. It's easy to see how the island's Port of Refuge Hotel got its name.

Among the places you'll want to visit by launch is the Swallows' Cave. Not far from Neiafu, it is a great cathedral-like chamber, nearly 100 feet high and 200 feet in circumference. The sun streams through an opening to light the caves in multi-color splendor.

Vava'u has some excellent swimming beaches, such as the ones at 'Ene'io, Keitahi, Toula, Talau Fanga, and the castaway island of Nuku. The Port of Refuge Hotel can give you details and arrange for any local sightseeing.

PRACTICAL INFORMATION

Entry regulations

To enter Tonga, you must have a valid passport, a smallpox vaccination certificate, and proof of on-ward transportation. In addition, you must have (in the words of a government spokesman), "an adequacy of funds for living in an appropriate manner for the duration of your stay."

Where to stay

In Tonga you'll find two modern, first-class hotels, and a scattering of smaller ones. The 50-room International Dateline Hotel in Nuku'alofa on Tongatapu faces out to a lagoon from its one-acre site on the waterfront. Built in 1966, the Dateline is not far from the Palace, Post Office, and the heart of downtown Nuku'alofa. It has a dining room and bar, swimming pool and tennis court, shops and service facilities. The hotel can make arrangements for you for skin diving, boating, surfing, aquaplaning, and sightseeing.

Tonga's newest first class hotel, opened in 1972, is the Port of Refuge Hotel in the town of Neiafu on Vava'u. Set on a five-acre site, the Refuge is the Kingdom's first major resort hotel. It has 30 Tongan-style thatched bungalows, a restaurant, bar and nightclub, swimming pool, shops, and service facilities. One of the Refuge's dramatic features is a stairway built of great limestone slabs that curve 200 feet down the cliff to the beach below. The Port of Refuge has facilities for water sports, big game fishing, cruising, car rentals, and bicycling. Village entertainments and feasts are held at the hotel. Another small hotel on Vava'u is Stowaway Village.

If you prefer a smaller hotel, there are several attractive possibilities. The Polynesian-style Moana Hotel, a mile from the center of town and just opposite Nuku'alofa's fishing harbor, is small and intimate; it has four double units. The Beach House, also in Nuku'alofa, is a large, colonial style wooden house with great atmosphere. Situated on the waterfront, it has nine double rooms. The Way In Motel, a quarter-mile from the center of town, has 18 double rooms, 8 with private baths. Two more small hotels are on the island of Eua: the Polynesian style Taha-Kae-Afe Lodge and the Leipua Guest House.

Climate

The climate on Tonga is surprisingly cool for the tropics. Average temperature varies from just over 60° in the winter (May to November) to about 90°

LARGEST HOTEL in Tonga, the International Dateline in Nuku'alofa, faces out to a lagoon.

in summer. The average rainfall is 67 inches; winter months are the dry season. From December to April (the summer season), the humidity is high.

Communications

Radio telephone and radio telegraph operate between Nuku'alofa and Suva, Fiji. A government-owned weekly newspaper, the *Chronicale*, is issued in two editions, Tongan and English.

Commercial radio station ZCO, known in the South Pacific as "The Call of the Friendly Islands," broadcasts in Tongan and English for three hours in the morning, two in the afternoon, and four and a half hours in the evening. On Sundays, broadcasts are confined to three hours in the evening.

Currency and banking

Tonga's local currency unit is the *pa'anga*. It is comprised of 100 *seniti* or cents. At the present exchange rate, one U. S. dollar equals T$.80. Tonga has no commercial bank, but travelers checks can be cashed at the Government Treasury and hotels.

Health and medical

Medical services—doctors, dentists, pharmacy—are available in Nuku'alofa, and a large hospital has recently been completed in the capital city.

Treated water at the large hotels is safe to drink. In other areas, be cautious.

How to get around

If you arrive in Tonga by air, you will land at Fua'amotu airport, about 14 miles southeast of downtown Nuku'alofa. If you arrive by ship, you will dock within a few blocks of the business section of Nuku'alofa. At the airport, a hotel bus or taxi can take you into town.

Transportation in Nuku'alofa itself is largely by *ve'etolu* (pronounced vee-toe-loo)—colorful three-wheeled vehicles, roofed but open-sided. Taking one of these will give an extra dimension to sightseeing. Taxis are also plentiful. Fares should be discussed in advance of the trip, but you can count on the cost of a *ve'etolu* being about half that of a private taxi.

Rental cars are available in Nuku'alofa; rates are similar to those elsewhere in the Pacific. A Tongan driving license is required. You can obtain one by showing your domestic driving license to the Police Traffic Department in Nuku'alofa. The amount of driving you'll do will be limited by the scanty 150 miles of either sealed or gravelled roads on the island of Tongatapu. Among the natural hazards on most roads outside of town are pigs—they are virtually ubiquitous.

Tours and excursions by private car on the island of Tongatapu are now offered by several major tour operators in Nuku'alofa. Tour buses operate organized tours on cruise ship days.

By boat, it's possible to sail from Nuku'alofa to the island groups north of Tongatapu: to Ha'apai (7 hours) and to Vava'u (17 hours). You can also make a day trip by boat to Eua, second largest island in the Tongatapu group (three hours each way).

Sailings to Ha'apai and Vava'u are scheduled twice a week (leaving Nuku'alofa on Mondays and Thursdays, returning on Tuesdays and Fridays). The recently purchased *'Olovaha*, a government-owned, inter-island ferry that makes these runs, has two double-berthed cabins, as well as space for deck passengers. Occasionally the ferry will sail on days other than those scheduled in order to meet its local commitments. You can get details in advance from either the Tonga Shipping Agency or Tonga Visitors Bureau in Nuku'alofa.

Several other vessels based in Nuku'alofa offer added opportunities for sailing. The 45-foot motor-sailboat, *Just David*, can be chartered for day trips or for longer journeys through the Tongan archipelago. The *Petu'a Moana*, a 30-foot, gaff-rigged cutter, operates six to eight-hour cruises with time for swimming, snorkeling, and diving. It also visits an isolated island village for a traditional feast. Another day-trip offering is a full or half-day glass-bottom boat trip for viewing marine life. For information about offshore tours and boat hires, get in touch with these agencies in Nuku'alofa: Ma'afu Enterprises, Tonga Tourist & Development Company Limited, Teta Tours, and Tonga Holiday Tours.

For boat hire on the island of Vava'u, make arrangements through the Governor's office or the Port of Refuge Hotel.

By air, a newly scheduled service connects Nuku'alofa with Neiafu on Vava'u Island, flying two round trips daily except Sunday. The trip takes about 90 minutes each way. Charter air service is also available between these two islands.

Tipping

Tongans do not expect to be tipped in routine situations. If some special service has been given, a modest tip is in order.

For information

Write to the Tonga Visitor's Bureau, P.O. Box 37, Nuku'alofa, Kingdom of Tonga, South Pacific.

The New Hebrides... a rare condominium

PRIMITIVE RITUALS, DRAMATIC LAND DIVERS, VOLCANOES THAT RISE OUT OF THE SEA

Shaped by the effects of a lingering British empire and the heavy overlay of a French presence, the New Hebrides have the distinction of being the world's only condominium government (one country ruled by two nations) still in existence.

In some ways, the New Hebrides seem farther away and more foreign than any of the other islands of the South Pacific. The volcanoes are still smoking; the natives are still performing primitive rituals; the marks of Melanesian culture are many. These islands seem lightly touched by the visible evidences of contemporary civilization.

For the tourist, the semi-forgotten, lonely New Hebrides are still an off-beat experience. Approaching them by air, the traveler sees islands conspicuous for their dense green jungles, occasionally slashed by winding roads, usually outlined by crescent beaches and fringes of cultivated land, clusters of leaf huts near their shores. You'll probably fly over at least one of the steam or smoke-shrouded volcanic islands—Tanna, Lopevi, or Ambrym—their slopes rising steeply from the sea.

If you're lucky, your visit will coincide with a performance of the dramatic ritual of land-diving on Pentecost Island, where men dive from the top of a 90-foot high, makeshift tower headlong toward earth, their falls stopped short by taut liana vines secured to the tower and tied to their ankles.

Geography

The New Hebrides' closest neighbor of any size is New Caledonia, 330 miles to the south. Fiji is 600

BLEAK, DESOLATE, AND DRAMATIC is the landscape on Tanna Island near the slope of Mount Yasur, a volcano that is constantly active.

miles to the east, the Solomons 640 miles to the northwest. By air it's a one-hour flight from Noumea, New Caledonia, by UTA; a two-hour flight from Nadi, Fiji, by Air Pacific; and an hour and three quarter flight from the Solomons by Air Pacific.

The New Hebrides' land mass totals 5,700 square miles, spread out over 13 large and 60 small islands stretching some 450 miles in a north-south direction. The terrain ranges from coral formations to rolling mountains, from jungles and grassy uplands to smoking volcanoes.

Port Vila (usually called Vila), on the island of Efate, is the capital of the Condominium of New Hebrides. Ranking next in importance is the town of Santo (also called Luganville) on the island of Espiritu Santo.

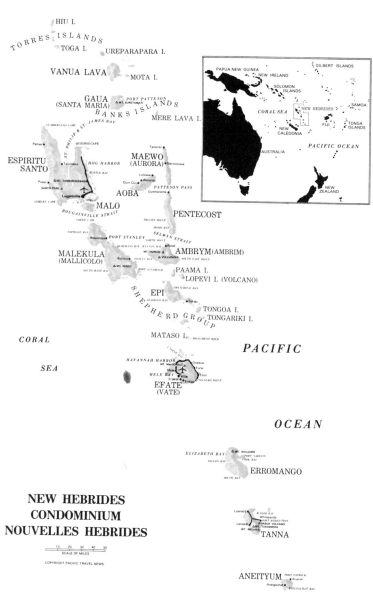

**NEW HEBRIDES
CONDOMINIUM
NOUVELLES HEBRIDES**

SCALE OF MILES

COPYRIGHT PACIFIC TRAVEL NEWS

History

On April 25, 1606, Pedro de Quiros, a Portuguese navigating for the King of Spain, became the first European to sight the New Hebrides. He dropped anchor off an island he named Espiritu Santo in the body of water he named St. Philip and St. James' Bay. Some 160 years later, the French navigator, Bougainville, landed on Aoba Island and then continued past other islands of the group. It fell to Captain Cook, in 1774, to discover, chart, and name the majority of the islands in the group. Following Cook came another navigator well known in the annals of the South Pacific: Captain Bligh, who in 1789 sighted several previously undiscovered islands in the group.

Not quite a century later, the unique condominium government had its origins. In 1871 an Irish settler, one John Higginson, finding British land and labor regulations too strict for his liking, asked the French Governor of New Caledonia to annex the New Hebrides. His request was refused. But his action set in motion various incidents involving the French, one of which was a proposal to allow liberated convicts from New Caledonia to settle in the New Hebrides. This prompted a protest movement in Australia, geared toward annexation of the New Hebrides by that country. There followed proposals, counter proposals, and divisive strategems until 1887, when Britain and France agreed to set up a Joint Naval Commission. So began the British-French connection that led to the establishment of the Condominium of the New Hebrides in 1906.

Lifestyle

The New Hebrides' population of 86,000 embraces a variety of cultures whose patterns change from island to island. Of the total population, some 78,000 are Melanesian or a mixture of Melanesian with Polynesian. The remaining 8,000 are European, Asian, and other Pacific peoples. Technically, each member of the non-indigenous population is classified as either "French and ressortissant" or "British and ressortissant." Ressortissants are people neither French or British who, under the terms of the Condominium Protocol, must elect to be governed by one or the other of the two systems of administration existing in the New Hebrides. Even the tourist, on arrival, can place himself under either French or British jurisdiction if required.

Nationality is less clear-cut for the indigenous population: having no national status, they therefore bear no allegiance to either the French or British; but they can request protection from either.

The complicated scheme of the Condominium Administration seems to work well enough despite its cumbersome aspects. In matters large and small,

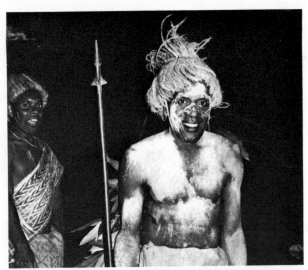

FEATHERS AND PAINT adorn a dancer from Pentecost Island. Two police forces, the French (far right) and the British (center) have jurisdiction in the New Hebrides.

a duality applies. Two flags — the Union Jack and the Tricolor—fly side by side. Two languages— English and French—are official (although pidgin English is commonly heard in these islands, where more than 200 languages and dialects are spoken by the indigenous population). There are two separate police forces (and two jails); and when it comes to judicial matters, four separate courts of law function: British; French; a third court for New Hebridean native affairs; and a fourth, the Joint Court, for dealing with matters of internal concern in the New Hebrides such as land claims. This multiple administration extends to public works, but medical services and education are the responsibility of the separate national administrations.

Outside the two centers of population, Vila (4,000) and Santo (2,750), most New Hebrideans live in small, scattered villages of leaf huts. Their culture, traditions, and everyday circumstances vary to such an extent that a "typical" lifestyle is virtually non-existent. The Melanesian woman on most islands tends her garden, shops in the village cooperative, and sends the children to schools run by missionaries. One of the chief occupations of the men on some of the islands is the raising of pigs that have fine circle tusks, used to make masks and other totems, primitive and symbolic.

Although new trends in politics, social advancement, and economics are slowly beginning to change these islands, the New Hebrides can still be considered primitive. To a large extent, the native population survives on subsistence farming. Copra is the chief export, followed by frozen fish,

beef, and food crops. Timber, tourism, cacao, coffee, and mother-of-pearl, along with some manganese mining, contribute to the economy.

A surprising number of overseas companies have established their headquarters' offices in the New Hebrides for the very good reason that there are no direct income or capital gains taxes. And thereby hangs a paradox: a basically primitive and underdeveloped country is becoming an important financial center.

Even though the missionary influence over the last century has been considerable, many native New Hebrideans have not been converted to Christianity. This is particularly true of the tribes living inland on the islands of Malekula, Espiritu Santo, Pentecost, and Tanna.

SIGHTSEEING

In and around Vila

Vila, capital of New Hebrides, is a mishmash of old colonial buildings, war construction of the 1940's, and new concrete structures. The business district straggles along a narrow reach of land beside a harbor punctuated by two picturesque inlets. Inland from the waterfront, narrow streets climb steep slopes graced with flowering bougainvillea and old buildings. The predominant impression of the town is French. And indeed the French, the more assiduous of the two ruling powers, overshadow the British in many respects.

BEACH YOUR BOAT on a deserted strand, here at Champagne Beach on Hog Harbour. Outside of Vila, you see typical Melanesian huts, and in town, paved streets, automobiles, and modern buildings.

Although small, Vila has some aspects of a sophisticated French city. It has at least two typically Parisian problems: traffic jams and a shortage of parking space.

The Cultural Centre on the Vila waterfront is a profitable place to while away an hour or so, looking at displays of primitive art, island crafts, shells, plants, birds and other wildlife. Guided by the shell exhibits at the Centre, visiting collectors are sometimes able to spot rare shells among those sold by local women at the Vila market. Bird watchers, after scrutinizing the exhibits, will be better able to identify such species as the Australian dabchick, the purple swamphen, the green palm lorikeet, and the Australian goshawk.

Shopping in the New Hebrides is enhanced by prices on imports that compare favorably with those in some free-port areas. (And no sales tax nibbles away at your wallet here.) Stores in Vila and Santo sell cassette recorders, stereo equipment, transistors, cameras, watches, French wines and perfumes, Chinese curios, and Tahitian fabrics. Look for bargain prices in the Chinese stores and for a wide selection as well as good prices at such well known establishments as Burns Philp.

Native handicrafts made in outlying Melanesian villages are becoming more readily available. Some of the shops in Vila and Santo sell grass skirts from Futana and Tanna, baskets and mats from Ambrym and Malekula, woodwork from Tongoa and Santo, pig tusk circles (rare and expensive) and necklaces of shells or colored seeds from villages around Vila.

If you're of a more active bent, you'll find at least a dozen different possibilities available at Le Lagon Hotel in Vila; tennis courts, snorkeling, water skiing, trimaran sailboats, outrigger canoes, pedal boats and glass bottom boats, a nine-hole golf course, rental bicycles, and clay-pigeon shooting. If you're a shell collector, you probably already know what many collectors know: the shores of the New Hebrides are a conchologist's paradise.

Beyond Vila, about 90 miles of all-weather roads stripe the island of Efate, their condition ranging from fair to poor by metropolitan standards.

Tours out of Vila

To make the most of your trip to the New Hebrides, consider touring some of the outlying islands. These include such far-famed attractions as the land-divers of Pentecost Island, whose performances are held sporadically and are now staged as much for a tourist attraction as for a primitive ritual.

On Malekula Island are the Big Nambas, a fairly primitive tribe known for their rituals and exotic dances. It takes eight hours' hiking to reach the village of Amok, where many of the Big Nambas live. Amok now has its co-operative store, and many of the Big Nambas listen to their transistor radios.

If you're up to a long and very arduous hike, you can trek to the south central part of Malekula—home of the Small Nambas. It takes two days' hiking on steep rugged terrain and difficult trail to reach them, and hiring a guide is essential. Few tourists have yet been in, for the Small Nambas do not welcome visitors, having successfully avoided much contact with missionaries and others of the outside world.

Far less demanding are the sightseeing flights over the volcanic islands of Tanna, Ambrym, and Lovepi. If you want a land-based view of a volcano, you can ride a Land Rover on Tanna right up the slopes of Mount Yasur, which is active enough to produce ash showers periodically.

In and around Santo

Santo, New Hebrides' second "city," lies along a six-mile stretch of shore fronting the Segond Channel on the island of Espiritu Santo. Though both the island and the town are also called Luganville, local residents use the name Santo.

Largest island in the New Hebrides, Santo is 76 miles long and 45 miles wide. Heavily wooded, it has many streams flowing out from an imposing range of mountains along its west coast. Mount Tabwemasana, 6,169 feet, is the highest peak in the New Hebrides.

The town of Santo has most of the amenities of a small tropical port. Despite being somewhat scruffy, undeniably it has some of the charm of the legendary South Seas.

PRACTICAL INFORMATION

Entry regulations

A tourist visa is required for anyone who is not a British or French subject. Visas must be procured in advance from any French or British consulate

TWO HOTELS in Vila: Le Lagon d'Erakor Hotel (left) on the beach of a lagoon; and Hotel Vate (above) in a downtown location.

and are good for three months. A smallpox vaccination and proof of onward transportation are also required.

At Vila's Bauerfield Airport, visitors are assisted through immigation by a bilingual hostess provided by the Tourist Information Bureau.

Where to stay

For tourists, three hotels in Vila, one in Santo, and some *bures* on the island of Tanna are the extent of accommodations in the New Hebrides.

In Vila, Le Lagon Hotel, with 130 rooms, is the largest. It has thatched Melanesian bungalows set on a narrow, white sand beach fronting Erakor Lagoon. The two other hotels in Vila are the Hotel Vate Vila (24 rooms) and the Hotel Rossi (32 rooms). Both are located on the main street of town.

In Santo, the Lokalee Beach Hotel stretches its 20 rooms out along a fine strand of beach about 30 miles from the airport.

On the island of Tanna, overnight accommodations can be arranged at Tanna Island Bungalows —six self-contained *bures* in Epul forming a village of leaf-houses a few miles from the airstrip. Facilities include bedroom, bath, and gas stove. Supplies are available at a nearby store.

Climate

New Hebrides has a pleasant, semi-tropical climate with two seasons. The cool, dry winter season runs from May through October; the warm, rainy, humid summer season lasts from November through April. Rainfall averages up to 120 inches a year. Humidity averages 83 per cent the year round.

Communications

No newspapers are published in the New Hebrides. The British administration issues a twice-monthly newsletter; the French, a weekly newsletter and a monthly bulletin in pidgin. Radio Vila broadcasts news, music, and features at noon and in the evening, Monday through Friday (in three languages).

Automatic telephones operate in Vila and Santo, and radio telephone service goes to Australia and Fiji, where cable relays connect with North America. Calls must be booked in advance.

Currency and banking

Two currencies are used, the Australian dollar and the New Hebrides franc. Combinations of both may be used—the Australian dollar, on the internal rate of exchange, is equal to 100 New Hebrides francs. Prior to departure, you must exchange francs.

As a result of its growing importance as head-quarters for a number of companies seeking the country's tax advantages, Vila has become a major banking center with eight banks (branches of major banks in Hong Kong, France, England, Australia, and New Zealand).

Health and medical

Malaria is the principal disease on these islands. Although the World Health Organization has recently begun a malaria-eradication program, it is still advisable to check with your doctor regarding preventive medications. Since you can expect to encounter more flies in the New Hebrides than in most places, you may want to take along some insect repellent.

Hospitals are established in Vila and Santo, and also on the islands of Tanna, Malekula, Aoba and Epi.

How to get around

Taxi service operates in Vila and Santo. Fixed fares are in effect; bargaining is not necessary.

Rental cars are available from three agencies (including Hertz and Avis) in Vila and one in Santo.

Guided tours are offered by several organizations in Vila. The variety of tours includes city sightseeing, visits to native villages, volcano viewing by airplane, and trips by sailing canoe.

By boat. The 29-foot cabin cruiser *Wiana* leaves from Port Havannah, North Efate, carrying up to six persons on day tours and fishing trips. Another craft, the trimaran *Jayel*, makes regular day trips to Mele Island and is also available for charter.

By air. Air Melanesiae, the local airline, flies out of Bauerfield Airport at Vila to Santo, Lamap and Norsup on Malekula Island, Walaha and Longana on Aoba Island, Lonorore on South Pentecost Island, and the islands of Tanna, Tongoa, Aneityum, and Erromango. Most flights are scheduled daily. Air Melanesiae also offers a variety of air-sightseeing tours—featuring volcano viewing, flights over the smaller islands in the vicinity of Vila, and a complete aerial tour of the island of Efate.

Tipping

Tipping is not customary in the New Hebrides; it offends the New Hebridean sense of hospitality.

For information

The Tourist Information Bureau of the Chamber of Commerce, Industry, and Agriculture is located in Vila. Address is B.P. 209, Port Vila, New Hebrides.

The Solomons...somewhat beyond the tourist routes

A MOUNTAINOUS CHAIN, FRINGED WITH VILLAGES, SCARRED BY WORLD WAR II BATTLEFIELDS

RUSTING REMNANTS of World War II still lie along the beaches where troops landed three decades ago.

Nowhere in the South Pacific is the sense of 20th century history stronger than in the Solomon Islands. Guadalcanal, Savo Island, Tulagi, the "Slot," Iron Bottom Sound, Plum Pudding Island—all are familiar names in the annals of World War II. It was on Guadalcanal in 1942 that the U. S. Marines succeeded in stalling the formidable Japanese offense and changed the course of war in the Pacific. It was on the tiny island of Olasana, now known as Plum Pudding Island, that John F. Kennedy and ten other survivors of PT-109 were marooned in 1943.

The vestiges of war remain: Sherman tanks overgrown with creepers; shell-torn landing craft ravaged by the seas; trenches pocking the land; redoubts rearing from the hillsides. Surrounded by the more gentle aspects of the land—exotic flowers, waving palms, blue lagoons, and coral atolls—the places of fierce fighting in World War II have lost some of their harshness. The Solomon Islands have slowly emerged to become a growing tourist attraction, appealing to travelers who have the inclination to visit old battlefields and to those who are lured to islands still somewhat beyond the standard tourist routes.

Geography

An extensive area, the British Solomon Islands Protectorate consists of 10 large islands and island clusters extending in a double chain for more than 900 miles, northwest to southeast. The boundaries of the Protectorate enclose a sea area of some 250,000 square miles. The Solomons lie about 1,100 miles northwest of Fiji, 675 miles northwest of the New Hebrides, and 875 miles due east of Papua New Guinea. Air Pacific schedules twice weekly BAC 1-11 flights to Honiara (the capital) from Nadi, Fiji, by way of Vila and Santo in the New Hebrides. Qantas and Air Pacific both have one flight a week from Port Moresby, Papua New Guinea.

Guadalcanal, 2,500 square miles, is the largest island in the group. Located on the northern side of the island, Honiara is the capital of the Protectorate and the main port of entry.

History

In 1567, Alvaro de Mendaña sailed from Callao, Peru, and reached the Solomon Islands the following year. He gave the largest island the name Guadalcanal after a town in Spain; tales of fabulous gold (wishful thinking rather than fact) in these islands prompted him to name the island group after King Solomon.

Over the centuries that followed came other explorers, British and French, who sighted the islands or stopped at them.

In the mid-1850's a period of massacre and murder beset the Solomons, largely a retaliation against "blackbirding" (the recruiting of labor by Europeans for plantations in Australia and Fiji). Because of this state of affairs, the South Solomons were declared a Protectorate by Great Britain in 1893. The remainder of the Solomons followed suit between 1898 and 1900.

Early in the 20th century, private companies started plantations, but in later years—up until 1940—the British Solomon Islands were largely neglected except for coconut planting.

Then came World War II. The Solomon Islands were the focal point of fierce battles before the mighty Japanese offensive was stalled and Guadalcanal airstrip, now known as Henderson Field, was completed by the Allies. In this chapter of history, many Solomon Islanders, fiercely loyal to the Allied cause, distinguished themselves in battle. The important naval battle of the Coral Sea was waged in nearby waters.

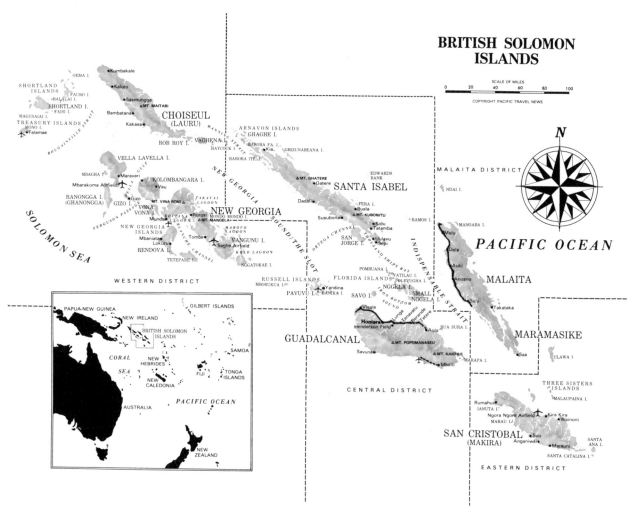

COOKING-FIRE SMOKE rising from community kitchen (above) is a kind of dinner call to villagers. On market day, natives gather around produce-laden canoe to buy food.

Lifestyle

Approximately 175,000 people live in the British Solomon Islands Protectorate. Of that number, close to 150,000 are Melanesian and more than 6,000 are Polynesian. The remainder includes Europeans, part-Europeans, Chinese, and Micronesians.

The largest concentration of the population (over 11,000) is in Honiara; but the island of Malaita, with some 51,000 Melanesians, is the most populous island.

The Polynesians—mainly from small islands such as Ontong Java, Sikaiana, Rennell, Bellona, and the Reef Islands—generally live on offshore islets and atolls. Darker-skinned Melanesians inhabit the villages on the larger islands. The peoples of the Solomon Islands are sometimes conveniently categorized according to residence: the "salt water people" live near shores, and the "bush people" live inland on the spurs of ranges.

Until World War II, the Solomon Islands' people did not have a great deal of contact with Europeans and others of the world beyond them. Some of the natives held engaging ideas about their world: some believed, it is said, that a tree could be killed by shouting at it every morning for a month. With a daily piercing yell aimed at it, the tree eventually lost its leaves and branches and died.

In any event, the Solomon Islanders certainly were not prepared for the advent of the aircraft that came in great numbers during World War II, let alone the wealth of material marvels that they brought. Canned foods, bottled drinks, kerosene lamps, radios, and tremendous supplies of weapons —these amazed the islanders. Many of them believed that an aircraft was a huge kind of bird that fed on petrol.

During this 20th century cataclysm, many of the Solomon Islanders served the Allied cause with particular distinction.

In governmental matters, the Western Pacific High Commission in Honiara administers the islands. As things exist at present, the Protectorate manages to appear economically flourishing. Private enterprise is prospering, and there is much new public and private building. The economy of the islands depends to a large extent on copra, rice, and timber production, and a limited amount of commercial fishing. Tourism, small but growing, is relatively new to the islands. The government-established British Solomon Islands Tourist Authority was launched in 1970.

No national language exists in the Solomons. Instead, at least 40 different languages and dialects are spoken. In most parts of the island group, however, the *lingua franca* is an Anglicized version of pidgin English.

HONIARA, THE CAPITAL

Before World War II, Honiara didn't exist; the site was a coconut plantation. Early in the war, the Japanese established a beachhead there and began building an airfield nearby. Then, after fierce fighting, the Allies moved in to establish an American

FRINGING THE SHORE-SIDE ROAD, a company of coconut trees is part of a coconut plantation.

base and complete the airfield. A place called Honiara and an island named Guadalcanal became well-known throughout the world. By the time the war ended, Tulagi, original capital of the British Solomon Islands Protectorate, had been demolished. Honiara, a name derived from *Nagh-oniara* (meaning "facing the southeast wind"), was selected as the new capital of the BSIP.

Any GI who remembers post-war Honiara—a collection of Quonset huts—would scarcely recognize the town today. And the first-time traveler is in for a surprise: Honiara doesn't have the typical look of a South Seas port.

Hemmed in between seafront and grassy ridges, Honiara displays a modern look with its air-conditioned buildings of concrete and glass. The headquarters of the High Court of the Western Pacific, the Secretariat, and the residence of the High Commissioner are handsomely designed buildings. Along Mendana Avenue, the main street has been turned into a tar-sealed thoroughfare; bright red buses rumble by its poinciana, palm, and tulip trees. In the hills back from shore are housing developments, and farther back, private residences are being built. Today, the visitor will find little more than a trace of the humble Quonset hut.

Sightseeing in Honiara

Pick up a map from your hotel desk or at the Tourist Authority if you want to take a self-guided tour. Drive along tree-lined Mendana Avenue, past the High Court, the Post Office, the General Police Station. Stop at the Solomon Islands Museum in Coronation Gardens, approximately across the avenue from the Hotel Mendana. The museum displays traditional artifacts, war relics, geological exhibits,

and collections of butterflies and shells. It's a good place to get an overview of the various facets of these islands. Continuing on along Mendana Avenue, you'll come to the duty free shops (see section on shopping) and then the Public Market, always worth a stop for a slice of local color. Near the market are two churches, the South Sea Evangelical and the United. A short distance farther, around the bend in the road, is the handsome contemporary Holy Cross Roman Catholic Cathedral. A little farther on, across the single lane bridge, is Chinatown, sprawling along the Mataniko River.

At the opposite (or west) end of town are the large Botanical Gardens, set in a sylvan valley through which a small stream meanders past a series of rocky pools. Early morning is the finest time for a visit. The gardens are about a quarter-mile inland from Mendana Avenue by way of a side road.

Shopping

The Solomon Islands are noted for excellent carvings with intricate patterns of pearl shell inlay. You find these in the shops, or, with a little perseverance, you can usually find a craftsman who markets his own work. A wide range of shells, woven baskets, and traditional shell money is also sold in shops. At the Solomon Islands Museum, the ladies sell handicrafts made by the Women's Clubs of the Solomon Islands.

A modified form of duty free shopping is available at five shops located in the area on or near Mendana Avenue and the road running out to Point Cruz. They sell everything from pearls to transistor radios to record players.

Most shops are open from 8 a.m. to 12:30 p.m. and 2 to 5 p.m., Monday through Friday; 8 a.m. to 12:30 p.m., Saturday. Some Chinese shops stay open longer.

Sightseeing outside Honiara

Guided tours, scenic flights to outlying islands, and cruises from Honiara all offer different views from different perspectives. Ask your travel agent about arrangements, or see a local agency in Honiara.

To give you an idea of the possibilities:

Among the shorter tours is a trip to Betikama Mission school where woodcarvers sing as they work and offer their carvings for sale.

Put the day trip to Savo Island on your list if you can afford a full day. About 25 miles from Honiara, this small island with its rounded volcanic crater is the home of the megapode birds. Even by tropical standards they are a curiosity: the megapode is a burrowing bird, and it lays its eggs at least two feet deep in the beach sand.

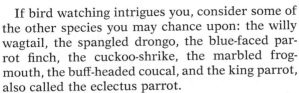

WRINKLED MOUNTAINS rise behind the town of Honiara, on Guadalcanal. Two hotels in the Solomons are the Mendana (upper right) in Honiara and the Tavanipupu Island Resort on Marau Sound (lower right), 65 miles from Honiara.

If bird watching intrigues you, consider some of the other species you may chance upon: the willy wagtail, the spangled drongo, the blue-faced parrot finch, the cuckoo-shrike, the marbled frogmouth, the buff-headed coucal, and the king parrot, also called the eclectus parrot.

A trip to Malaita Island's Alite ,located in Langa Langa Lagoon by plane, motor vehicle, and launch gives you a new insight into the islanders' way of life. Here, natives build their own islands out of coral and construct over-water leaf huts. You'll see traditional dances performed and the making of shell money demonstrated. (Shell money, long a medium of exchange, is now used only in certain "custom" or traditional situations.) A similar tour may be made to Laulasi, also in Langa Langa Lagoon.

For those interested in visiting or re-visiting the battlefields of World War II, various options are open: anything from a 2½-hour battlefield visit to all-day tours that fly to Auki and other islands that are of historical interest.

For scuba divers, there's another aspect of exploring the historical past: a 2½-hour underwater and diving tour to inspect the hulls of sunken Japanese warships.

PRACTICAL INFORMATION

Entry requirements

A passport and visa are required of United States citizens. The visa may be obtained from the nearest British Consulate; proof of onward transportation is required before it will be issued. A visitor's permit, issued on arrival, allows one to stay in the Solomons for a period up to four months.

An international certificate of vaccination for smallpox is required of United States travelers.

Cholera and yellow fever shots are required if a visitor is arriving from an infected area.

Where to stay

In all of the scattered islands of the British Solomon Islands Protectorate, you'll find only five hotels, along with a few guest houses.

In Honiara, three hotels are located in the central part of town: the Hotel Mendana (66 rooms), the Honiara Hotel (53 rooms), and Blum's Hometel (14 units). About 30 miles out of town (from the airport, an hour and a quarter drive) is the Tambea Village Tourist Resort (20 bungalows). The Tambea Village offers such resort facilities and attractions as snorkeling, boating, coral viewing in glass bottom boats, shelling, fishing, Melanesian music, dancing, and, occasionally, feasts. Just off the southeast tip of Guadalcanal is Tavanipupu Island Resort, a few cottages situated on the shore of Marau Sound. About 65 miles from Honiara, it is reached by a 25-minute flight and a 10-minute boat ride. Bungalows are fully equipped, including kitchens. Since there is no central dining room, however, guests must bring their own food supplies.

Although the Solomon Islands do not yet attract great numbers of tourists, hotel space is always at a premium. Reservations should be made well in advance of a visit.

Climate

Hottest from November through April, the islands register daytime temperatures in the high 80's and nighttime ones in the 70's. The summer season is the period when torrential rains fall, but they are often short, sharp bursts, followed by sparkling sunshine. From the end of April until November, southeast trade winds cool the air, and rain squalls are shorter and farther apart. Average annual rainfall at Honiara is more than 80 inches. As a rule, it's too hot and humid to wear a raincoat, but an umbrella (or lacking one, a banana leaf) comes in handy.

Communications

No newspapers are published in the Solomon Islands, but a Protectorate News Sheet is issued fortnightly by a Government Information Officer.

The Solomon Islands Broadcasting Service transmits 83½ hours a week, the programs presenting news, interviews, and various types of features.

An automatic telephone exchange operates in Honiara. Overseas radio-telephone circuits go to Suva, Fiji, where they connect with most countries in the world.

Currency and banking

The British Solomon Islands Protectorate uses Australian currency, and two banks—the Commonwealth Bank of Australia and the Australia and New Zealand Bank Ltd.—have branches in Honiara.

Health and medical

Hospitals are located in Honiara and at Auki on Malaita; Gizo, on Gizo Island; and Kira Kira, on San Cristobal.

Malaria is still prevalent, although anti-malarial measures in the last decade have considerably reduced the incidence. It is advisable to ask your doctor about preventative medications.

How to get around

If you enter the Solomon Islands by cruise ship, you will anchor at Point Cruz in the bay fronting Honiara. If you arrive by air, you will land at Henderson Field, about eight miles out of Honiara.

Taxis are available at the airport and in town for trips in and around Honiara. Paved roads extend for a distance of about 30 miles on either side of Honiara.

Car rentals can be arranged in Honiara or at the agency desks at Henderson Field and the Hotel Mendana.

Boat trips along the Honiara coast and canoe trips up the Mataikau River can be arranged at your hotel.

Air travel between the widely scattered islands is provided by the Solomon Islands Airways Limited, locally known as Solair. The airline operates scheduled services from Honiara to some 18 airstrips in the Protectorate, including Avu Avu and Marau on Guadalcanal; to Kira Kira, on San Cristobal; to Auki, on Malaita Island; to Yandina, on Banika Island in the Russels; and to Sege, Munda, Gizo, and Barakona, all in the New Georgia Islands.

Tipping

Tipping in any situation is discouraged in the Solomon Islands.

For information

Get in touch with the British Solomon Islands Tourist Authority, Box 321, P.O. Honiara, B.S.I.P.

Papua New Guinea...land of seven hundred cultures

SECOND LARGEST ISLAND IN THE WORLD, LAND OF SING-SINGS, WIG MEN, AND MUD MEN

Seven hundred tribes, 700 languages, 700 cultures—that, in essence, is Papua New Guinea, a place where the primitive holds a a strong appeal.

Papua New Guinea has emerged only recently from a dominant Stone Age culture, and even today this culture persists in the fastnesses of secluded valleys and high plateaus, places where tribes, still isolated, are insulated from the impact of the 20th century.

Until the arrival of the first Australians in the early 1930's, the mountains known as the Highlands of Papua New Guinea remained virtually an unknown territory to outsiders. Even now, first contacts are still being made with these dwellers among the high ranges.

Touring, especially in the Highlands, is accented by the unscheduled and the unexpected, whether a gathering to mourn a death or a singing and dancing festival known as a sing-sing. The people are fascinating: each tribe has its peculiarly distinctive personality. There are wig men, topheavy with huge, elaborate wigs; and mud men, grotesque with baked earthen masks and bodies caked with mud. There are dwellers in the mountains whose huts have openings no larger than a dog's kennel; there are river dwellers who build towering palm leaf temples.

And there are other compensations for the intrepid tourist in Papua New Guinea: leaping, boulder-strewn streams and mile-wide, muddy rivers; 14,000-foot peaks and alpine forests; mangrove swamps where crocodiles lurk and jungles with the exotic bird of paradise and king of Saxony.

THE TOWERING, DECORATED haus tambaran, *a native spirit house, is common to the Sepik River region of Papua New Guinea.*

In its remote reaches, the scenic splendors of Papua New Guinea are still unspoiled by man. With its kaleidoscopic facets, it is one of the Pacific's intriguing but as yet virtually untapped travel destinations.

Geography

Papua New Guinea is about 900 miles west of Honiara, British Solomon Islands, and 1,700 miles north of Sydney, Australia.

Second largest island in the world (after Greenland), the island of New Guinea is 1,306 miles long. The districts of Papua New Guinea comprise the eastern half of this island and include the mainland and several islands to the east and northeast (New Britain, New Ireland, the Admiralty Islands, the Trobriands, Bougainville, Buka, and various small archipelagoes). Altogether, Papua New Guinea covers 183,540 square miles. The western half of the island of New Guinea is the entirely separate country of West Irian, held by Indonesia.

The central part of mainland New Guinea, known as the Highlands, is a massive mountain spine—a splendid and verdant chain of knife-edged ranges, high plateaus and valleys, and forest choked ravines that extends for more than a thousand miles from one end of the island to the other. More than a dozen of its peaks rise to heights of 10,000 feet or more. The highest, Mount Wilhelm, soars to 15,400 feet. The Highlands' main centers are Mt. Hagen, Goroka, and Kundiawa.

Draining the ranges are a great many streams. The two largest are the Sepik River, more than a mile wide in places, flowing north, and the Fly River, flowing south to form a broad delta where it empties into the Gulf of Papua. Each of these rivers is navigable for about 500 miles.

Papua New Guinea's capital, as well as its main harbor, is Port Moresby. Other harbors are located at Madang and at Rabaul in New Britain. Fringing much of the coastline of Papua New Guinea are coral reefs. Dense jungles and broad mangrove swamplands cover a large part of the lowlands.

History

Because the Moluccas, the rich "Spice Islands," lie to the west of New Guinea, many 16th century Spanish and Portuguese ships sailed in the vicinity of New Guinea. A Portuguese governor of the Moluccas by the name of Meneses was the first

STILT HOUSES in the coastal villages, such as this one at Madang, contrast with tent-like huts that are typical in the Highlands.

European to land on the shores of western New Guinea. He called the island "Ilhas dos Papuas," meaning "Island of the Fuzzy-Haired Men," and its people eventually came to be known as Papuans. In 1546 a Spanish navigator, de Retes, gave the island the name of Nueva Guinea (probably because it reminded him of Portuguese Guinea in Africa).

Things simmered along without great incident until 1828, when the Dutch annexed the western half of New Guinea. In 1884 the British claimed the southeastern portion of the island, calling it British New Guinea and later, Papua. In the same year, Germany annexed the northeast part of the island, naming it German New Guinea. Thus the island was divided into three parts.

After World War I, Australia became the administrator of New Guinea as well as Papua.

Change, swift and inevitable, has swept Papua New Guinea in the 20th century; the islanders have become increasingly aware of the world beyond. Nationhood, with independence, is an emerging reality—possibly in the mid-1970's.

Lifestyle

Papua New Guinea's population is close to 2¾ million persons. Of that number, more than 2 million are indigenous, the remainder largely Australian, European, and Chinese.

To characterize the indigenous population is difficult. They are loosely described as Papuans or Melanesians, with some elements of the Polynesians. But in fact there is such an extraordinary range of physical types and languages that no general terms are an adequate description of the people of Papua New Guinea.

A startling multiplicity of languages—over 700—means that the natives cannot necessarily talk to others outside their own tribe. Even within groups of similar racial characteristics, language is a barrier because of the many different dialects. This is the reason that pidgin English flourishes. Pidgin sounds foreign to the ear of an English-speaking traveler. But pidgin dictionaries and pidgin phrase books make the going somewhat easier in this polyglot language. English, however, is being taught in all Papua New Guinea schools and is therefore spoken by the majority of younger people.

As with language, there is much diversity in ways of living among the Papua New Guineans. No brief description can cover the subject.

Touring from the coast to the Highlands, the traveler will notice differences in living quarters: along the shores, natives live in houses set on stilts high above the ground or over the water. Up in the Highlands, the hut is tent-like, on the ground, with a conical thatch roof on a rounded structure.

The thatched *haus tambaran* (or spirit house) is common in the Sepik area of Papua New Guinea. Usually a tall structure, as much as 60 feet high, it has a distinctive peaked roof and an elaborately ornamented facade. The natives hold to many beliefs about spirits, and much of their lives are patterned around such beliefs or superstitions.

Often as not, the native women do the heavy work involved in the sustenance economy. They gouge the earth and plant their corn with pointed sticks, using these primitive implements to plow with as well. You often see the women carrying the

THINGS TO SEE AND DO in Papua New Guinea: shopping at Koki Market, Port Moresby (upper left); cooling off near Madang (middle left); watching natives come to Madang market (lower left); visiting botanical gardens (upper right) and downtown Lae (lower right).

heavy burden of produce to the market, while the men walk along relatively unencumbered, perhaps driving a pig or two in front of them.

One conspicuous characteristic among the peoples of the Highlands never fails to intrigue travelers: the Highlanders decorate themselves profusely for their sing-sings—more so, perhaps, than any other people in the world. Cosmetics and costumes, paint, feathers, and shells are applied.

SIGHTSEEING

Port Moresby area

This gateway city to Papua New Guinea is seen briefly by most visitors to the country. Scruffy and undistinctive, it gives little more than a hint of the wonders that lie in the hinterland. Port Moresby is an administrative rather than a tourist city, a little too westernized, a little too much like many Australian towns in its setting to be overwhelmingly interesting. Nonetheless, you'll appreciate the fine views from the hills and a harbor of some beauty.

With a bit of time in Port Moresby, you should visit the Port Moresby Museum, where you will come upon the first real inkling of the brilliant folkloric world that is in store for you beyond the city. Here are river canoes 60 feet long, magic flutes that measure 10 feet, great water drums (drums, open on one end, that are placed on the water and pounded) that were used to call upon the Great Spirit.

It won't take long for market fanciers to find the outdoor Koki Market—and every day is market day. Expect to see a kaleidoscope of people, produce, exotica of Papua New Guinea: big green eggs of the cassowary bird, parrot fish strung on a rack, yellow and orange cucumbers, and all manner of curious wares.

Among the many excellent shops are Trobriand Crafts (a good selection of carvings and artifacts from the Trobriand Islands), and Sepik Primitive Art (Sepik River region artifacts). At the latter shop, you'll see many fine examples of the valuable New Guinea hook artifact. Important in the Sepik culture, a decorated hook is suspended from the rafters of a hut; on it are hung foodstuffs, babies, and—until fairly recent times—human skulls.

Papua New Guinea's stamps are among the world's most delicately designed, and philatelists will relish a stop in the efficient Philatelic Bureau (the shop next to the Post Office).

Lae and Madang area

Usually featured in itineraries of the Highlands and the Sepik are the big, westernized towns of Lae and Madang. Lae is very modern and well laid out: supermarkets, offices, hotels, and clubs border its tree-lined streets. Lae's Botanical Gardens, covering 140 acres (30 of them untouched jungle), contain thousands of species. Next to the gardens is the impressive War Cemetery.

Madang, on the coastline of lagoons, has one of the most beautiful settings in Papua New Guinea —hibiscus and bougainvillea blossom along its tree-lined streets. Here you'll see the great landmark, the Coastwatchers Memorial. (Coastwatchers were men of many nationalities who spied for the Allies during World War II from strategic points along the coast.) The memorial, shaped like a bomb, is a beacon that guides ships from miles away into Madang Harbor. Other sights around the harbor include natives paddling rough-hewn canoes and many other war relics—a number of half-submerged barges and at least one airplane still embedded on the beach where it fell. Take a harbor cruise, while you're in Madang, or a district drive to see, among other things, the famous potters of Madang.

The Highlands

You have to travel upland to reach primitive Papua New Guinea, the region of masks and feathers, birds of paradise and bare breasted women, spirit houses, and other marks of lifestyles that are altogether different from those elsewhere in the South Pacific.

Mt. Hagen. Known all over the world for its Highlands Show (see page 126), Mt. Hagen, the town, is really more like an extended market. It has only three streets; but on market days its population swells to 10,000 or more, with natives coming in from the outlying districts.

Two great attractions in this area are the Baiyer River Bird Sanctuary (where birds of paradise can be seen in captivity) and the Wabag wig men. The men's wigs are sometimes more than a foot across and are made from hair clippings—their own, their women's, and that of their relatives living and dead. Some are mushroom shaped, others like the horns of a bull; still others are in the shape of a diamond. Often their wigs are covered with bark cloth, beaten lace-thin and worn like a hairnet to keep the coiffure intact. When it rains, they protect their precious wigs with the pandanus leaf umbrellas they all carry.

Other tours from Mt. Hagen run to Minj and the Wahgi Valley. Minj is a social center for farmers and plantation owners. A sing-sing or festival is usually underway somewhere around Minj—a great place to see natives in ceremonial dress. The costumes in this area outshine all others in the Highlands.

SING-SING IN THE HIGHLANDS

You'll hear a sing-sing here and a sing-sing there, every now and then up in the Highlands of Papua New Guinea; but the sing-sing that outshines all others in its own extravagant, spectacular way is the annual song and dance festival known as the Highlands Show. It's held annually—in Mt. Hagen at the end of August or the first of September in odd-numbered years; in Goroka in mid-May during even-numbered years.

The ingredients that make this two-day sing-sing a spectacular thing are highly unusual. Something like 80,000 tribesmen, from all over Papua New Guinea, participate. Some come on foot, traveling for weeks to get there; others come by plane from the outlying islands. Most of them bring the best of their crops, livestock, and handicrafts to display in exhibits. The judging of these starts off the show. Then come the singing and dancing, with as many as 40,000 natives, swaying to the sound of ancient chants and the beat of lizard-skin drums.

To describe their costumes as fantastic would be an understatement. A typical performer wears a huge headdress of brilliantly colored bird of paradise plumes. Tail feathers of the rare king of Saxony bird hang from his nose; pieces of possum fur dangle from his ears. His face and body are painted in brilliant yellow, blue and red, and around his waist he wears a band of snail shells and irridescent June beetles. Certain tribes have characteristic costumes. The Porgera wig men wear Napoleon-style hats of woven human hair. The basket men of Minj encase themselves from head to foot in cones of wicker cane. The mud men of Goroka don grotesque head masks of baked mud and smear white clay on their bodies.

It's all part of the sing-sing—and there's nothing like it in all the world.

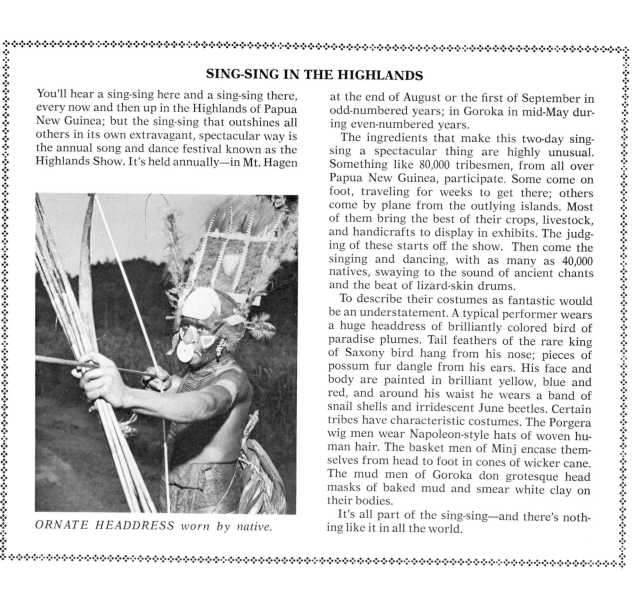

ORNATE HEADDRESS worn by native.

An interesting trip from Minj is to a Swiss Mission Station hidden in the mountains.

Goroka. The largest town in the Highlands, located at 5,000 feet in the Bismarck Range, Goroka is set among market gardens and coffee plantations. It has the climate of an exotic summer capital—warm days, cool nights.

On market days, thousands of natives come from the surrounding district, most of them wearing native dress. They bring in local vegetables, yams, sweet potatoes, pigs, and often small furred and feathered creatures from the bush.

The real attractions of Goroka, however, are outside the town. Foremost are the mud men of Asaro Valley. For a small fee, the Asaros will cover themselves with river mud and put on mud masks. They will even simulate an attack with bows and arrows, and the women will perform a sing-sing.

Tours from Goroka generally aim to give visitors a glimpse of various aspects of life in Highland villages, including visits to coffee plantations.

Kundiawa. In the heart of the Chimbu District, Kundiawa can be reached by a ragged road from Goroka or more comfortably by a 15-minute spectacularly scenic flight.

It's been less than 50 years since the first white men explored this very primitive and thickly populated region, where in the more remote parts warriors still travel with their weapons. Even today the inhabitants occasionally fight and kill with axes or arrows. Yet the Chimbus are hard working people and their patchwork gardens climb up the steep mountains to as high as 8,000 feet.

One tour to this area includes the opportunity to see Chimbu bush plays in a village about 15 miles from Kundiawa. These are spectacular performances of mime, dance, and song depicting scenes of everyday tribal life.

OMKALAI AIRSTRIP (above) is sliced into the mountains near Goroka. Strips of cloth, on which coffee beans will be spread out to dry, near Minj. A Highlands native holds up two pieces of shell money.

The Sepik

Winding its way for a thousand miles, the Sepik River runs through one of the most primeval parts of Papua New Guinea. Along this waterway live swamp dwellers, a people entirely different from the Highlanders. Their houses are on stilts; their usual means of transport is the dugout canoe. An artistic and intelligent people, they produce ceremonial wooden masks that are probably the best known symbols of the country.

One way to visit the Sepik is to take an air tour from Mt. Hagen north to Angoram, a government outpost with a population of 30 Europeans and 1,500 natives. Angoram is the old head-hunters' territory. Up until World War II, a native could not achieve the status of manhood until he had killed an enemy and brought back his head.

In Angoram there is an attractive *haus tambaran* (traditional home of the spirits, center of culture and worship, and treasure house of sacred drums, bamboo pipes, weapons, and masks). The main floor, reached by a wooden ladder, is 12 feet or more above ground, supported by carved poles depicting animals, birds, and men. This *haus tambaran* now houses the work of native craftsmen who have formed a cooperative. It holds a vast number of artifacts: bone-tipped spears, flint axes, wooden bowls, and masks.

From Angoram, organized trips proceed along the Sepik River in canopied, motorized canoes. These boat rides provide visitors with the opportunity to see the river scene and the native life supported by the river. Every so often you pass natives paddling dugouts, going to and from their tiny settlements of huts perched on stilts over the river.

Another way to see the Sepik is to fly to Wewak, north of Angoram, on the scheduled services and make this a base for touring. The town itself offers little for the tourist other than the setting. Its most famous landmark is Wom Point, where the Japanese 18th Army surrendered in World War II. But

POTTERY MAKERS *in the Sepik district sell their work in village stores. In Madang, the first-class Smugglers Inn has 30 rooms on a shore-side location.*

Wewak is the stepping-off point for a three-day houseboat cruise on the Sepik, one of the special experiences for tourists to this region.

By road the great trip from Wewak is to Maprik, if one can stand the 80 miles of bends on a well-surfaced but unpaved road. The road climbs from the lowlands, where people live in stilt houses, into the hills, where they live in tent-shaped huts.

You can also fly to Maprik, a busy little town where the native people take great pride in their spirit houses—and Maprik has the most famous of them all. Built like a pyramid, 100 feet high, it used to be off limits to visitors but is now open to them to watch the carving and painting of ceremonial masks.

New Britain Island

The largest island outside of Papua New Guinea, New Britain lies due east of Madang. Crescent shaped, it is 370 miles long and about 50 miles wide at its widest point. Its center of activities is Rabaul, the island's busiest port and principal airport. Rabaul's spectacular setting, along with its harbor, surrounding hills, and plantations, makes it a distinctive destination.

Special features of tours in Rabaul include a harbor cruise, a climb to the summit of Matupit Volcano, and trips to see remnants of World War

II, including the tunnels dug into the hills around Simpson Harbor by the Japanese.

Trobriand Islands

The largely isolated Trobriand Islands have great natural beauty and a carefree, sociable population. They resemble Polynesia more than Papua New Guinea. The airport building is a thatched roof structure; and sure enough, just as it happens in Polynesia, you're greeted by elated islanders, bringing with them their exquisite carvings.

The 22 islands in the Trobriand group are all coral islands—some of them only a few feet above the ocean. Largest in the group is Kiriwina Island, with its main village being Losuia.

Village tours feature a sing-sing, men and boys performing. A typical dance depicts a mother bird teaching the little ones to fly: performers wear large white hats made of parrot feathers and circles of shells around their necks and calves.

PRACTICAL INFORMATION

Entry regulations

To enter Papua New Guinea, you need a passport, visa, and Entry Permit Form, all of which may be obtained from the nearest Australian consulate or embassy. You will also need a smallpox vaccination certificate.

Where to stay

In Port Moresby, gateway city to Papua New Guinea, accommodations are available at the Davara Hotel on Ela Beach and at the Gateway Hotel near the airport. The Papua Hotel, in the heart of the city, is old but has a large number of modernized rooms. In a quieter hillside setting a short distance from the city, the Outrigger Motel is quite good. Other more modest accommodations can be found.

In Lae, the best known hotels are the Melanesian, one of the best in Papua New Guinea, located on a hill overlooking the bay, and the Huon Gulf Motel. Other accommodations include the Klinkii Lodge and Transair Lodge— all with very modest appointments.

In Madang, the most stylish hotel is the first class Smugglers Inn, located on the water a half-mile from the center of town. The Hotel Madang is old and typical of the South Seas hotel, and the Coastwatchers Motel, overlooking Astrolabe Bay and the Coastwatchers Memorial, is very comfortable. The CWA (for Christian Women's Association) Lodge is one of the best in the country. Farther out of town (about 40 miles from the airport) is the small Plantation Hotel.

In Wewak, the small Sepik Hotel is 15 minutes from the airfield; the Windjammer Hotel fronting the beach is five minutes from the airfield; and the delightful CWA Lodge has inexpensive rooms.

Angoram, a government station about 60 miles up the Sepik River, has one modernized hotel, the Angoram. In Ambunti, still farther up the Sepik, the Karawari Lodge is the outpost for tourist accommodations on this river. At Maprik, farther upcoast from Wewak, the Maprik Hotel offers overnight accommodations.

In Goroka, the best known accommodations are in the modern, functional Bird of Paradise Motel. The Goroka Hotel is old, and though some of its rooms have no private baths, others are new and modern. For travelers on a shoestring budget, the Minogere Hostel, formerly a boarding school, has clean and inexpensive rooms.

At Kundiawa, in the heart of the Chimbu District, the modern accommodations of the Chimbu Lodge are close to the airfield. The Kundiawa Hotel, mainly a drinking pub, also has rooms.

In Mt. Hagen, accommodations are available at the modern Hagen Park Motel, the Mount Hagen Airport Hotel, and the Mount Hagen Hotel (an old hotel with a new block of public rooms). Newest hotel is the Kimininga (13 rooms), on the outskirts of town. At Minj, on the road between Mount Hagen and Goroka, the Minj Hotel and the Shangri-La Hotel are the only accommodations. At Kainantu, between Goroka and Lae, the new Kainantu Hotel is three hours up the road from Lae. In Wabag, also in the Highlands, is the King of Saxony Hotel.

On Bougainville Island, the Hotel Bougainville is a small resort; a new motel, the Davara, is outside Kieta at Toniva Beach and the Arovo Island Resort, on an island by itself, is offshore from Kieta.

On New Britain Island, several hotels are located in Rabaul. Most modern and luxurious is the TraveLodge, between the main street and the harbor. The Kaivuna Motel is also first class, and the Cosmopolitan Hotel has some attractive new units. Other accommodations are in the old Hotel Ascot, now renovated; the small Kulau Lodge, across the harbor from town; and the Jolly Roger Mini-Motel, 10 miles out of Rabaul.

On the Trobriand Islands, the Trobriands Hotel at Losuia has rooms without bath in the main unit and a few poolside units with bath.

Climate

Because Papua New Guinea lies within the tropics, the climate is typically monsoonal. There are two principal seasons, designated according to the prevailing winds: the season of the northwest monsoon (from December to April)—hot, with sudden squalls, heavy rains, and high winds; the season of the southeast trade winds (from May to November)—drier, cooler, breezier.

PEAKED ROOFS, like so many coolie hats, add style to cottages of Shangri-La Hotel in Minj.

*A PICNIC STOP in the Highlands (upper left).
Among places to stay in Papua New Guinea are the
Hagen Park Motel (center left) in Mount Hagen
and the Papua Hotel in Port Moresby (lower left).
Tourists (below) shop for hand-woven blankets.*

Rainfall in coastal regions varies from 60 to 300 inches a year (in Lae, it averages 180 inches per year; in Port Moresby, 40 inches). The average temperature ranges from a minimum of around 75° to a maximum of 86°. Humidity varies from 73 to 90 per cent.

In the Highlands, the days are sunny and pleasantly warm, the nights refreshingly cool, and the humidity low. Throughout the year, the climate is similar to late spring in a temperate region.

Communications

The English language *Papua New Guinea Post Courier* is published five days a week in Port Moresby. A pidgin English newspaper, *Nu Gini Tok-Tok*, is published in Lae.

Radio stations in Port Moresby and Rabaul broadcast programs of news, features, and entertainment from 6 a.m. to midnight.

Overseas telephone communication facilities are available in Port Moresby, Lae, and Rabaul, and radio-telephone links these places with Sydney, Australia.

Currency and banking

Papua New Guinea uses Australian currency. Banks with offices in Port Moresby and branches in various towns include the Reserve Bank of Australia, the Commonwealth Bank, the Bank of New South Wales, the Australia and New Zealand Banking Group, the National Bank of Australasia, and the Papua New Guinea Development Bank.

Health and medical

Hospitals are established at Wewak, Mt. Hagen, Goroka, Madang, Lae, Rabaul, Port Moresby, and other towns in Papua New Guinea. There are dentists in Lae and Port Moresby.

Because malaria is prevalent, preventive medication is advisable. Other recommended precautions: typhoid, tetanus, and cholera inoculations.

How to get around

Moving around within the country is no problem. More than 150 airports and landing strips are scattered throughout Papua New Guinea. The practical way to see as much as you can is to fly. Roads in Papua New Guinea are practically non-existent. The Highlands Highway links Lae/Goroka/Mt. Hagen, but sections are often closed due to climatic conditions.

Taxis operate in the main centers—Port Moresby, Lae, and Madang. You'll also find car rental agencies in all main towns. You need an International Driving License to drive in Papua New Guinea.

Many tours by air, bus, boat, and private car are offered—up the Sepik River, into the Highlands, and out to the offshore islands. Consult your travel agent about these or make local inquiry at the agencies in Port Moresby, Lae, and Madang.

Calendar of events

January or February. Chinese New Year celebrations in Rabaul and Lae on the date determined by the lunar calendar.

January. On the weekend closest to New Year's Day, a sing-sing at the Lae Showgrounds.

Easter weekend. Annual yacht race from Port Moresby to Yule Island.

May. In even numbered years, the Highlands Show at Goroka (see page 126).

June, July, August. Yam festivals—a type of festival—on the Trobriand Islands; ceremonial exchanges of decorated yams, traditional feasts, and dancing in the villages.

July. Kavieng Show, New Ireland; an annual agricultural show that draws people from all over the island.

August. In the odd-numbered years, the two-day Highlands Show held at Mt. Hagen (see page 126).

August to November. Pig killing season in the Highlands; natives hold village feasts and festivals, especially in the Chimbu and Lufa areas to celebrate the occasion.

September. Kokopo Show, New Britain; a large agricultural show held at Kokopo, about 20 miles from Rabaul, attracting people from all over the island.

September. Rabaul Art Show; the biggest display and sale of art, amateur and professional, in the Territory.

Tipping

As on many of the islands of the South Pacific, tipping is not necessary and officials do not encourage the practice.

For information

Get in touch with the Papua New Guinea Tourist Board, Box 773, Port Moresby, Papua New Guinea.

A TOUR BUS in the Highlands makes a stop for photographers in the shade of a tree.

UNSPOILED CHARACTER of Micronesian islands is typified by clean sweep of sand at Laura Beach on Majuro (above), by Ponapeans at work in village of Net (at left), by peaceful charm of village of Umatac on Guam (where Magellan landed in 1521).

Guam and Micronesia...
a coral necklace

2,141 SPECKS OF LAND, TRACES OF ANCIENT CIVILIZATIONS, DEEP SCARS OF WORLD WAR II BATTLES

The islands of Micronesia stretch like a coral necklace across more than three million square miles of the western Pacific Ocean. Though bearing some of the deepest scars of World War II, they are among the most unspoiled and varied groups of islands in the Pacific. Most of them are unknown to outsiders; however, a few—like Guam, Saipan, Truk, Yap, Peleliu, Kwajalein, Ulithi, and Majuro—would stir the memories of many Pacific war veterans.

What is the secret of the islands' solitude and lack of development? Simply the fact that they were off-limits to the casual visitor for many years—and then, once restrictions began to be lifted, the would-be visitor faced an impossible lack of transportation and accommodation. But in 1968, Air Micronesia began flying into the area out of Honolulu, and travel development got underway.

Now there are frequent flights into the area, a smattering of hotels ranging from just adequate to excellent, a variety of boat services (so necessary in this watery expanse), minibuses and jeeps and taxis for local transport, as well as a well-developed assortment of packaged tours. Yet even with this development, islands still almost outnumber tourists.

You'll find that the Air Micronesia flight from Honolulu via Midway, Kwajalein, Majuro, Ponape, and Truk to Guam is one of the great air trips in the Pacific. The Boeing 727 crews are well-schooled in the lore of the area, and they combine this knowledge with enthusiasm and their personal experiences (exploring, scuba diving, fishing, etc.) to make the flight a giant aerial sightseeing experience. Part of the enjoyment of the flight is the side show at each airport along the way. Plane arrivals are well attended by locals of all ages whose dresses, *lavas lavas*, and *maramars* (circlets of fresh flowers worn on the head) provide vivid splashes of color. When lips part in a betel-nut-red

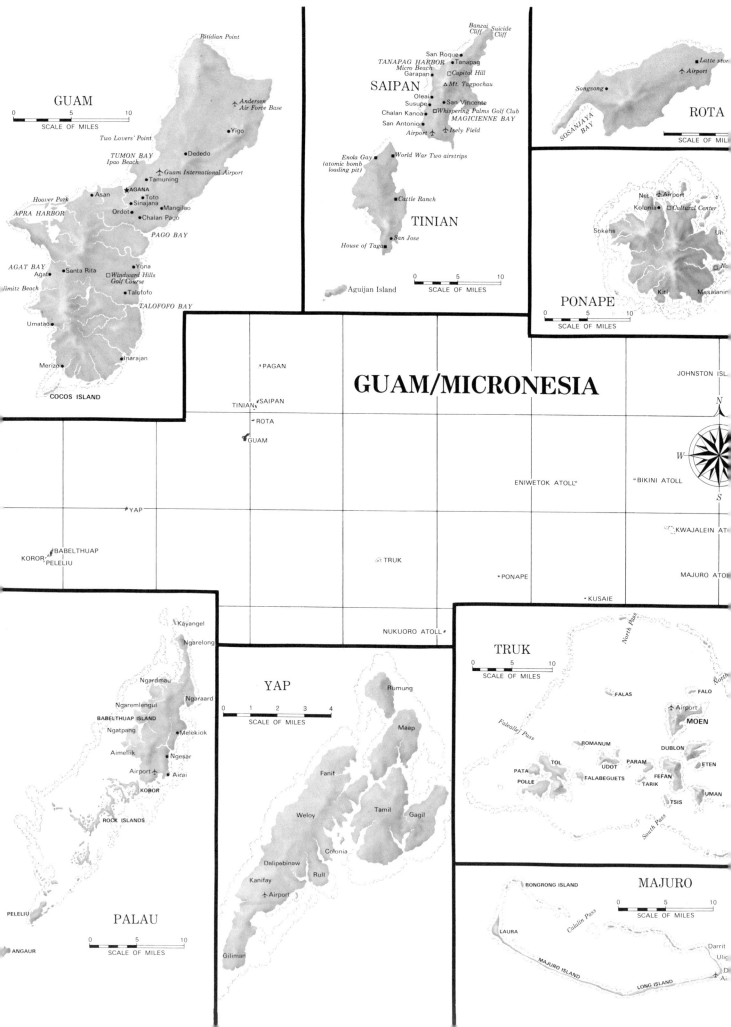

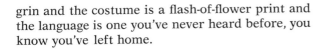

HISTORY OF ISLANDS shows itself in crumbling bridge on Guam (above), built by Spaniards in 1800; in Japanese fortifications (above right) on Saipan; in German bell tower, built on Ponape in late 1800's.

grin and the costume is a flash-of-flower print and the language is one you've never heard before, you know you've left home.

Geography

Micronesia's islands wind down through vast reaches of ocean for a distance of about 1,300 miles from north to south, about 2,300 miles from east to west. Included in the group are some 2,141 specks of land divided among three island groups: the Marshalls, Carolines, and Marianas.

Total land area is only about 900 square miles, of which Guam (the largest island in Micronesia) comprises 209 square miles. Guam, as the center for exploring the other islands, sits more than 3,700 miles west of Hawaii, about 1,300 miles south of Japan. Palau, in the far south of the Micronesian complex, is less than 600 miles east of Cebu in the southern Philippines.

Government

Politically, all the islands but Guam are part of the Trust Territory of the Pacific Islands, a United Nations trusteeship administered by the United States since 1947. Guam is a U.S. Territory and has been under U.S. rule since 1898.

History

First sighted by early explorers in the 16th century, Micronesia has survived successive waves of outsiders (Spanish, Germans, Japanese, and American). The Trust Territory islands were mandated to Japan in 1920 and reached their peak of development under the control of the Japanese. They planted sugar cane, rice, and pineapple; laid out attractive towns; built massive fortifications and aircraft facilities; constructed roads, railroads, docking facilities, water and electrical systems,

RECONSTRUCTED abai *on Koror in Palau group retains ancient architectural style, unique story board facade. (Below) copra production on Ponape—still a village occupation on many islands.*

and hospitals. In fact, the Japanese colonized the islands; the 100,000 Japanese used the Micronesian labor force of about 40,000 to develop the islands for the war effort and for food for Japanese home consumption. The bombed-out buildings and other facilities and the extensive roadway systems throughout the islands, almost all jungle covered now, are all that remain of that extensive development.

The imprint of Japan's more than 25 years in the area is still felt: Japanese remains as the *lingua franca* of the pre-war generation. English is being taught in the school system today and is the second language of the post-war youngsters.

Until the 1960's the islands remained in a state of post-war status quo. But then the United States began turning its interest and funds to developing the area for the Micronesians. In 1966 the Congress of Micronesia was convened. An elected body representing all the island groups, it has exercised more and more legislative authority over the islands, even though the Trust Territory is still the concern of the U.S. Department of the Interior. Under the Department, the Territory is governed by a High Commissioner appointed by the President.

Lifestyle

Micronesia is actually an umbrella term for a collection of people with some similarities but also with striking differences. One thing they all share is the usual life patterns of villagers on small tropical islands. The indigenous inhabitants originally came from Southeast Asia (probably Malaysia) as long ago as 1500 B.C.

Nine distinct languages and many more dialects are spoken in the territory. The Chamorros in the Marianas group and the Palauans speak a language that is similar to Malay; the language of Yap, Ulithi, Truk, Ponape, Kusaie, and the Marshall Islands is considered to be Micronesian; and the Kapingamarangian and Nukuoroan people in the Ponape district speak a Polynesian tongue.

Customs differ from island group to island group —with strong allegiances in each group to local folklore, ancestors, leaders, and their own social structure. Isolated islands have produced local adaptations and inventions of their own—even down to different ways of putting canoes together. Stone money is unique to Yap. The traces of an advanced civilization as evidenced by Nan Madol are unique to Ponape. Only Chamorros erected *latte* stones, and the bas-relief carvings of Palau are not duplicated elsewhere. Social organization may be matrilineal in one group, caste conscious in another, and chief-dominated in a third. Catholicism, introduced by the Spanish, is embraced by perhaps 50 per cent of the population.

Copra is the only cash crop in Micronesia's basically subsistence economy. The sugar cane fields and pineapple plantations on which the Micronesians worked for the Japanese were allowed to revert to jungle following the war. Attempts are now being made to diversify agriculture and to develop a fisheries industry. Overlaying the agricultural economy are government, tourism, and the military; these activities provide by far the largest source of money oriented jobs. Wages from the private sector have finally exceeded government payrolls.

You won't find much distinctive traditional architecture such as you find in the Samoas or Fiji —except on Yap. Old ways of building have been supplanted by tin, plank, plywood, and concrete. Towns on the district center islands are generally a straggle of buildings concentrated near the port area. Occasional devastating typhoons are a menace to all construction. On Moen in the Truk District, for instance, many families now dwell in typhoon relief houses, simple plywood rectangles supplied by the government after one of the last big blows.

With the exception of Yap, traditional dress has largely disappeared from the district center islands. Shirts, T-shirts, and trousers are male garb, and bright print dresses are common women's attire.

For all their sameness in terms of island orientation, economy, and ethnic background, the islands of Micronesia offer great contrasts for the visitor who makes the circuit and takes the time to explore. Here briefly are some of the features of each of the accessible main islands.

GUAM

Between Hawaii and the Philippines, the largest land mass (8 by 32 miles) is Guam, the hub of U. S. development in this part of the Pacific (even though the Trust Territory administrative headquarters are on Saipan). Although about one-third of the island's real estate is occupied by the military, there's still plenty of open space for its residents (112,000, including the military).

Guam is a hilly island, with savannah-like expanses punctuated by jungle-filled valleys and ravines and a ragged coast of bays, beaches, and rocky cliffs. Its reputation as a "crossroads of the north Pacific" (gained in the days when Spanish galleons plied the hemp routes between Acapulco and Manila) is once again valid: more than 80 planes arrive each week at Guam's International Air Terminal.

Located about mid-way on the west coast of the island, the main town of Agana resembles any other small town in America that is caught up in an era of scrambling growth. Small shops line Marine Drive, the main highway into town from the airport; substantial buildings are beginning to show

themselves; and hotel builders are busy making two-mile-long Ipao Beach on Tumon Bay look like a miniature Waikiki Beach.

Guam's indigenous residents are descendants of the Chamorros, a brown-skinned, black-haired people whose ancestry goes back to the Malays. Over the centuries, they have intermarried with Spanish, German, Filipino, Chinese, Japanese, and Americans. As a result, the Chamorro today is quite different from his tall, large-boned ancestor. In names, in their Hispanized-American culture, and in appearance, the modern Chamorros resemble—in the eyes of the casual traveler—the Filipinos.

Guam is currently the favorite honeymoon spot for the Japanese—a sort of Hawaii for them in terms of reasonable flight-time and air fare. They come there because Guam has a year-round warm climate, warm surf and miles of beaches, smog-free air, and lack of crowding, and because Guam's tourist facilities are set up for them. Menus, signs, tour folders, hotel instruction pamphlets—almost everything—is bi-lingual. And Japanese-owned hotels do a booming business (Japanese visitors enjoy their *saki* and *sashimi* away from home just as we enjoy our hamburgers and milkshakes).

For the traveler from the United States, Guam is an excellent stopover for sun and rest before or after a temple-touring trek through the Orient or Southeast Asia (a return home stop, incidentally, that offers a familiar language, a return to U. S. currency, water you can drink, hamburgers, ham and eggs, and other traditional American fare).

SPANISH CHURCH on Guam provides background for young carabao racers at annual Inarajan Carnival.

Guam is also the best base from which to explore the other islands of Micronesia.

Sightseeing

Agana. Though much of downtown Agana is new (the result of reconstruction following the war), you can still catch glimpses of some of the island's heritage. The town centers on the Plaza de Espana, a wide expanse of tree-shaded gardens and government buildings bordered by an arched coral wall. Latte Stone Park, across the street from the plaza, is a monument to an ancient civilization whose only traces are huge rough-hewn columns of coral rock similar to those in the park. More than 200 groups of these *latte* stones, which date back to 1500 B.C., may be found on the island, each site consisting of a double row of the stones that seem to have been used as foundation stones for housing.

Nearby is Fort Santa Agueda, built by the Spanish in 1671, stormed by Chamorros in early uprisings, and used by the Japanese for gun emplacements during World War II.

Round-the-island. Paved highways follow the coast around the southern tip of the island, loop north (but miss the northern tip of the island), and provide several cross-island drives. The best road trip is the loop around the south end of the island. It takes you by Apra Harbor where the cruise and navy ships anchor; Agat Bay, landing site for both Japanese and American invasion forces; Nimitz Beach, an excellent camping and picnicking spot; and an old bridge built by the Spanish in 1740.

At Umatac, a picturesque little village clustered on the shores of a magnificent cove, a monument testifies to Magellan's landing in 1521. An old Spanish sentry box still stands guard on a headland above the bay and the town. On the hillside overlooking Umatac, you can visit Fort Nuestra Señora de la Soledad, only the walls of which remain.

Near the south end of the island, Merizo boasts the oldest Spanish buildings in Guam (the monastery alongside the village church). Merizo is a water-sports base with boats to take you waterskiing, scuba diving, fishing, or sightseeing along the coast or out to nearby Cocos Island (good hiking, picnicking, and an isolated sunning spot). Glass-bottom boats operate out of Merizo for coral garden viewing.

Along the east coast on the loop back, you go through Inajaran, another old village with narrow streets, old buildings, and a lovely setting. The rock cliffs north of Inajaran are worth exploring: Gadao's Cave in the cliffs has some interesting petroglyphs. Farther north is Talofofo Bay. With no protective reef to break the ocean's surge, it is the best surfing spot on the island. And nearby Talofofo Village is the take-off point for a trail that leads upriver to beautiful Talofofo Falls.

North from Agana, the road takes you to Two Lovers' Point, combining a lovers' legend with one of the island's finest view points; by the remains of a number of Japanese fortifications; and around the skirts of the Strategic Air Command's huge Andersen Air Force Base.

Things to do

Natural features combine with man-made facilities to make almost any activity possible:

Shell collecting. Collectors have catalogued nearly 1,000 varieties of gastropods in the area. The best beaches along the west coast are at Tumon Bay, Gun Beach, Agana Bay, the lagoons between Agana and Asan Point, Hoover Park, Agat Bay, and the lagoon between Merizo and Cocos Island. On the east coast, Pago Bay is one of the few safe places.

Fishing. Game fish—including tuna, skipjack, mahi-mahi, marlin and sailfish—abound in the waters off Guam. A 1,153-pound world record Pacific blue marlin was caught off Ritidian Point in 1969. Charter boats are available in Agana and Merizo. Surf casting and reef fishing along the western coast and spear fishing along the more rugged east coast are excellent.

Hunting. The rugged northwest part of the island offers a variety of hunting opportunities for fruit bat, deer, wild pig, dove, quail, and rail. Details are available from the Department of Agriculture in Mangilao.

Hiking. You'll find a number of trails in the vicinity of most of the popular scenic and historic sites. If you want to try taking off into the boondocks, arrange for a guide through one of the tour companies.

Golf. Visitors are welcome at the 18-hole Windward Hills Golf and Country Club in the highlands inland from Talofofo Bay. A par 72 course, it has club house, snack bar, and swimming pool; carts and clubs may be rented.

Swimming. Strong currents make some of Guam's enticing looking beaches hazardous, but you'll find the following to be safe, diverse, and excellent: Ipao Beach in Tumon Bay; Nimitz Beach, south of Agat; and Besbes Beach, five miles east of Merizo.

Camping. Nimitz Beach Park near Agat and Santos Park in Piti have water, barbecue pits, and toilets.

Permits for camping must be obtained from the Department of Land Management, Government of Guam, Agana.

Cockfighting. Once a sport illegally held in the villages, cockfighting has now been legalized to operate in the Sport-O-Dome in Tamuning, a few miles north of Agana. Fights—held every Saturday, Sunday, and legal holiday—are wild, high-betting affairs.

Shopping

Guam's duty-free-port status makes it a bargain center for shoppers for products from all over the world: pearls, cameras, and electronic equipment from Japan; watches from Switzerland; handicraft, fabrics and tailored goods from Micronesia, the Philippines, and Hong Kong. Most of the shops cluster in a two-mile area along Agana Bay, and most are open every day, including Sundays.

Where to stay

U. S. and Japanese hotel interests have constructed six major hotels (most of them with more than 200 rooms) along Ipao Beach on Tumon Bay about 10

SPANISH RECTORY in Merizo (above right) built in 1856, is still in daily use by parish priest. Most of Guam's hotels, like Guam Tokyu Hotel (above), are located on Ipao Beach. Latte stones (right), ceremonial limestone columns erected by ancient Chamorros, are found in jungle groupings in many places on Guam, other Mariana Islands.

Guam and Micronesia 139

minutes from the airport. Since almost all of them have been built within the last two or three years, they are still sparkling new and boast all the amenities of modern resort hotels.

The beach-front hotels are the Guam Hilton, the Guam Tokyu, the Guam Continental, the Guam Dai-Ichi, the Fujita Guam Tumon Beach, and the Guam Okura. Another major hotel, the Cliff, sits on the hillside overlooking Agana. In addition a scattering of smaller hotels and motels lies in and around Agana, and several new ones are under construction or at the drawing board stage.

Dining and entertainment

You'll find a surprisingly wide choice of cuisine—Oriental, European, American, or "native"—at Guam's hotels and restaurants. The volume of Japanese tourists to the island has, of course, resulted in the establishment of a number of excellent Japanese restaurants: the Kurumaya teppan-style restaurant in the Dai-Ichi Hotel, the Genji steak house in Tamuning, the Fujiya in downtown Agana, and the dining rooms at the Guam Tokyu, Guam Okura, Fujita Tumon Beach, and Cliff hotels.

For Chinese fare, try the House of Chin Fee or Chin's Shangrila in Aniqua, the Panciteria Far East and the House of Wong in Tamuning, or the China House next to the Dai-Ichi Hotel. The Crow's Nest, a nautically-styled restaurant atop a hill about eight minutes from downtown Agana, is new and very stateside in size, decor, and menu. Casa de Flores, located in Agana Heights, is as elegant a Spanish restaurant as you'll find anywhere.

Familiar American dishes are served in attractive surroundings in the dining rooms and coffee shops at the Hilton, Continental, and Cliff hotels.

Ask your hotel if any of the villages plan a fiesta during your stay. Usually held in honor of the village's patron saint, they are all-day affairs and offer a great variety of local foods: spicy chicken, fish, rice, breadfruit, taro, and island fruits.

SAIPAN AND THE NORTHERN MARIANAS

The Marianas Islands stretch northward from Guam for about 400 miles. Largest in the group and the only ones with airstrips are Saipan, Rota, Tinian, and Pagan. Their inhabitants are similar in ancestry and appearance to the people of Guam.

Saipan, the largest of the northern Marianas, is 14½ miles long, about 5 miles wide, and has a population of nearly 11,000. As the headquarters island for the Trust Territory government, it is the second busiest island in Micronesia after Guam.

Shrub-covered, Saipan is bounded on the west by gentle beaches, on the east by a rugged rocky coast, and on the north by dramatic inland and coastal cliffs. Practically palmless as a result of wartime bombardments, much of Saipan is now covered in a mass of *tangan-tangan*, a nondescript shrub-tree with good soil-holding attributes.

Like Guam, Saipan was visited by Magellan in 1521. On his charts he labelled the area as *Islas de Ladrones*, the islands of thieves.

Sightseeing

Touring on Saipan has a special poignancy, for the basic things to see are the relics of war: tanks, landing craft, gun emplacements, ghost towns, the old Japanese Command Post, and memorials to war dead.

Garapan, once a major seaport for the Japanese with a population of about 15,000, is now overgrown by *tangan-tangan*, but you can see the ruins of the prewar Japanese hospital and the old Japanese jail where Amelia Earhart may have been imprisoned. A red engine, once used to haul rail cars from the cane fields, and the statue of the man who helped develop Saipan's pre-war sugar industry stand in Garapan's Sugar King Park.

Near the northern end of Saipan above Marpi Point, you can see the concrete-reinforced natural cave which was the last Japanese command post on the island to fall to American forces in one of the most bitterly fought amphibious battles of World War II. Here, too, you can see 800-foot-high Suicide Cliff, towering above the command post, and Banzai Cliff. Hundreds of Japanese, including entire families, plunged to their deaths from these cliffs rather than be taken prisoner in the 1944 battle for Saipan. Two starkly simple marble memorials, recently erected by the Japanese, now stand atop the cliffs. You'll find other traces of Japanese fortifications alongside almost any road or trail you choose to follow on the island.

In the center of the island, Capitol Hill is the complex where the Trust Territory government and the offices of the Congress of Micronesia are located. If you're interested in finding out more about how such a far-flung island territory is governed, you would be welcome to the Trust Territory offices. Nearby (reached by driving along a doubtful road or by hiking) is Mt. Tagpochau, at 1,545 feet the highest point on Saipan.

If your time schedule permits a few days on Saipan, there are many more things to do than to look at the relics of war. The rugged eastern shore is marked by cliffs, rocky shores, and secluded pocket beaches that are excellent for sunning, swimming, snorkeling, shelling, or spear-fishing. The reef-protected western coast offers long

SAIPAN'S EAST COAST, without sheltering reef, is buffeted by wind and ocean, has pocket beaches, tidal pools, blow holes. Sugar cane train (above right) was used during Japanese occupation of Saipan. Japanese jail on Saipan, possibly where Amelia Earhart was imprisoned before war.

stretches of superbly empty beach. You should also visit one or more of Saipan's eight villages, even though you'll find relatively new and typhoon-resistant houses instead of the thatch huts you might be expecting. You can also see some of the ancient *latte* stones on Saipan.

Little nightlife enlivens Saipan except what generates itself at the hotel cocktail lounges and dining rooms or at one of the dozen or so village bars. The Sunday cockfights are exciting. You can play golf at the island's 9-hole Whispering Palms Golf Club. Car rentals are available at the airport or through the hotels. Boats may be rented along Beach Road or through your hotel.

Rota, Tinian, and Pagan

From Saipan, you can arrange excursions to Rota, Tinian, and volcanic Pagan, islands with populations of about 1,700, 780, and 55 respectively. Mod-

est accommodations are available at the 16-room Blue Peninsula Hotel or the 12-room Rota Hotel on Rota and at the Fleming and Tinian hotels on Tinian.

Rota has a number of excellent beaches and is another place where you can see some of the ancient *latte* stones used by the early Chamorros. Tinian, with its crumbling airstrips, was the take-off place for the Enola Gay, the B-29 that dropped the atom bomb on Hiroshima in August, 1945. Pagan, the exposed top of a volcano that rises 30,000 feet from the ocean floor, is popular with skin divers who camp overnight so they can explore the coastline, relax on the island's black sand beach, or bathe in one of the hot springs or warm lagoons.

Where to stay

Saipan's Royal Taga Hotel, on the beach at Susupe, is an excellent small hotel with 70 air conditioned rooms with a very good dining room, its decor making attractive use of native artifacts. At Garapan near Micro Beach is the 38-room Hafa Adai Hotel, whose dining room offers pleasant *alfresco* dining by the water. Two new hotels—the 200-room Saipan Continental and the Saipan Inter-Continental Inn will be completed in 1974 (the Inter-Continental Inn will be a 200-room hotel) on a cove near Micro Beach; their rooms will offer a view out toward Tanapag Harbor. Two other small hotels, Abel's Apartments with 10 rooms and the Mariana with 10, complete the Saipan hotel picture.

MAJURO

Majuro is the District Center for the Marshall Islands, a collection of 29 low-lying atolls and 5 small coral islands that are meagerly scattered over about 500,000 square miles of the Pacific. Even though there are more than 1,000 islands circling these 29 atolls, their total land area is only 70 square miles.

Majuro itself is a meandering thread of reef and palm-studded islands surrounding a huge turquoise lagoon. Some consider it to be the gem of the Marshall Islands. Outside the reef, the ocean pounds in a ceaseless boil; inside, the waters of the lagoon lap gently on the purest white sand beaches; the lagoon itself sparkles like a lake. At their highest point, the islands that surround the lagoon are only a few feet above sea level.

At its widest point, Majuro's strip of land is only half a mile wide, but it stretches so far along the western edge of the lagoon that Majuro boasts the longest road in Micronesia: 35 miles from near the airport to the beautiful little mission village at Laura Point at the northern tip of the island. Though the atoll is inhabited by only about 2,000 persons, the area has six churches.

Sightseeing

Swimming, shelling, snorkeling, scuba diving, and fishing are among the prime attractions of Majuro. Small boats may be rented through the hotels, and a new 32-foot Grand Banks cruiser is available for deep-sea fishing charter. You'll find the airport swarming with taxis when you land, so there's no problem if you want to explore the full 35 miles of atoll roadway. Seaplanes and small trading vessels operate out of Majuro to the other islands in the Marshall group. Details can be obtained and arrangements made through the tour operators in Majuro.

On the way to or from Majuro, you stop at

AN ISLAND HOPPING ADVENTURE . . . ON FIELD TRIP VESSELS

A highly romanticized (but rugged and uncertain) way to travel in the Trust Territory is by field trip vessel. These are 100-foot vessels that sail from the district center islands to outer islands on voyages that may take from three days to a month or more. The varied missions of the service include loading copra, maintaining an informal census, delivering mail, giving medical aid, pulling teeth. Stops are short—sometimes a few hours, sometimes as much as a day. But each stop is an experience: islanders gather at the dock with songs, flowers, and food to welcome a crew they may not have seen for several months.

Departure dates are always uncertain, and you have to stand by in one of the District Centers in order to board a vessel. Priority space goes to those with official business, so there's no guarantee that you'll get on the first vessel into the District Center. Accommodations range from sleeping on deck (bring your own sleeping bag) to sharing an unadorned cabin. Cuisine—in this case, perhaps more appropriately called "chow" —is not exactly cruise fare, but food that you get ashore may compensate.

The cost of travel, however, is undoubtedly a bargain—about $4 per day—and the trip certainly qualifies as high adventure that can take you to some of the most remote, seldom-visited islands in the Pacific.

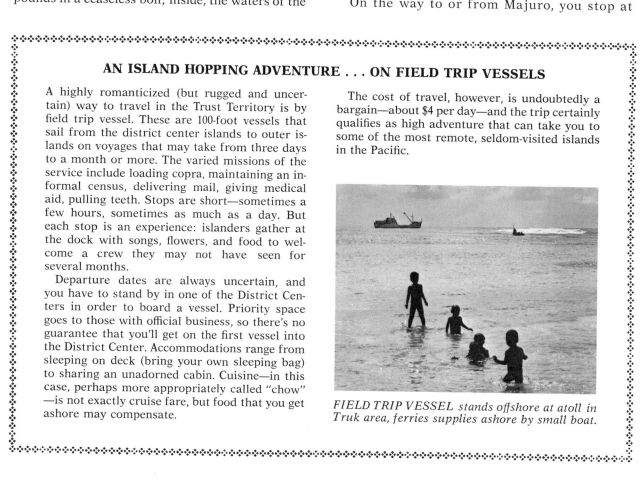

FIELD TRIP VESSEL stands offshore at atoll in Truk area, ferries supplies ashore by small boat.

Kwajalein, the largest atoll in the world. Its fringe of reef and land encloses an 840-square-mile lagoon. Kwajalein is a Strangeloveian oddity, a fine example of what a battle, followed by modern technology, radar domes, and wall-to-wall concrete can do to an atoll that looked much like Majuro before the war. The island is a major U.S. missile tracking facility, the lagoon a splash-down point for missiles launched from Vandenberg Air Force Base in California. You see Kwajalein only from the air as you circle to land. It is off-limits to visitors; no photos are allowed from plane or on the ground.

Where to stay

Two hotels provide accommodations in Majuro: the Eastern Gateway Hotel, within walking distance of the airport, has 18 breeze-cooled rooms and a bar and dining room open to the lagoon's beach front. The older Mieco Hotel, with 19 rooms, occupies the second story of a three-story concrete building in the center of Darrit-Uliga-Dalap, the principal community in the atoll. It also has a bar and dining room. A half dozen small restaurants and bars in the area serve Micronesian and American meals.

PONAPE

Two very high islands, Ponape and Kusaie, and eight atolls (all but one sparsely populated) make up the Ponape District. The only island in the district that has an airstrip and hotels is Ponape. And Ponape has a touch of Moorea or Tahiti about it, with its towering mountains rising almost from the sea. As Micronesian islands go, Ponape is big: 117 square miles, about one tenth of Micronesia's entire land mass.

Ponape Island is actually the slightly submerged remains of a classic shield-shaped volcano, now encircled by a coral reef that protects a narrow lagoon. Its rugged central mountains, seventeen of which are more than 1,600 feet in elevation, taper off to the sea, their flanks cut by long, deep valleys. The island receives more than 350 inches of rain annually, and the valleys provide the courses for turbulent rivers cascading in dramatic waterfalls that bejewel the island.

Dense, mossy rain forests, almost perpetually in the clouds, clothe the upper elevations. The lowlands are planted with breadfruit and coconut trees. Extensive swampy areas and coastline are tangled with mangrove; some of the swamps are planted with taro.

The more than 20,000 persons who live on the islands and atolls of the district are Micronesians, except for those who live on Nukuoro and Kapingamarangi, two atolls inhabited by Polynesians.

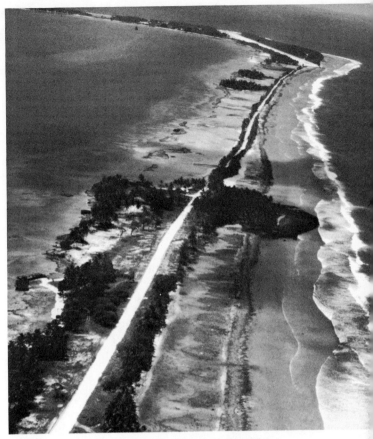

CORAL HIGHWAY on Majuro stretches 35 miles from the airport (far background) to Laura Village.

ON PONAPE, you paddle your own canoe to get to the newly developed cultural center at village of Net.

NAN MADOL . . . ARTIFICIAL ISLETS IN A WORLD OF ISLANDS

In terms of their age, engineering achievement, and sheer mystery, the ancient ruins of Nan Madol off the coast of Ponape certainly rank alongside the great stone heads of Easter Island, the ancient *maraes* of Tahiti, and the menehune's fish ponds of Hawaii.

Nan Madol is a series of artificial islets built on the tidal flats and reef that border Temwen Island, one of Ponape's small satellite islands. It is estimated that the islets were built sometime in the early 13th century by the Saudeleurs, a dynasty of Ponape rulers. Using slabs and log-shaped pieces of basalt, the Saudeleurs built royal houses, temples, tombs, ceremonial halls, an administrative center, an artificial lake, a playing field, special bathing rooms, feast houses, and pools to keep fish, turtles, and eels. The size of the complex is amazing: the islets stretch along the flats for more than a mile. Pahn Kadira, the islet thought to have been the Saudeleurs' administrative center, covers nearly 20 acres. Manmade channels wind through the complex, navigable by boat at high tide, traversable by foot at low tide.

For 16 generations the Saudeleurs reigned over Ponape. They were succeeded by the Nahnmwarki dynasty, a descendant of which lives today after 21 generations. Known as the Nahnmwarki of Madolenihmw, he resides on Temwen Island and is still considered by Ponapeans to be the reigning chief of this section of Ponape. Respect is still paid to him in behalf of visitors; either you ask his permission to visit Nan Madol or you remain silent and seated as your boat passes his residence.

The last residents of Nan Madol are thought to have left the islet city three or four hundred years ago. Descendants have lived on Temwen Island since then. The life and activities of the rulers of the two dynasties still live in the folklore of present day Ponapeans.

Although the erosion of time and the sea have taken a heavy toll on Nan Madol, the ruins are spellbinding, particularly if, stimulated by the guide's recounting of the legends surrounding the ruins, you spice your exploration with a little imagination.

You can reach Nan Madol by boat from Kolonia in about 40 minutes. The trip should be scheduled to take full advantage of high tide, and you should plan to spend at least half a day on the trip. Tide charts are available at the hotels and the docks. An excellent historical booklet on Nan Madol is available from the office of the District Tourist Commission in Kolonia, Ponape.

LOGS OF BASALT, piled log-cabin style, were used to build ancient royal village of Nan Madol. You explore area by boat, winding through man-made channels constructed in tidal flats off island of Ponape. Ruins stretch for more than a mile.

Some of the latter, transplanted from Kapingama-rangi, live at Porakiet village, just down the road from the Hotel Ponape on Ponape. Their houses and customs are quite distinct from those of the Micronesians. The village crafts store at Porakiet is one of the best you'll find in Micronesia.

Sightseeing

Ponape's only town, Kolonia (not to be confused with Colonia on Yap), is the government and commercial center for the district and for the more than 14,000 residents of Ponape Island. Across the lagoon that fronts the town can be seen the profile of Sokehs, a soaring promontory that has become known as the "Diamond Head" of Ponape.

In or near Kolonia you'll find a few fragmentary overlays of former governing powers: a moss-covered Spanish fort, an agricultural station started by the Germans, an encircling road and fortifications built by the Japanese.

On Ponape the visitor turns inland rather than to the sea. Since mangrove swamps are more common than white sand, beaches are negligible. The big rivers flowing out of the mountains, however, offer refreshing pools for freshwater swimming.

Prime target for most visitors to Ponape is Nan Madol (see opposite page). Plan to spend a half day there as a minimum, a full day to really explore.

You can easily spend at least another half day at Ponape's cultural center in the village of Net. Inspired by Oahu's Polynesian Cultural Center, a young Ponapean came home and organized his island's own center with the cooperation of people in his community. You get to the center by canoe (you do the paddling); there the Ponapeans demonstrate various crafts, show you some of their local dances, and pound and serve you some *sakau*, Ponape's tongue-numbing, potent brand of *kava*. The center is a simple collection of thatched sheds set in a shady spot beside the river.

Taxis, rental cars, motor scooters, and four-wheel drive vehicles available through the hotels allow you to explore the island's rather limited roadways. You can also make arrangements to go to the far side of the island to spend a day or two in villages that have been visited by very, very few tourists. The island has a surprisingly wide variety of flora and fauna: more than 40 kinds of birds, monitor lizards that grow to 6 feet in length, deer, and more than 30 varieties of fruits and vegetables, including giant yams that weigh more than a ton.

Where to stay

Ponape boasts one of the most charming little hotels in Micronesia—the Hotel Pohnpei, a cluster of nine thatch bungalows clinging to a forested hillside with vistas out toward the lagoon and Sokehs. The Pohnpei has hot water but no electricity and no restaurant; but each cabin is spotless and has a modern toilet and garden shower. Each evening at dusk you are given three lanterns: one for the bedroom, one for the bathroom, and one for the porch.

For meals the Pohnpei guest can stroll down the road to the Cliff Rainbow Motel, consisting of eight little cottages, a four-story unit, and a restaurant building overlooking the shore.

Downtown is Kaselehlia Inn, a two-story structure having 10 rooms upstairs and a restaurant/bar combination downstairs. Inland a few miles is The Ginger House, recently built along the lines of the Pohnpei by local residents. It has 12 thatch cottages with bath, a restaurant and bar, and a small swimming pool is to be constructed in 1973 by diverting one of Ponape's fresh-flowing rivers. Six other small hotels and inns complete the Ponape hotel picture.

TRUK

A collection of verdant islands, Truk is enclosed in an 822-square-mile lagoon that measures 40 miles from reef to reef at its widest. As you circle the lagoon for landing on the island of Moen, you see Truk's high islands rising out of the immense

OUTRIGGER CANOE off Namunuito Atoll in Truk area. Boat design differs from district to district.

lagoon and the more than 100 small coral islets that dot the lagoon or crop up along the 140-mile long barrier reef.

The lagoon and the world beneath its surface are Truk's key attractions. For the scuba diver, the lagoon holds a dual fascination: the natural world of coral and fish counterbalanced by the World War II wreckage of more than 60 ships of the Japanese Imperial Fleet. Most of the ships were sunk in a surprise bombing attack in February, 1944. For Truk was Japan's mightiest naval installation outside of the Japanese homeland. Here they had airfields, seaplane ramps, underground hangars, submarine pens, huge docking facilities, hospitals, extensive communications installations, gun emplacements, and all the buildings, roadways, and other facilities necessary to provide the base and support for Japan's combined fleet.

Sightseeing

Though you land on Moen Island and stay in a hotel on Moen, most of the attractions in the Truk area are elsewhere. To see them, you have to take to the water. Moen itself has only a few points of interest. The Truk Department Store, a huge warehouse quonset that is famous throughout Micronesia for the variety and quantity of its merchandise, is certainly worth a visit. You'll find everything from kerosene lanterns to washtubs to ladies' ready-to-wear to handicrafts arranged on 15-foot-high racks lining both sides of a series of narrow aisles. You should also go inside some of the island's charming churches, visit Xavier High School for boys, and climb to the top of the old Japanese lighthouse in Sapuk village for a view of the whole lagoon.

Scuba divers find Truk Lagoon and the many ships resting on the lagoon floor so fascinating that special diving tours are booked into Truk each year in growing numbers. The super-structure of hulls rest just below the surface of the water (some masts are above water), so the surface-bound traveler can share a little of this world by snorkeling or by cruising over the wrecks in a glass bottom boat. The water in the lagoon is so clear you can see 50 or 60 feet into its depths.

Because these extensive relics on the lagoon floor have been declared a monument, salvage and souvenir taking are prohibited by law. A permit to dive around the ships is available from the Truk Office of Tourism. A contribution is solicited which goes into a local fund for a decompression chamber, equipment that will eventually be added to until Truk has a complete diving service.

Another popular water excursion at Truk is a visit to Dublon Island, former Japanese naval command headquarters. Once a thriving community of more than 40,000 Japanese, the island has been swallowed up by the jungle, its roads and buildings almost lost under the vines and trees. A walking tour from the docks will take you along one of the overgrown roads past the ruins of a Japanese hospital, an elaborate geisha house, stronghold caves, and other installations that partially survived the bombardment.

Half-day and day trips can be taken to other islands to see additional interesting vestiges of the Japanese era, for visits to quiet villages, and for swimming and picnicking on isolated beaches. The other islands are more unspoiled. On them you can stroll through peaceful villages (where men still wear loin cloths and women wear grass skirts) and watch the processing of copra. Osakura, one of the smaller uninhabited islands, makes an ideal spot for a picnic and a day of swimming, snorkeling, sunning, and dozing.

Boats are available at Moen, including a 44-foot sailing trimaran that goes on tours of the lagoon or can be chartered.

Where to stay

Newest hotel on Moen is the Truk Continental, a low-profile cluster of buildings on a palm-shaded point that is edged by one of the best beaches on the island. Downtown, the 17-room Maramar is a low, rustic building with a good island atmosphere, tasty food, and an excellent craft shop. Christopher Inn, also downtown, has 31 clean but plain rooms on the second floor above a store and coffee shop. Several other small, rather rough-and-ready establishments complete the hotel picture.

YAP

The District Center for a group of 18 islands and atolls, Yap is probably the least developed in terms or tourism of any of Micronesia's districts. It also seems to be the least interested in such development. Traditional culture is deeply ingrained in the Yapese way of life; customs, architecture, and dress remain as they have for centuries. The wearing of the *thu* (loin cloth) by the men is still commonplace, a fact you become aware of quickly when the airline's ground crew meets the airplane. In the villages, women can still be seen in the voluminous Yapese grass skirts.

To some extent, Yap resembles New Caledonia—red earth, a coastal fringe of mangrove swamps, beaches, and palm groves, and interior stretches of dry uplands clothed in grass, ferns, and scrub. The island called Yap is actually four islands separated by streamlike stretches of sea. The "urban center" is Colonia with the island's one hotel, the Rai View.

Sightseeing

On Yap the general sightseeing pattern is to visit those villages where you can see examples of Yap's famous doughnut-shaped stone money and some of the traditional *failus* (men's houses). Yap's road system extends for only 17 miles; but the roads are good, and taxis or rental cars can be obtained through the hotel or at the airport. Another, perhaps better, way to get around is by boat. This opens up more sightseeing possibilities, including a visit to O'Keefe's Island, once the home of an Irish-American adventurer who made his fortune on Yap and lived there for more than 30 years.

A number of well-preserved *failus* can be seen in various parts of the main island. Centuries old in design, the *failus* sit on stone foundations, the floor three or four feet off the ground. Open sided to allow in the cooling trade winds, the *failus* have steep, thatched roofs towering forty or fifty feet high. Symbolic decorations mark the thatch above the entrance.

Northernmost in the cluster of Yap's four islands is the island that claims to have the largest piece of stone money: 12 feet across. Balabat village, on the south edge of Colonia, has Yap's largest stone money bank (two *failus* are in the same area). The quiet village of Dalipebinaw on the west coast of the main island claims to have some of the oldest and most valuable stone money.

Other villages worth visiting are Gachapar and Wanyan, to the east of Yap's main island. These are the traditional seats of power, the highest places in Yap's caste system. The villages of Gagil, seven miles north of town, and Giliman, nine miles south, are located on beautiful beaches and are two of the loveliest of Yap's traditional villages.

Yap's airport itself is somewhat of a sightseeing experience: more than a dozen torn and rusted Japanese Zero fighter planes lie along its edge and in the bush nearby, caught on the ground in a surprise raid more than 25 years ago.

No self-respecting visitor should leave Yap without buying a packet of betel nut, the mildly narcotic nut wrapped with dry lime in a hot pepper leaf and chewed by young and old alike on Yap.

Where to stay

Yap's only hotel, the Rai View, perches its ten rooms on a hillside. Rooms—spartan and clean—all share the bath and are located in the second story of the building over the lobby-dining room and the kitchen. Water is rationed out during dry periods of the year. Food is plain and served family style, though you can also order local fare (in advance) which includes fish, pig, turtle, taro, and tapioca served in a palm-frond basket.

MEN'S MEETING HOUSE under repair on Yap gives you a skeleton-view of traditional architecture.

STONE MONEY, here being transported by truck, is still seen in many of the villages on island of Yap.

DESERTED BEACHES on outer fringes of
Rock Islands in Palau District (left) offer
Robinson Crusoe-like chance to explore. Wood
carvers on Koror still practice ancient art
of carving story-boards.

Across the road from the Rai View is a handi-crafts shop, and up the hill is the simple Yap museum, housing artifacts in a *failu* and presided over by an articulate old Yapese gentleman. Next to the museum is an elementary school where the uniform of the day for young boys is a bright red or royal blue *thu*.

Down the hill from the hotel is Yap's main water-ing hole: O'Keefe's, a membership club where off-island visitors seem to be welcome. You'll find beer and mixed drinks there—none at the hotel.

PALAU

In the Palau District, you'll see a fascinating collec-tion of impenetrable and black-green jungle-clad heights, coastal mangrove swamps, and an almost endless number of clear, placid channels that thread their way between more than 200 small greenery-smothered islands, Palau's famous Rock Islands (see page 149).

Flying into the Palau District, you land on the big island of Babelthuap and travel by bus to neigh-boring Koror Island, traversing the narrow water-way between them by a small cable ferry.

Babelthuap, 27 miles long, is the largest island in the Trust Territory (though smaller than Guam). Despite its intriguing appearance, most visitors to the Palau District bypass it in the interest of spend-ing their time exploring the Rock Islands. In many respects this is unfortunate. Babelthuap has attrac-tions of its own that any self-respecting island col-lector would certainly want to see: the Japanese communications center, so massive in its construc-tion that American bombing never did destroy it; fascinating caves, some part of island legends, others used as hangars for Japanese seaplanes; villages that have preserved Palauan culture in an almost unchanged state; jungle waterfalls that may be among the most beautiful in all of the tropical Pacific; the stone pillars that mark the ruins of what may have been a giant *abai* (tradi-tional men's meeting house) large enough to shelter more than a thousand persons; and other vestiges of ancient man that remain a riddle to today's stu-dents of the Pacific Islands. Most of Babelthuap's attractions, however, have to be reached by boat; what remains of the old Japanese road system is negligible.

Koror is the busiest and most progressive look-ing of the Territory's District Centers; it has sub-stantial stores, handicraft shops, nightclubs, boat docks, and busy fisheries. Sprawling over flats and up and down hills, it is nearly submerged in lush greenery.

The Palau District is becoming famous for its Rock Islands, which provide enough variety of scenery, wildlife, and activity to keep you busy for several days (see page 149). Other musts on Koror include the museum, founded in 1955, and its *abai*. The museum is housed in the former Japanese communications center that sits in a garden-like setting of lawns and an unpretentious arboretum. Its collection includes artifacts from a number of the Micronesian islands, relics of the war, as well as some fascinating photographs of the area as it looked at the height of its development under the Japanese.

Similar to the *failus* of Yap is the *abai* on the grounds, except that the Palauans decorate the thatch above the entrance with their intricately carved and decorated storyboards. These boards are long wood planks that illustrate scenes from local legends. The carving of the storyboards is not a lost skill. Many artisans still make the boards, including some of the inmates of the town jail. You can even visit the jail and see the men at work. Storyboards may be purchased from the men in jail or at the town handicraft center.

Found also on the museum grounds (in pools behind a wired-off area) are a number of the saltwater crocodiles that inhabit the mangrove swamps along the coasts of Koror and Babelthuap. Since they're night feeders and pretty well stay in the swamps, they're of little concern to the area's skin divers.

For the active traveler, the Palau District offers boundless opportunities for water sports—swimming, water-skiing, snorkeling, and scuba diving. Boats, tanks, and air are available for divers. As a visit to the fish market at the docks in the morning will verify, fishing is excellent.

Most of the species of shell fauna of the Indo-Pacific region can be found in the Palau District. So prolific are these waters that most of the shells in the famous Micronesian collection at the Philadelphia Academy of Sciences were collected around Palau. The water is crystal clear; even in December and January it is warm enough for long sessions of snorkeling.

PALAU'S ROCK ISLANDS ... THE LOCALS CALL THEM CHALBACHEB

When the airplane circles for its landing at Babelthuap in the Palau District, look south. Almost as far as the eye can see, the waters are dotted with huge pincushions of green: Palau's Rock Islands. They lie in clusters, 200 of them, creating a labyrinth of channels and protected bays.

The islands are rounded knobs of limestone, smothered in trees, shrubs, and vines that grow in an impenetrable mass right to the waterline. And the waterline is unique, for almost every island has been undercut by centuries of tidal action, a phenomenon that lends itself to the common description of the islands as toadstools or knob-like. The Palauan name for them, Chalbacheb, means "small islands made of rock."

Because of the dense growth, the steep rise of rock out of the water, and the sharp undercut that makes landings impossible, only a few of these islands are inhabited. Some have caves; some have been cut in half; some have been cut through leaving huge rock arches.

These are the unique attraction of the Palau District. And they're easy to explore. Boats are available in Koror to take you zooming through the channels, stopping to explore a grotto, to snorkel over a downed Japanese zero fighter, to dive for clams, to watch the birds soar, to study the jungle that smothers the islands, to watch a huge sea turtle swim along just below the surface. It's so remote, so untouched that you should insist on your boatmen giving you periods to drift in silence.

Beaches are in short supply; but on the outer limits of the Rock Islands stretch several islands with long stretches of white coral sand: just the place to pull ashore, go swimming, snorkeling, beach-combing, picnicking. The water is warm and crystalline clear; the life below the surface an incredible show of coral and colorful fish.

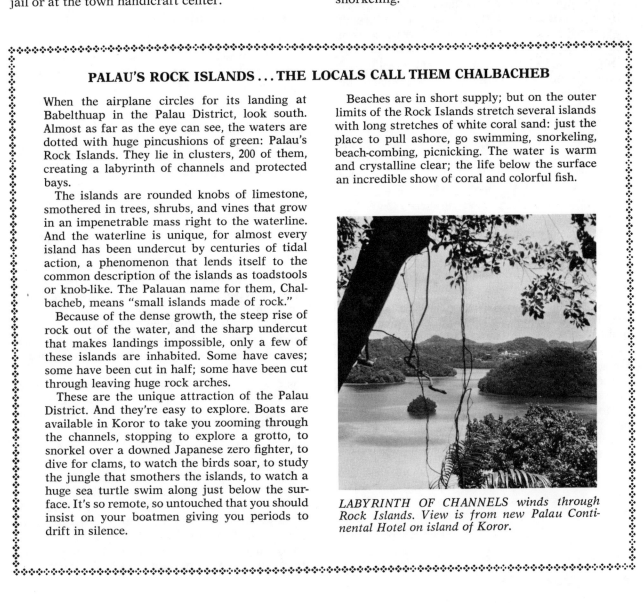

LABYRINTH OF CHANNELS winds through Rock Islands. View is from new Palau Continental Hotel on island of Koror.

Where to stay

Four hotels are available on Koror, among them the new 56-room Palau Continental, which perches on a hillside overlooking a sheltered bay dotted with some of the district's Rock Islands. Rooms are in a group of two-story blocks staggered down the hillside so that every room is assured of a view of the bay and the verdant islands. A small swimming pool, cocktail lounge, picture-window dining room, and gift shop are among its comforts. The other Koror hotels are older and more back-water islandish in their atmosphere: the Blue Lagoon, Paradise, and Royal Palauan, all having 20 rooms or fewer.

On the hillside near the Palau Continental are the remains of a pre-war Shinto shrine. Stone lanterns and stone slabs with Japanese characters etched into them mark the way to the shrine. A broad stone stairway edged with low rock wall, until recently completely overgrown, has now been cleared so you can ascend the hill to the shrine site. (Don't be surprised if you find Japanese sailors there from one of the tuna clippers that works out of Koror.)

Koror's night-time scene is about the liveliest in the Territory. Bright lights, drinks, music, and dancing are to be found at such spots as the Cave Inn (built in a limestone cave), the Factory, Boom Boom Room, and Peleliu Club.

On Babelthuap, a village meeting house, about 20 miles from Koror, has been converted into the five-room Melekiok Village Inn. Village families take turns cooking the food for each meal.

PRACTICAL INFORMATION

How to get there

To get to Micronesia, you can fly directly to Guam on Pan American or TWA transpacific flights and use that main island as a base from which to explore nearby Saipan, Tinian and Rota to the north, Yap and Palau to the southwest, and Truk, Ponape, Kwajalein and Majuro to the south and east.

Another way to get into the area is to take Air Micronesia's thrice weekly Boeing 727 service out of Honolulu and island hop your way to Guam (see page 133). Coming from the Orient, you can also fly directly from Tokyo to Guam on either Pan American or Japan Air Lines. Or from Hong Kong or Okinawa on TWA. Or you can even reach the area from the lands to the south: out of Fiji on Air Pacific or out of Australia on Air Nauru. Both flights take you to the island nation of Nauru where you can connect with an Air Micronesia or Air Nauru flight to Majuro.

Several steamship lines make regular or occasional calls at Guam: American President Lines from the U.S. West Coast; and Micronesia's own shipping company, Transpacific Lines, Inc. The latter offers a passenger-carrying freighter service out of San Francisco and Honolulu to the District Center islands.

Entry regulations

United States citizens and permanent residents of the U. S. do not need a passport or visa to enter Guam or the Trust Territory. However, some other proof of identity may be necessary. A valid international certificate of vaccination for smallpox is required. And if you are coming from an area infected with cholera or yellow fever, you should have those shots. Typhoid, paratyphoid, and tetanus shots are strongly recommended, along with gamma globulin (for hepatitis).

Customs regulations

No restrictions are placed on what you may bring into Micronesia. Returning home to the U. S. mainland, you are entitled to receive a customs exemption of $200 (an extra $100), provided that not more than $100 of this exemption is applied to merchandise purchased elsewhere than Guam. You may also take home four more fifths of liquor from Guam than if you returned directly from a foreign country. The duty free shop at the Guam airport is well supplied with this merchandise.

Climate

Micronesia's Islands share a common climate: tropical and hot, with high humidity. Rainfall varies from Ponape's 350 inches per year to a scant 20 inches on some of the Marshallese atolls. Temperatures rarely drop below 70 or go above 90 degrees, but humidity can make it seem higher. The best months are from January through June. Trade winds decrease and rains start in July, becoming monsoonlike in September, October, and November. Typhoons are possible almost anytime, but those of consequence usually come in November.

Health and medical

Micronesia is one of the healthiest climes in the world; happily, it has none of the diseases and maladies often found in the tropics. As a rule, though, it is wise wherever you go in the Trust Territory to be sure of the source of water you are drinking. Water in Guam and all the District Centers of the Territory except Majuro is potable, though it may be brackish in some places. Water in a stream may or may not be potable. In outlying areas, you would be wise to substitute coconut water for the local water supply.

You'll find hospitals in Guam and the District Centers of the Trust Territory. Where there are no hospitals, dispensaries can take care of first aid and other minor problems.

For information

For information on the islands of the Trust Territory, write Chief of Tourism, Trust Territory of the Pacific Islands, Saipan, Mariana Islands 96950. For information on Guam, write the Guam Visitors Bureau, Box 352, Agana, Guam 96910. For specifics on each of the island groups in Micronesia, write to the District Tourist Commissions as follows: Saipan, Mariana Islands 96960; Majuro, Marshall Islands 96960; Koror, Palau 96940; Kolonia, Ponape 96941; Moen, Truk 96942; Colonia, Yap 96943. Other good sources are: Micronesia Tours, Box 2050, Tamuning, Guam 96910 (this company offers ground arrangements on all the islands); Air Micronesia, Saipan, Mariana Islands 96950; any office of Continental Airlines (Air Micronesia's parent company).

PALM-LINED BEACH on Truk Lagoon (above right) is site of new resort hotel, Truk Continental. Auto ferry (above) links islands of Koror and Babelthuap in Palau District. Truk Department Store on Moen is part of corrugated metal complex of warehouses, stores, and public buildings.

CALENDAR OF EVENTS

Residents of Guam and Micronesia observe all United States national holidays, but they also celebrate a number of local events each year:

IN MICRONESIA:

March 1. Yap Day. Ceremonies honoring the tradition and history of Yap.

May 1. Law Day. Observed throughout the Territory with public gatherings and speeches stressing citizen relationship to law. Ceremonies and sports.

July 4. Saipan Liberation Day. Commemorates release of Saipanese from wartime civilian camps. Several days of festivities including parades, floats, sports, dancing, and queen coronation.

July 12. Palau Fair. Koror, Palau. Villagers prepare for months ahead to display and sell their story boards and other fine carvings, shell and woven handicrafts for which Palau is famous. Sports events, game booths, Palauan dances.

July 12. Micronesia Day. Observed throughout the Territory; commemorates opening of the Congress of Micronesia.

August 23. Legislative Day. Ceremonies and sports events at Moen, Truk.

October 24. United Nations Day. Celebrated throughout the Territory. Parades, floats, sports events.

ON GUAM

Almost every month one or more of the villages on Guam will hold a religious festival honoring their patron saint. Everyone is welcome to go to the homes in the villages to participate in a buffet with all kinds of Guamanian foods, visit and meet friends, hear the language spoken, and have a wonderful time among the people. In the village church, a solemn religious procession is held on Saturday and a mass in honor of the patron saint on Sunday. Ask the Guam Visitor's Bureau when you arrive if any religious festivals are scheduled during your stay. Other major celebrations on Guam:

January 1. New Year's Day. Open house at Government House, traditional prewar pranks at Umatac after Midnight Mass.

February. Inarajan Carnival. Featuring street dances; horse, carabao, and bicycle races; float parade; tuba drinking; coconut husking contest. Coronation of queen, fun in the old tradition.

February. Mardi Gras Ball. Featuring costumed participants, excellent food, superior entertainment in the last fling before Lent. Sponsored by the Guam Women's Club.

March. Discovery Day at Umatac. Commemorates Magellan's discovery of Guam in 1521. Pleasure boat flotilla and fiesta atmosphere.

June. Navy Relief Community Fair. Featuring carnival atmosphere, concessions, fishing derby, entertainment, fireworks.

June. Merizo Water Festival. Featuring skindiving, water skiing, boat races, games, dances, carnival.

July. Liberation Day festivities. Includes colorful parade with floats from different villages and civic organizations, coronation of queen by Governor, ball, exhibitions, carnival, recreation activity, fireworks, boat and fishing derbies.

November. Chamorro Night. A gala evening in tropical atmosphere with traditional Guam food, dancing, and native Guam entertainment, at the Recreation Center in Agana.

December. Procession of Our Lady of the Immaculate Conception. Beautiful procession, where image of Our Lady is carried through the streets to Cathedral. Women dressed in best, many wearing traditional Spanish *mantilla*. Older women wear *mestiza* dress.

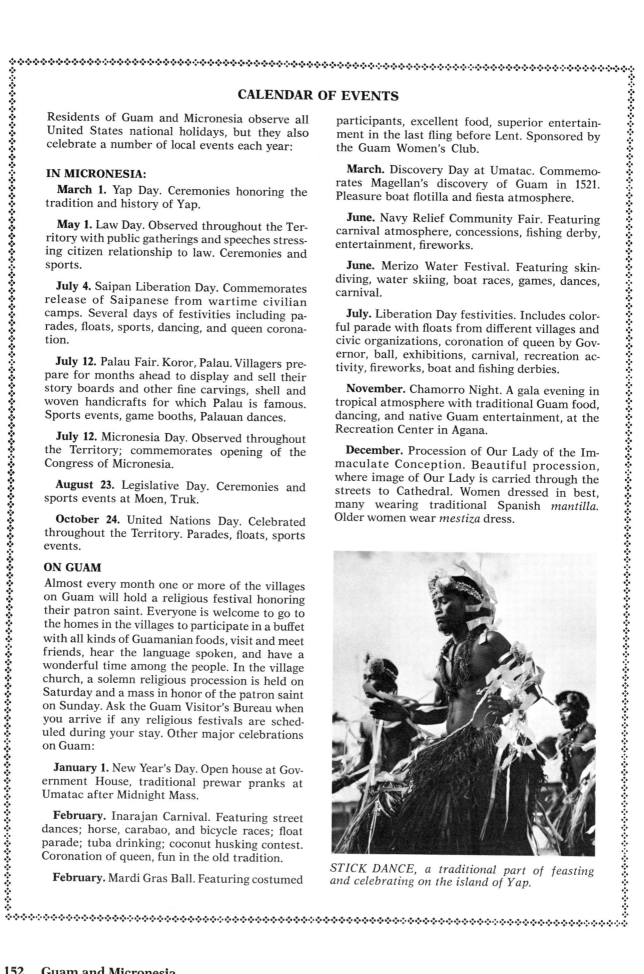

STICK DANCE, a traditional part of feasting and celebrating on the island of Yap.

Newcomers...islands you can help to discover

PREVIEWS OF THE COOKS, EASTER, GILBERT AND ELLICE, LORD HOWE, NAURU, AND NORFOLK ISLANDS

LORD HOWE ISLAND has dramatic heights, almost deserted beaches that are protected by the most southerly coral reef in the world.

As the inveterate island collector knows, a "new" island appears on the travel horizon almost every year—"new" in the sense that the island emerges, complete with hotels, as a reachable tourist destination. And each year a few island collectors go out of their way, by plane or cruise ship, to reach these new destinations "ahead of the tourists."

Among the recent newcomers are the Cooks, Easter, Gilbert and Ellice, Lord Howe, Nauru, and Norfolk islands. Some day these island groups will have become familiar household names in the South Pacific lexicon. At the present time, although they are served by scheduled air or sea services, frequency of service is generally too limited to accommodate many tourists' timetables. And although they have accommodations comfortable enough to be described as adequate, there are as yet no resort-style hotels able to take care of tourists in any great volume.

Most of these new islands are some distance from the well-traveled routes, but to discover one or more of them can become the highlight of a trip to the South Pacific. Here are brief glimpses at some of these newcomers—a sort of preview of coming attractions:

The Cook Islands

A former New Zealand dependency, the Cook Islands are comprised of 15 islands—some atolls, some high islands—scattered over approximately 850,000 square miles of ocean. Located about 1,500 miles east of Fiji, the Cooks have a population close

RAROTONGA HARBOR in Cook Islands (left),
as townsfolk await arrival of cruise-ship passengers.
Stone statues on Easter Island (lower left) are
principal attraction on this remote bit of Polynesia.
Thatch hut (below) on Tarawa; low profile of island
is typical of Gilberts. Choir girls (below right) in
Sunday best for performance at special event in
Rarotonga in Cook Islands.

to 20,000, of which more than 19,000 are Polynesian (classified as Maori in the Cooks.)

The island of Rarotonga, port of entry and administrative center for the Cook Group, has an airstrip presently being upgraded to take big jets in 1973. Currently Air New Zealand schedules flights into Rarotonga (and out via Aitutake) from Auckland, via Nadi, Fiji. Most tourists who reach Rarotonga at present come in on the occasional cruise ships that drop anchor offshore for the day.

Blessed with a glorious climate, Rarotonga grows pineapples and oranges on plantations almost in the shadow of its craggy volcanic peaks and not much more than a stone's throw beyond its white beaches and blue lagoons.

The few tourists who do arrive in Rarotonga find an unspoiled island where natives give them a memorably warm welcome—a hula band performing on home-made instruments, a choir of powerful voices singing hymns learned from the missionaries, and dancing by some of the best performers in the South Pacific.

Although there are no tourist-type hotels in the Cooks, the Otera Rarotonga, on the island of Rarotonga, affords accommodations in a kind of boarding house (often filled with public service personnel and airport construction workers).

For more information, get in touch with the Cook Islands Tourist Authority, P.O. Box 14, Rarotonga, Cook Islands.

Easter Island

One of the more isolated islands of Polynesia, Easter Island, a dependency of Chile, is 2,300 miles from Santiago, Chile, and 2,500 miles from Papeete, Tahiti.

Easter Island—or Rapa Nui, as it is called in Polynesian—is about 64 square miles in area and has a population of approximately 1,400 Polynesians. Sheep raising is their main occupation.

An almost treeless island, Easter is a vast storehouse of archeological treasures—more than 1,000 huge monoliths called *Moai*, stone statues weighing as much as 90 tons, towering as high as 25 feet, the work of an ancient civilization dating back to approximately A.D. 857. Here, too, are great stone quarries, petroglyphs, towers, and roads, built for reasons still not clearly understood, by a people of extraordinary achievement.

The Chilean airline, LAN-Chile, flies to Easter Island from Santiago and from Papeete. Cruise ships occasionally include the island among their ports of call.

Hosteria Honsa, the island's one hotel, has 60 rooms with private baths, an air conditioned restaurant, and a swimming pool.

The Gilbert and Ellice Islands

A British Crown Colony, the Gilbert and Ellice Islands are comprised of 37 widely scattered islands and atolls: the Gilbert, Ellice, and Phoenix Groups, as well as the islands of Christmas, Fanning, Ocean, and Washington. Altogether they cover a land area of 376 square miles scattered over two million square miles of seas. The population of almost 54,000 is made up of Micronesians (the Gilbert Islanders) and Polynesians (the Ellice Islanders). Capital of the Colony is Bairiki, on Tarawa, 1,365 miles north of Suva, Fiji.

Most of the low atolls of the Colony afford a lean existence at best: bits of coral rock, they are covered with about eight feet of hard sand, and topping it, a very scanty supply of soil—just enough to grow taro, coconut, and pandanus.

The islands' meager economy depends to a large extent on the phosphate deposits of Ocean Island. By the late 1970s, it is anticipated that these will be exhausted—a prospect that has impelled the Colony to consider the possibilities of attracting tourists to bolster the soon-to-be-sagging economy. These islands are presently in the category of out-of-the-way places; and for some travelers they provide the magnetic attraction of seeing islands with a mix of Polynesia and Micronesia before large numbers of tourists arrive.

You can reach the Gilbert and Ellice Islands from Suva or Nadi, Fiji, by way of Air Pacific's flights that go to Tarawa in the Gilberts and Funafuti in the Ellice Group. Accommodations consist of the Otintai Hotel (11 rooms) at Bikenibeu, Tarawa, and the Vaiaku Laugi (7 rooms) on Funafuti.

Lord Howe Island

Qualifying as a hideaway haven is Lord Howe Island, 435 miles off the coast of New South Wales, Australia. No telephones jangle, fewer than 50 motor vehicles move on the roads; a population under 300 enjoys the unindustrialized tranquility.

A high island with two massive mountains soaring to more than 2,500-foot heights, Lord Howe is small: seven miles long, a mile and a half wide.

A dependency of the Australian state of New South Wales, Lord Howe Island derives its name from the lord who was Secretary of State for the Colonies in the British Cabinet in 1788, the year the island was discovered.

Lord Howe Island's chief distinction—aside from its peace and quiet—is its coral reef, the most southerly one in the world. It has a beautiful lagoon on the western side and many fine stands of the Kentia (or Howea) palms and banyan trees. The palms reach heights up to 70 feet; the great banyans cover acres of ground.

Until a projected airstrip is completed, no jets fly into Lord Howe Island. You come in from Sydney on a three hour flight on one of those big beautiful Sandringham Flying Boats operated by the Airlines of New South Wales. The time of high tide influences the hour of arrival and departure from the lagoon; there are generally three flights a week.

Once you get there, what? There are seven guest houses. Bicycling is the best way to get around the island, and rentals are available. Half-day trips in a glass-bottom boat give you an idea of the richness of the lagoon. Skin diving, snorkeling, swimming, and fishing are popular.

For further information about Lord Howe Island, get in touch with the New South Wales Government Tourist Bureau, Challis House, 8 Martin Place, Sydney 2000, Australia.

The Republic of Nauru

Three and a half miles long and two and a half miles wide, the Republic of Nauru is one of the smallest sovereign states in the world and probably the only one in the world with no capital and no urban development. About 400 miles west of the main Gilbert and Ellice Groups, Nauru boasts other distinctions that set it far apart from the tropical lotus lands of the South Pacific. For one, it has the highest per capita income in the world—nearly twice that of its two closest rivals, the United States and Kuwait. The income derives from the mining of phosphate deposits covering some 85 per cent of the island. About a half-mile back from the shore and the narrow green belt where the natives live lies a barren phosphate-rich plateau. No trees, no shrubs, no flowers grow on this landscape, whose very harshness gives it a peculiar fascination.

For the sightseer, the phosphate area—especially the grotesque looking coral pinnacles left after the phosphate has been mined—is a feature you view with mixed emotions. The devastation is total. By night the pinnacles resemble a stark graveyard, acre upon acre of stones as high as 60 feet, all that is left after the phosphate has been ripped away. You can't help but wonder what the Nauruans will do when the phosphate gives out.

A sealed road, 12 miles long, circles the island, but you won't have it to yourself: more than 1,000 registered vehicles circulate on Nauru. The island population of close to 7,000 is predominantly Nauruan, racially most closely related to the Polynesians.

The Republic of Nauru has its own airline, Air Nauru, that flies between the island and the Mar-shalls, the Gilberts, New Caledonia, and Australia. Air Pacific flies to Nauru from the Gilbert Islands, and Air Micronesia provides a link to the north and Guam and Micronesia.

Nauru's newest tourist facility is the Meneng Hotel. The only hotel on the island, it has 32 rooms.

For further information, get in touch with the Secretary for Island Development and Industry, Republic of Nauru, Central Pacific.

Norfolk Island

All who have read James Michener's *Tales of the South Pacific* know of Norfolk Island which lies 900 miles off the east coast of Australia. It can be reached by plane from Auckland, New Zealand, or Sydney, Australia.

With a population of less than 1,500, the island is 5 miles long and 3 miles wide (or as the natives put it, 20 minutes long by 5 minutes wide.) A Territory of the Commonwealth of Australia, its administrative center is at Kingston.

At first glance, you might think you're in Cornwall when you set foot on Norfolk: its greenness, its pastoral qualities, and its peaceful atmosphere are reminiscent of England. Not all of this is accidental. The island, uninhabited when Captain Cook discovered it in 1774, became a penal settlement for convicts from the British Empire in the 18th and 19th centuries. After the settlement was closed, descendents of the mutineers of *Bounty* fame came to Norfolk to settle because Pitcairn Island had become overcrowded.

Norfolk Island has a high, irregular coastline of rugged basalt cliffs. An island of green hills, its ridges are crowned with the famous Norfolk Island pines. This species, planted by convict laborers, towered along a straight mile known as Pine Avenue; but this avenue of trees had to be cut down in 1942 in order to build a World War II airstrip. A new avenue of 100 pines has been planted on Kingston's Middlegate Road.

Among Norfolk Island's charms are the quiet friendliness of the islanders, their attractive houses and gardens, their individuality, and their hospitality. Tourism is now their main industry, and they make it clear that tourists are welcome. Hotels, inns, and lodges, and guest houses—all of them small—cater to those travelers who find their way to Norfolk Island. Besides its natural charm, the main attractions are golf (9-hole), tennis, swimming, hiking, superb fishing, water skiing, and duty-free shopping. Cars and motor scooters are available for rent.

For further information, get in touch with the Norfolk Island Tourist Board, P.O. Box 123, Norfolk Island, Pacific Ocean.

BARREN PHOSPHATE PLATEAU on Nauru
(upper left) contrasts with lush growth surrounding
Nauru's Buada Lagoon (upper right). Norfolk
Islanders gather (center left) to celebrate Bounty Day,
in memory of Pitcairn Island forebears. Emily Bay
on Norfolk (lower left) is edged by characteristic
Norfolk Island pines. Ruins from convict era (above)
are much in evidence today on Norfolk.

Supplementary Reading

Descriptive Atlas of the Pacific Islands, edited by T. F. Kennedy. Sixty-four maps and accompanying text cover Micronesia, Polynesia, Australia (A.H. & A.W. Reed, New Zealand).

Fiji in Colour, by James Siers. Photographs and text of personal experiences and general information (A.H. & A.W. Reed, New Zealand).

Fiji Islands, photographs by Hank Curth, text by Sue Wendt. A portrait of Fiji (Thomas Nelson, Australia).

The Golden Haze: With Captain Cook in the South Pacific, by Roderick Cameron. An illustrated reconstruction of Cook's voyages from the point of view of the author's travels (World Publishing Co.).

Guam Past and Present, by Charles Beardsley. A general handbook covering the island's discovery, history, culture, and geography (Charles E. Tuttle Co.).

Isles of the South Pacific, by John Cockroft. Photographs and text covering Papua New Guinea (Angus & Robertson, Australia).

Isles of the South Pacific, by Maurice Shadbolt and Olaf Ruhen. Photographs and text covering Polynesia and Melanesia (National Geographic Society, Washington, D.C.).

Melanesia: Isles of the South Pacific, by John Cockroft. Photographs and text covering Melanesia (Angus & Robertson, Australia).

Micronesia: The Breadfruit Revolution, by Byron Baker and Robert Wenkam. Text and photographs covering Micronesia (East-West Center Press, Honolulu).

Pacific Islands Literature: 100 Basic Books, by A. Grove Day. A selective annotated bibliography (University Press of Hawaii).

Pacific Islands Year Book, edited by Judy Tudor. Standard reference book on the islands of the Pacific (Pacific Publications, Australia).

People of Paradise, by David Attenborough. A journey of discovery through Fiji, Tonga, and the New Hebrides showing peoples and their customs (Harper & Row).

Polynesia in Colour, by James Siers. Includes text and photographs on Fiji, The Samoas, Tonga, the Cooks, New Caledonia, and Tahiti (A.H. & A.W. Reed, New Zealand).

Polynesian Isles of the South Pacific, by John Cockroft. Photographs and text covering Tonga, Tahiti, American and Western Samoa, Cook, Pitcairn, and Easter islands (Angus & Robertson, Australia).

Samoa in Colour, by James Siers. Photographs and text covering general information (Charles E. Tuttle, Tokyo).

South Pacific, by Jack and Dorothy Fields. A pictorial with 320 photographs covering 14 island groups in Melanesia, Micronesia, and Polynesia (Kodansha International, Tokyo and Palo Alto, Calif.).

The Story of Fiji, by G. K. Roth. Covers history, geography, and present-day Fiji (Oxford University Press).

Tahiti, by Barnaby Conrad. Presents Tahiti as a way of life, and includes chapters on history and hints to travelers (Viking).

Tales of the South Pacific, by James A. Michener. A Pulitzer Prize-winning collection of short stories (Macmillan).

Traveller's Guide to Papua New Guinea, by Ann Malliard. Sightseeing guide book with historical background covered (Jacaranda Press, Milton, Australia).

Vikings of the Sunrise, by Sir Peter H. Buck. An important work covering early migrations of the Polynesians (Lippincott).

PHOTOGRAPHERS

American Airlines: 49 (right). **Mike Ashman:** 136 (right), 144 (left). **Nancy Bannick:** 86 (right), 101 (bottom), 105 (bottom left), 106 (bottom left). **Dave Bartruff:** 38 (bottom), 45 (left), 51 (top right), 52 (right). **David Beal:** 124 (top left), 130 (middle, bottom left). **Boisnard-Guiter:** 72 (left), 76 (bottom right, left). **W. Brindle:** 126. **British Solomon Islands Tourist Authority:** 119 (top right). **I. Calé:** 74 (bottom left), 80 (top right). **Noël Calé:** 71 (bottom left), 74 (right). **Gordon J. Clear:** 103 (right), 154 (top right). **Frances Coleberd:** 4 (top), 9 (left, right), 11, 12 (top), 15 (top, bottom), 16 (bottom right), 23 (top, bottom right, top left), 24 (right), 27 (bottom left), 29 (bottom), 30 (right), 68 (top right, left), 71 (right), 78, 79, 82 (right), 96 (left). **Dolly Connelly:** 28. **Continental Airlines:** 8 (right), 132 (top), 147, 152. **D. Darbois:** 12 (bottom). **Extension Service Photo:** 130 (right). **Fiji Visitors Bureau:** 42 (bottom right), 50 (right), 61 (right). **Shirley Fockler:** 7 (bottom right), 8 (left), 19, 20, 21 (left, right), 27 (top right, left, bottom right), 29 (left), 35, 49 (left), 55 (bottom left), 64 (top, bottom), 80 (left), 81 (bottom left), 83 (left), 87, 101 (top right), 102, 105 (top left, bottom right), 106 (right), 112 (right), 113 (left), 115, 118, 123 (left), 124 (top, bottom right, middle left), 127 (top, bottom right), 128 (right), 130 (top left), 131, 132 (bottom), 135 (top right), 141 (top, bottom right, left), 143 (bottom), 148 (right). **J. Genest:** 13, 16 (top left, bottom left), 23 (bottom left). **Paul Genest:** 29 (top), 65, 76 (top right), 82 (left). **Government of American Samoa:** 84 (top). **Government of American Samoa-Kay Purinton:** 90 (left). **Government Tourist Department Tahiti:** 15 (left). **Malcolm Holmes:** 74 (top left). **George Holton:** 154 (bottom left). **Robin Kinkead:** 89 (left), 90 (right), 93, 95 (top, bottom right), 107, 154 (bottom right, top left). **Nitin Lal:** 5, 42 (bottom left), 45 (top, bottom right), 46 (top left), 48 (right, left), 51 (top left), 53 (left), 55 (top left), 57 (top right), 58 (top, middle left). **A. Maillard:** 67. **Matson Lines:** 16 (top right). **Milton Mann:** 89 (bottom right), 91, 92 (right), 95 (left). **Ted Marriott:** 117 (right, left), 119 (left). **C. Mitride:** 111 (left). **New South Wales Department of Tourism:** 153. **Office du Tourisme de la Nouvelle Calédonie:** 7 (top, middle), 74 (middle), 80. **Photo Marco:** 32. **Photomic:** 68, 73 (left). **Qantas:** 81 (right), 127 (left), 157. **Frederic M. Rea:** 50 (left), 51 (bottom right), 143 (top), 149, 151 (bottom right). **G. Reithmaier:** 86 (left), 96 (right), 99, 106 (middle left). **Nelson Shreve:** 31 (bottom). **Larry Smith:** 30 (bottom left), 151 (top). **Mary Benton Smith:** 43, 101 (left), 105 (top right). **J. Neil Stebbins:** 10 (left), 29 (right), 61 (left). **Stinsons:** 51 (bottom left), 53 (right), 57 (bottom right). **A. Sylvain:** 4 (bottom left), 7 (top right), 24 (left), 30 (top left), 31 (top), 34 (bottom left), 37. **T. Takahara:** 109, 112 (bottom left). **Michael Terry:** 58 (right). **Tonga Visitors Bureau:** 106 (top left). **Dankwart Von Knobloch:** 123 (right). **Charles Wechler:** 57 (left). **R. Wenkam:** 10 (right), 133, 135 (bottom right, left), 136 (left), 137, 139 (top, bottom right), 142, 144 (right), 145, 147 (top), 148 (left). **Withers of Fiji:** 7 (bottom left). **Rob Wright:** 38 (top), 42 (top left), 55 (top, bottom right), 60, 62, 63. **Rob Wright, Jr.:** 46 (top, bottom right, bottom left), 52 (left).

Index

Authors, 5, 13
American Samoa, 88-94
    Climate, 88
    Currency & banking, 88
    Customs regulations, 92
    Entry regulations, 92
    Fagotogo, 91, 92
    Geography, 85-86, 89
    Government, 86
    History, 85-86, 90
    Hotels, 89, 93
    How to get around, 93
    Information services, 94
    Lifestyle, 86-87
    Map, 88
    Night life, 93
    Museums, 90
    Pago Pago, 89-91
    Religion, 88
    Restaurants, 93
    Shopping, 91-92
    Sports, 92
Bougainville, L.A. de, 13, 85, 110
Coconut palm, 9, 60, 100
Cook, Captain James, 5, 11, 13, 67, 75, 99, 110
Cook Islands, 7, 11, 153-155
Copra, 9, 44, 67, 111
Coral reefs, 8, 41, 67
Easter Island, 7, 11, 154, 155
Fiji Islands, 38-63
    Beqa Island, 41, 53
    Bures, 41-43, 50, 54
    Castaway Island, 41, 54, 58
    Climate, 4, 41, 55
    Communications, 56
    Cumming Street, 39, 48
    Currency & banking, 56
    Customs regulations, 56
    Entry regulations, 56
    Events, 63
    Feasting & festivities, 43-45, 47, 53, 61
    Firewalking, 53
    Geography, 41, 47, 50
    Glass bottom boat, 54
    Government, 43
    Health & medical, 56
    History, 41, 43, 45
    Holidays, 56
    Hotels, 48, 50, 54, 58
    How to get around, 39, 59
    Information services, 54, 56

Fiji Islands, (cont.)
    Kadavu Island, 41, 54
    Koro Island, 54
    Korolevu, 57
    Language, 41, 44
    Lau Islands, 41
    Lautoka, 41, 44, 49, 50
    Lifestyle, 39, 41-43, 45
    Malololailai Island, 41, 54
    Mamanuca Islands, 52-54
    Map, 40
    Nadi, 39, 44-45
    Navua River, 52
    Night life, 61
    Ovalau Island, 41, 54, 61
    Parks & gardens, 47
    Religion, 41
    Shopping, 44, 45, 47, 49
    Somosomo, 55
    Sports, active, 44, 47, 52, 61, 62
    Sports, spectator, 44, 61
    Sugar cane, 44-45, 50
    Suva, 41, 43, 45, 46, 47-48, 49, 57
    Tai Island, 58
    Taveuni Island, 41, 54
    Toberua Island, 58
    Train, sugar cane, 50
    Vanua Levu, 41, 54, 55
    Vatulele Island, 41, 58
    Wayaka Island, 54
    Yanuca Island, 41, 58
    Yaqona, 44, 50, 60-61
    Yasawa Islands, 41, 52-54
Gauguin, Paul, 5, 13, 24
Gilbert & Ellice Islands, 7, 8, 154, 155
Guam, 133, 135, 137-152
    Agana, 137, 138, 139, 140, 151
    Chamorros, 137, 138, 139
    Climate, 137
    Entertainment, Events, 137, 140, 152
    Geography, 135, 137, 140
    Government, 135, 136
    History, 135-136
    Hotels, 139-140
    How to get there, 133, 150
    Inajaran, 137, 138
    Ipao Beach, 137, 138, 139
    Language, 137
    Map, 134
    Merizo, 138, 139
    Restaurants, 137, 140
    Shopping, 139
    Tamuning, 139-140, 151
    Transportation, 133, 137-138

Guam, (cont.)
    Tumon Bay, 137, 138, 139
    Umatac, 132, 138
High islands, 8
Kwajalein, 133, 143
Lord Howe Island, 153, 155-156
Low islands, 8
Magellan, Ferdinand, 11, 140
Majuro, 132, 133, 142-143
    Accommodations, 143
    Geography, 142-143
    History, 143
Map, Pacific area, 6
Melanesia, 5, 7, 43, 67, 75, 109, 111, 117, 123
Micronesia, 5, 7, 117, 132-152 (See also: Majuro, Palau, Ponape, Rota, Saipan, Tinian, Truk, Yap)
    Caroline Islands, 8, 135
    Chamorros, 136, 139, 141
    Climate, 137, 150
    Customs regulations, 150
    Economy, 137
    Entertainment, Events, 152
    Entry regulations, 150
    Geography, 135
    Government, 135-136, 140
    Health & medical, 150-151
    History, 135-136
    Information services, 151
    Kusaie, 8, 136, 143
    Language, 136
    Latte stones, 136, 138, 139, 141
    Lifestyle, 133, 135, 137
    Map, 134
    Marianas Islands, 135-136, 139, 140-142
    Marshall Islands, 135-136, 142
    Midway, 133
    Pagan, 141
    Peleliu, 133
    Religion, 136
    Ulithi, 133, 136
Nauru, Republic of, 156, 157
New Caledonia, 64-83
    Aquarium, 69, 71
    Amedée Island, 76, 79
    Climate, 75, 77
    Communications, 77
    Currency & banking, 77
    Customs regulations, 77
    Entry regulations, 77
    Events, 83

New Caledonia, (cont.)
    Feasting & festivities, 69, 75, 82-83
    Geography, 4, 65-66, 75
    Government, 67
    Health & medical, 77
    Hienghène, 74, 78
    History, 65, 76
    Holidays, 77
    Hotels, 74, 75, 77, 78-80
    How to get around, 72-75, 80-82
    Information services, 77
    Isle of Pines, 67, 75-76
    Language, 69, 75, 78
    Lifestyle, 67, 73, 75
    Loyalty Islands, 67, 76-77, 80
    Map, 66
    Museums, 68, 69, 70
    Nickel mining, 65, 67, 70
    Night life, 82
    Nouméa, 68, 69-72, 80, 81, 82
    Ouen Island, 77, 79
    Ouvéa Island, 82
    Parks & gardens, 70, 74
    Religion, 69, 75
    Restaurants, 74-75, 77, 80, 82
    Shopping, 69, 70-72
    Sports, active, 70, 72, 76
    Sports, spectator, 70, 72
    Touho, 74, 82
    Yaté, 74
New Hebrides, 109-114
    Ambrym Island, 109, 112-113
    Climate, 114
    Communications, 114
    Currency & banking, 114
    Efate, 110, 114
    Entry regulations, 113
    Espiritu Santo, 110
    Geography, 109-110
    Government, 109-110
    Health & medical, 114
    History, 110
    Hotels, 113, 114
    How to get around, 114
    Information services, 114
    Land divers, 109, 113
    Language, 110-111
    Lifestyle, 110-111
    Lopevi Island, 109, 113
    Luganville, (See Santo)
    Map, 110
    Pentecost Island, 109, 111, 113
    Port Vila, 110-113
    Religion, 111
    Santo, 110-113
    Shopping, 112
    Sports, 112

New Hebrides, (cont.)
  Tanna Island, 109, 113
  Vila,
    (See Port Vila)
Norfolk Island, 156, 157
Palau, 148-150
  Accommodations, 150
  Babelthuap, 148, 151
  Geography, 135, 148,
    149
  History, 148, 149
  Koror Island, 136, 148,
    149, 151
  Rock Islands, 148, 149
Papua New Guinea, 121-
131
  Angoram, 127
  Baiyer River Bird
    Sanctuary, 126
  Bougainville Island,
    122
  Buka Island, 122
  Chimbu District, 126
  Climate, 129-130
  Communications, 130
  Currency & banking,
    131
  Entry regulations, 128-
    129
  Events, 131
  Feasting & festivities,
    125, 126
  Geography, 122
  Goroka, 126
  Government, 123
  Haus tambaran, 121,
    123, 127-128
  Health & medical, 131
  Highlands, The, 125-126
  History, 122-123
  Hotels, 128, 129
  How to get around, 131
  Information services,
    131
  Kundiawa, 122, 126
  Lae, 124, 125
  Language, 123
  Lifestyle, 121, 123
  Madang, 124, 125
  Map, 122
  Maprik, 128
  Minj, 125-126
  Mt. Hagen, 125
  Mud men, 126
  New Britain Island,
    122, 128
  New Ireland Island,
    122
  Port Moresby, 124, 125
  Rabaul, 128

Papua New
  Guinea, (cont.)
  Sepik River, 121, 122,
    125, 127-128
  Shopping, 125, 127
  Sing-sings, 126
  Trobriand Islands,
    122, 128
  Wewak, 127-128
  Wig men, 125
Polynesia, 5, 7, 12-38, 94,
117, 154
Ponape, 132, 133, 136,
143-145
  Accommodations, 145
  Climate, 143
  Cultural center, 145
  Geography, 8, 143
  History, 135, 136, 144
  Hotels, 145
  Kapingamarangi, 136,
    143
  Kolonia, 144, 145
  Nan Madol, 144
  Nukuoro, 136, 143
Rota, 140, 141
Saipan, 133, 140-142
  Accommodations,
    141-142
  Banzai Cliffs, 140
  Capitol Hill, 137, 140
  Entertainment, 141
  Garapan, 140
  Geography, 140, 141
  History, 135, 140, 141
  Marpi Point, 140
  Mt. Tagpochau, 140
  Suicide Cliff, 140
Solomon Islands, 115-120
  Climate, 120
  Communications, 120
  Currency & banking,
    120
  Entry regulations, 119
  Geography, 115-116
  Government, 117
  Guadalcanal, 115
  Health & medical, 120
  History, 115, 116
  Honiara, 116, 117-118,
    119
  Hotels, 119, 120
  How to get around, 120
  Information services,
    120
  Language, 117
  Lifestyle, 117
  Map, 116
  Shopping, 118
Tahiti, 12-38
  Art galleries, 19

Tahiti, (cont.)
  Bastille Day, 37
  Bora Bora, 12, 13, 15,
    26-28
  Botanical gardens, 22
  Churches, 19
  Climate, 33
  Communications, 33
  Currency & banking,
    33
  Customs regulations,
    33
  Entry regulations, 33
  Festivities & feasting,
    19, 26, 30, 31, 32
  Firewalking, 31, 32
  Food & drink, 19, 22
  Gauguin, Paul, 22-24
  Geography, 15
  Government, 17
  Health & medical, 34
  History, 11, 17, 31
  Hotels, 12, 27, 29, 30,
    34-35
  How to get around,
    18, 35
  Huahine, 13, 15, 28
  Information services,
    34
  Language, 18
  Lifestyle, 15-17
  Local regulations, 33
  Map, 14
  Maraes, 23, 28, 30, 32
  Marquesas, 11, 15, 36
  Moorea, 12, 13, 15,
    29-30
  Museums, 20, 22
  Night life, 20, 22
  Papeete, 17-22, 34
  Raiatea, 13, 15, 30-32
  Rangiroa, 13, 32
  Religion, 17
  Restaurants, 19-20
  Shopping, 21, 28, 31
  Sports, active, 22-25, 29
  Sports, spectator, 26
  Tahaa, 32
  Tahiti-iti, 15, 22
  Tamaaraa, 30, 32
Tinian, 140, 141
Tonga, 99-108
  Climate, 107
  Communications, 108
  Currency & banking,
    108
  Entry regulations, 107
  Eua Island, 106
  Flying foxes, 106
  Geography, 99

Tonga, (cont.)
  Government, 99-100
  Ha'apai, 99
  Health & medical, 108
  History, 100, 104
  Hotels, 107
  How to get around, 108
  Information services,
    108
  Language, 100
  Lifestyle, 100
  Map, 100
  Nuku'alofa, 101-104
  Religion, 100-101
  Shopping, 104
  Sports, 104
  Transportation, 8-10
  Vava'u, 99, 107
  Whale hunting, 103
Truk, 145-146
  Accommodations, 146
  Dublon Island, 146
  Geography, 8, 145
  History, 146
  Moen Island, 137, 145,
    146, 151
  Osakura Island, 146
Trust Territory of the
  Pacific Islands, 135, 136
Western Samoa, 94-98
  Apia, 95-96, 97, 98
  Climate, 88
  Communications, 98
  Currency & banking,
    98
  Customs regulations,
    97
  Entry regulations, 97
  Geography, 4, 85, 95
  Government, 86
  History, 85-86
  Hotels, 97-98
  How to get around, 98
  Information services,
    98
  Lifestyle, 86-87
  Map, 94
  Night life, 98
  Religion, 87-88
  Savai'i, 96
  Shopping, 95
  Sports, 97
Yap, 146-148
  Accommodations, 147,
    148
  Colonia, 146
  Geography, 8, 146
  History, 146, 147
  Lifestyle, 136-137,
    146-147, 152
  O'Keffe's Island, 147